Capital, State, Empire:
The New American Way of Digital Warfare

Scott Timcke

UNIVERSITY OF WESTMINSTER PRESS

University of Westminster Press
www.uwestminsterpress.co.uk

Competing interests

The author declares that he has no competing interests in publishing this book

Published by
University of Westminster Press
101 Cavendish Street
London W1W 6XH
www.uwestminsterpress.co.uk

Text © Scott Timcke 2017

First published 2017

Series cover concept: Mina Bach (minabach.co.uk)
Printed in the UK by Lightning Source Ltd.
Print and digital versions typeset by Siliconchips Services Ltd.

ISBN (Paperback): 978-1-911534-36-5
ISBN (PDF): 978-1-911534-37-2
ISBN (EPUB): 978-1-911534-38-9
ISBN (Kindle): 978-1-911534-39-6

DOI: https://doi.org/10.16997/book6

This work is licensed under the Creative Commons Attribution-NonCommercial-NoDerivatives 4.0 International License. To view a copy of this license, visit http://creativecommons.org/licenses/by-nc-nd/4.0/ or send a letter to Creative Commons, 444 Castro Street, Suite 900, Mountain View, California, 94041, USA. This license allows for copying and distributing the work, providing author attribution is clearly stated, that you are not using the material for commercial purposes, and that modified versions are not distributed.

The full text of this book has been peer-reviewed to ensure high academic standards. For full review policies, see: http://www.uwestminsterpress.co.uk/site/publish/

Suggested citation:
Timcke, Scott 2017 *Capital, State, Empire: The New American Way of Digital Warfare* London: University of Westminster Press. DOI: https://doi.org/10.16997/book6. License: CC-BY-NC-ND 4.0

To read the free, open access version of this book online, visit http: https://doi.org/10.16997/book6 or scan this QR code with your mobile device:

Dedicated to Rick Gruneau

Contents

Acknowledgements	ix
Introduction	xi
Chapter 1. A Material Critique of Digital Society	**1**
1.1 Radical Political Economy as an Organizing Intellectual Framework	7
1.2 The Need to Jettison Idealism	10
1.3 The Labour Regimes of Digital Capitalism	12
1.4 The State of Data	19
Chapter 2. Extraction, Expansion and Economies of Bondage	**25**
2.1 European State Formation	26
2.2 American State Formation	32
2.3 Intra-Ruling Class Struggle and Bargained Settlement	37
2.4 Consolidation and Collapse, Contention and Cooperation	44
2.5 Neoliberalism and the Great Recession	48
Chapter 3. Calculation, Computation, and Conflict	**55**
3.1 Cold War Social Science	57
3.2 The Strategic Return to Centres of Calculation	59
3.3 Automated Lethal Robotics	60
3.4 Extrajudicial Drone Strikes	65
3.5 The Order of the Internet of Things	67
Chapter 4. Internal Rule and the Other America	**77**
4.1 The Atrophy of Opposition and the Truly Disadvantaged	78
4.2 The War on Blacks	82
4.3 The Daily Ugliness of Police Militarization	86
4.4 The Universality of Black Lives Matter	91

Chapter 5. External Rule and 'Free Trade' — 99

   5.1 Induced Under- and Combined-Development — 100
   5.2 Contradictions of Global Rule — 105
   5.3 Bases for Commodities and Containment — 111
   5.4 Securing International Circuits of Production — 116
   5.5 The Military Response to a 'Global Power Shift' — 121

Chapter 6. Minds, Brains, and Disciplinary Programs — 125

   6.1 The First AI Revolution and the Legacies of Political Behaviourism — 127
   6.2 The Second AI Revolution and Embodied Computation — 129
   6.3 The Role of Economics and Psychology — 131
   6.4 Computing Means and Social Ends — 134
   6.5 Lazy Definitions and Weak Epistemology — 136
   6.6 The Psychologism of Abstracted Empiricism — 141

Conclusion. Digital Coercion and the Tendency Towards Unfree Labour — 145

Notes — 149

References — 155

Index — 179

Acknowledgements

I am deeply indebted to Rick Gruneau and Gary McCarron. Their friendship and guidance has forever improved my life and work.

Conversations and correspondence with all my colleagues and companions at Simon Fraser University helped form the core of the argument. Though I single out Matthew Greaves, Graham Mackenzie and Nawal Musleh-Motut, everyone at SFU deserves gratitude. Dal Yong Jin and Jay McKinnon provided vital comments in the conceptual stages of this project. Nearer to the end, Michelle Roopnarine was a cheerful student assistant. Throughout, both Derek Kootte's and Graeme Webb's comments greatly helped tie many chapters together. The Press's anonymous reviewers were generous and exacting. All made this a better product.

Levi Gahman, Priya Kissoon, David Mastery, and Annita Montoute have become excellent new colleagues at The University of the West Indies. Thanks go to my Head of Department, Maarit Forde who has supported me in ways too numerous to elaborate.

I am grateful to Christian Fuchs, the editor of this series, and to Andrew Lockett, Press Manager at the University of Westminster Press for supporting this project, but especially for their ongoing commitment to open access publishing. Most of this manuscript was written while working in the Global South where global inequalities and paywalls limit access to scholarship. For these and other reasons, efforts like theirs will change international research for the better.

My deepest appreciation is for my partner, Mariana Jarkova and my parents, Dennis and Diana Timcke. All three have provided care and understanding as part of my daily life during the completion of this book.

Introduction

The United States presents the greatest source of global geopolitical violence and instability. Much of this comes from the state's security apparatuses. For example, just in the early part of the twenty-first century, 150,000 troops and thousands of contractors did little to build regional stability in Iraq. Instead, around 10 million Iraqis require humanitarian assistance, another 3.4 million are internally displaced, and according to the Lancet Study, between 2003 and 2006 around 650,000 violent deaths can be attributed to the US invasion (Burnham et al. 2006). In fiscal terms, the Congressional Budget Office estimates that by 2017 the Iraq War will have cost the US over $2.4 trillion, while the Watson Institute at Brown University arrives at a figure of $4.79 trillion and counting, when one includes US wars in Syria, Afghanistan, Pakistan, as well as Homeland Security (Crawford 2016). This outcome was worse than most anti-war protestors predicted. The scale of this disaster is even greater when one considers that this destabilization is a contributing factor in the Syrian Civil War.

Domestically, in direct violation of legal limitations, the National Security Agency (NSA) has conducted mass surveillance to assemble electronic dossiers

---

How to cite this book chapter:
Timcke, S. 2017 *Capital, State, Empire: The New American Way of Digital Warfare.*
    Pp. xi–xvii. London: University of Westminster Press. DOI: https://doi.org/10.16997/
    book6.a. License: CC-BY-NC-ND 4.0

on nearly every US citizen. It is almost impossible not to do so, given that the agency scrapes 1.6 per cent of all internet traffic (*The Economist* 2016). When confronted with evidence, the agency denies these programs in front of elected representatives. Assisted by extraordinary rendition, the Central Intelligence Agency (CIA) undertook torture programs at black sites, lied about it, then wiretapped and attempted to erase Senate investigators' records (US Senate Select Committee on Intelligence 2014). The Justice Department has refused to charge the officials involved therein. Similarly, Homeland Security and the State Department's various security projects have blurred the lines between foreign and domestic populations, thereby eroding civil liberties. In contradistinction to their treatment of whistleblowers who have revealed the extensive civic harm caused by these activities, these departments are hostile to public accountability and open court proceedings.

On the theme of prosecutorial inaction, the Justice Department has refused to prosecute the bankers involved in the widespread financial fraud that triggered the 2008 recession: 'Too Big to Fail' became 'Too Big to Jail'. Yet, between the Troubled Asset Relief Program, the Emergency Economic Stabilization Act 2008, the Presidential Task Force on the Auto Industry, the American Recovery and Reinvestment Act 2009 and quantitative easing, the US has spent around $6 trillion to limit the harms caused by the financial sector. However, most of this public spending went to the already rich. Between 2010 and 2012, the US experienced the greatest ever increase in social inequality, drastically increasing the wealth gap between the 0.1 per cent and everyone else.

This jump is worrying, but it is also a continuation of a longer trend leading simultaneously to capital concentration and pauperization. Aided by productivity gains born from information technology, the US economy has doubled since 1980. So relative to 1960, a typical US worker is twice as productive, but real median wages are almost flat, if not declining in some sectors. About a quarter of US jobs pay an hourly wage that could not support a family of four above the poverty level. Millions of Americans can hardly afford either suitable healthcare or adequate food. Effectively, labour's situation has worsened since the 40-hour work week was established in the 1940s because for many occupations a 40-hour work week does not provide a living wage.

Not only are workers paid less, capitalists have structured and manipulated their relationship with the state to ensure they pay minimal taxes. One major consequence of this arrangement is that the state cannot undertake sufficient welfare redistribution, nor provide sufficient public goods, and this has facilitated a massive transfer, an appropriation even, of wealth to the ruling class. The degree to which the US is committed to private property cannot be disentangled from the comparatively weak institutional social welfare system. Instead, families, civil society, and charity carry the welfare burden. As the adage goes, 'God and guns fill in for the welfare state.' But Homeland Security is not social security. So while workers are producing more value, the benefits of their labour cannot be seen by them, and it has not been evenly translated into broad socio-economic upliftment.

This is unsurprising given that American party politics is in the pockets of Wall Street and districts are gerrymandered into stalemate. Campaign finance regulations mean that the ruling class controls the barriers of entry to political office, and so running a campaign is so costly that even well intentioned advocates bend to the wishes of funders and donors. The electorate know this and so consistently regard politicians with distain. Nevertheless, they are so ill-informed about first causes, that they cannot even comprehend how these various parts fit together to form a whole oppressive social structure, meaning they are hard pressed to resist class warfare 'from above'.

With such conditions, policy discussions have degraded to the exchange of talking points, misrepresentation, and disinformation. American party politics is nothing but a parade of wilful ignorance, avoidance, and hawkishness. Take environmental issues for instance. While nearly 70 per cent of Americans acknowledge that Earth's average temperature is increasing, less than half attribute this to human activity. Conversely, as of April 2013, only a third of Americans believe that global warming is a very serious problem (PEW 2013). This finding came in the same month as CO^2 passed 400 parts per million (NOAA 2013,) and the most comprehensive study of near 12,000 papers found that of the articles that took a position on Anthropogenic Global Warming, 97 per cent endorsed the theory (Cook et al. 2013). Similar dynamics are in play in almost any social issue. Capital speaks while the working class is silenced.

The Supreme Court of the United States is of little help. The 2009 Citizen's United decision, while holding that political speech is 'the means to hold officials accountable to the people' and 'indispensable to decision-making in a democracy', perverts it by adding that 'this is no less true because the speech comes from a corporation'. Couched in the rhetoric of rights, but aware of the consequences, the Court justified its decision in the utility of corporate speech to the public exchange of reasons. But this is nothing but an alibi for increasing corporate influence in political affairs. For instance, 50 senators who stalled gun control measures in 2015 received a combined total of over $27 million for political expenditures from firearms lobbyists.[1]

Elsewhere, Silicon Valley is producing tools for mystification and oppression. By stock market value Amazon, Apple, Facebook, Microsoft and Alphabet are some of the most valuable firms in the United States.[2] But this wealth comes from massive unpaid labour as users unwittingly turn themselves into commodities.[3] As Farhad Manjoo (2017) notes, it also comes, 'from their control of the inescapable digital infrastructure on which much of the rest of the economy depends—mobile phones, social networks, the web, the cloud, retail and logistics, and the data and computing power required for future breakthroughs.' Knowing this, in 2015 the Department of Defense (DoD) established a venture capital fund, the Defense Innovation Unit, to help accelerate the production and testing of specific kinds of artificial intelligence research. It is these kinds of software that are intended for robotic humanoids like the Atlas, a robot produced by Alphabet-owned Boston Dynamics (Markoff 2016).[4] Publicly, it stated that these autonomous robots are intended for disaster response scenarios or space travel. However, given that Boston Dynamics is a weapons manufacturer that tests technology with DARPA (Defense Advanced Research Projects Agency), the door is open for military uses. So not only do these digital technologies companies shape everyday perception, collude to suppress wages and destroy public good, they cooperate with state security forces and are becoming arms manufacturers. This aspiration is of utmost concern because it leaves the US ripe for tyranny.

Making sense of the devastation in American social life requires seeing how a coercive security apparatus marching to the metronome of capital rules over those US citizens battling the civil powers that oppose it. And because of the central place of the US in the international political economy, this dynamic is at the heart of a global 'democratic recession' occurring in the early twenty-first century (cf. Diamond, 2015). Granted, there are virtues in American social life, much as in many societies, but they stand adjacent to these social developments. In part, this is indicative of the great American tragedy; a society founded on freedom but built on slavery. The reproduction of this contradiction haunts American history and it appears in the fever of property rights but constant dispossession, or extraordinary wealth with immiserating poverty.[5]

* * *

Presently, US security apparatuses are dramatically reconfiguring. This is for several reasons, many of which I will discuss in the coming chapters, but the most important is what I call the deployment of *digital coercion*. When I use this term I am referring to the various processes facilitated by digital technologies that greatly enable American rule. This is because these kinds of technologies acutely illustrate how the machinery of governance is developed for—or co-opted by—the state to manage subjects and processes at near unprecedented scale and scope. Working from a position that the constellation of digital coercive practices is central to the social life in capitalism, paying attention to these active relationships, as they are shaped by class struggle, both 'from below' and 'from above' can tell us much about the tendencies of capital's rule as it unfolds in the early twenty-first century.

Although present in many places, digital coercion can certainly be seen in the changing nature of warfare. Let me explain. In 1960 Russell Weigley described the 'American way of war' a mode of modern industrial warfare employing strategic attrition. First deployed in the American Civil War and constantly refined until the Second World War, this mode of warfare drafted and mobilized citizen-soldiers to leverage and deploy mass-industrial output as unprecedented firepower. However, the development and strategic deployment of nuclear weapons made total industrial strategic attrition unfeasible between nuclear-armed states. Subsequently, nuclear weapons initiated the shift from the industrial mode of warfare to the political nature of limited asymmetrical warfare.

Along with many others (Boot 2003, Echevarria, 2004), I call this reorganization of military strategy the 'New American Way of War'. I suggest it has several formal features. These are the quest for minimal democratic oversight, computationally aided global dragnet surveillance, automated attempts to avert internal dissent, internal repression of vulnerable populations, and protracted conflicts abroad. While I shall add to these observations in the coming chapters drawing attention to their military nature and political ramifications, my central proposition is that the totality of imperial relations, both foreign and domestic, are geared towards accumulating value, and amongst other process, comes about through dispossession, extraction, and exploitation, themselves *amplified* by digital coercion that allow for unprecedented reach. I contend that these processes can explain many of the empirical observations about state security apparatuses with which I began this book.

This central line investigating military and information technology is an uncommon albeit one of the most urgent topics for Communication Studies. Sadly, disciplinary stalwarts have made this argument for decades but to little avail. Consider how in the mid-1980s, Vincent Mosco lamented how this area was 'ignored' (1986, 76). In early 2017 he has good grounds to come to the same conclusion; that 'scholars who study media and new communication technology tend to ignore the military in favour of examining social media' (2017, 1). This oversight is more perplexing considering that the US Department of Defense, with upwards of 1.3 million active service members and augmented with near 750,000 civilians, is one of the world's largest employers, and certainly the biggest single employer in the US (DoD 2017).[6] Moreover, with a budget of $600 billion in 2015, the DoD is the single biggest purchaser of information and communication goods, and so this is a labour process that warrants focus and critical attention. It is a 'bureaucratic colossus'. If anything, it is fair to say that Herb and Dan Schiller along with a handful of other researchers are the exceptions to this other disciplinary 'blindspot.' All in all, Mosco is quite correct to chastise communication researchers for this general neglect. And so what is required is an analysis of the military that understands battlefields as a product of the relationship between war and society as those things themselves are coloured by historical forces. To the extent that this book can do that, I aim to contribute something to this research agenda.

Aside from the aforementioned themes, and to reiterate, the most important area of investigation in this book is the relationship of *capital and constraint* as it is digitally mediated. Selected aspects of constraint are addressed throughout my coverage of the various topics in this book, and illustrated by cases like state capture, calculated conflict, ghettoization and disposability, uneven-development, and techniques of ideological manipulation. A focus on cases like this is not necessarily chronological for the simple fact that not all regions are integrated at the same time, nor do all regions require the same kind of control at any given point. Jettisoning periodization allows a methodological suppleness that has the advantage of seeing how various institutional arrangements function within a synthetic whole (cf. Wood 1997, 549).

Accordingly, the aim of this book is simple. It is to plot selected features of the American social structure, demonstrating how a capitalist state creates structural injustices, stratifications, and inequalities. Examining these 'laws of motion' further involves a treatment of how intense extraction and exploitation creates surpluses that are then used to fund global indirect and informal rule to ensure American paramountcy and ultimately conducive conditions for capital accumulation. In short, the question of how American capitalism reproduces. Accordingly, it is important to resist bifurcating domestic and international affairs since these rarely act in isolation of one another; instead, this scope can tell us much about the relationship between rulers and ruled irrespective of whether these groups live in the US or elsewhere on the planet.

In the opening chapter, I outline my theoretical approach and defend a materialist critique of digital society, one sensitive to the various components of digital rule like new and emerging labour regimes. In the second chapter, I use a historical narrative of US state formation to discuss selected aspects of state theory. This involves some preliminary discussion of European colonialism in the Americas. Throughout this exercise, I try to balance my attention between dispossession, inter- and intra-class struggle and changing labour regimes. Violence receives a central role because of how it supports the accumulation and dispossession process. A subsidiary goal is to demonstrate the expanding accumulative drive that seeks to get ahead of inevitable capitalist crises, irrespective of whether they occur in fifteenth-century Spain, nineteenth-century Britain, or the twentieth-century United States.

Drawing upon an assessment of recent US military budgets and policy statements, the third chapter examines how the security state configures its security forces for the twenty-first century. Digital technologies like automated lethal robotics such as drones and dragnet surveillance enable the US to increase force projection and the maintenance of an imperial system. Chapter Four turns towards internal patterns of subjugation. While I touch upon recent activism such as Black Lives Matter, prison abolitionists, and the Movement for Black Lives, my main purpose is to look at the salient longstanding repressive elements in the United States, the very structures which these activists contest, all the while demonstrating how the American security state is responsible for, and condones this harassment. In Chapter Five I discuss how imperial organization creates uneven development and then examine the warfare that arises from these conditions. Here I pay attention to how territories contended and defended for access to resources and markets, were then finally incorporated into imperial domains. Topics in this chapter include the administration of zones of violence and zones of pacification.

As code conditions the possibilities of so much of social life, it is important for contemporary material analysis. Accordingly, the last chapter addresses what Vincent Mosco termed 'digital positivism'. Herein, I focus on paternalistic 'nudges' predicated upon behavioural economic calculations and bureaucratic approval of big data analysis that informs algorithmic regulation. Injunctions and interjections drawing upon social theory are therefore required to assess how digital technologies of governance and control are used to further capitalist state rule. I conclude with some thoughts on the impact of digital coercion on a labour regime, suggesting that there will be an increase in unfree labour.

I anticipate that American scholars will likely receive this work in similar ways to which European scholars view American studies of their continent, or the ways Africans view European studies of theirs: there is certainly a politics of outsider observation. Still, while I may not have the knowledge of an insider, or be privy to all the subterranean politics within the US social structure, it is nevertheless worthwhile continuing to produce, and insist upon, a Southern literature that makes the North the subject of study, but on Southern terms. This is not because the North is the sole site of history. On the contrary, to my mind, this is a complimentary component of understanding the imperial experience in the South. As many Southern theorists have shown, colonized spaces were (and are) experimental sites for rule, military techniques and scientific practice, or have made clear that underdevelopment is an intended by-product of capital interests in the dominant metropoles (cf. Connell 2007). Insights like this underscore that the South has a capacity to write directly and plainly about the sites where global oppression and exploitation is initiated. So all this said, my interest lies less in satisfying a US audience by pursuing a pure inquiry into concepts, and more as an exercise of the South 'writing back' identifying some of the very features that oppress almost all of us.

In a short book like this one, I cannot marshal all the evidence required to prove conclusively the aforementioned propositions. What I do hope to do is advance them enough that others might find the general conjecture sufficiently compelling to subject it to more scrutiny, lending support where appropriate and pruning where necessary. Discarding and reconfiguring select elements are likely too. In this spirit, there are items I have left unattended lest this become a spiralling multi-volume project. For instance, I hardly raise issues of gender in the US social structure, nor do I discuss domestic gun violence, debates on reparations, or arms manufacturing. The same is true of many more things. This is not absolute neglect stemming from a belief that they do not warrant attention, but rather because of a momentary focus elsewhere. Currently it is the examination of how digital components of the US social structure exacerbate de-democratizing social inequality, jeopardizing basic values and diminishing prospects for human flourishing.

CHAPTER 1

A Material Critique of Digital Society

In a Marxist vernacular, capital should not be mistaken for an asset class that can generate income.[7] Rather, historical in nature, capital is a relation found sometimes in the exploitation of labour power, sometimes in the products they make, sometimes in private property but certainly not limited thereunto. Its sole drive is to 'valorize itself' and so accordingly, identifying capital requires indirect observations to find a 'specific social character' appearing in 'a definite social production relation' in discrete social roles. One common way to study capital and the ramifications of its reproduction is to examine the transactions and circulation of commodities. A complimentary avenue, and the one explored in this book, is to study the social structure that emanates from the uneven pace of extraction and accumulation of value, and how this is underwritten using violence greatly enabled by digital technologies. This involves analysing the legacies of how 'civilized horrors of over-work are grafted onto the barbaric horrors of slavery, serfdom' (Marx 1977, 345). In both cases, there is a concern for particular kinds of relations, ones driven by the self-expanding drive of value.

Granted, some scholars analyse capitalism strictly as a mode of economic organization, presuming it to be a natural manifestation emanating out of humans' trucking, trading, and bartering. Even setting aside this historical inaccuracy (cf. Polanyi 1957, Wolf, 2010, Graeber 2011), the preoccupation with the hard distinction between the political and the economic must necessarily wither in advance of a more insightful study of the growth of capitalism and the uneven development it creates. In the case of the capitalist mode of production, it is motivated by the dynamic interplay of capital accumulation and labour power. Furthermore, recalling one of Karl Marx's many insights, it is not the things that can be exchanged that is ultimately important, but the ability and authority to decide that they can be exchanged in the first place. The ability to make a market and extract profits demonstrates the imbalance of

---

How to cite this book chapter:
Timcke, S. 2017 *Capital, State, Empire: The New American Way of Digital Warfare.*
    Pp. 1–24. London: University of Westminster Press. DOI: https://doi.org/10.16997/
    book6.b. License: CC-BY-NC-ND 4.0

power between capitalists and labour. Again, capitalism is a particular kind of relationship. This imbalance also reveals that economics is how modern politics is conducted.

In social analysis, one misses a considerable amount if there is a general neglect of how capital sustains a particular structure of power, maintains contradictions, and aggressively conceals itself. Still, even then, the accumulation drive is not a smooth or simple expansion. The 2008 Great Recession is a good example of how setbacks and crises do occur, but this is a temporary barrier until new things are commodified, exploitation is intensified, or resources are seized and incorporated into the economy. Each of these processes allows for a new phase of expansion, much like nearly a decade after the Great Recession, the Dow Jones Industrial Average is at record highs.

At present, capitalism prevails globally despite a culturally heterogeneous world and different local politics. This is to say that whatever variety of capitalism one confronts, whatever configuration it constructs, whatever veneer it creates is just particular local contouring. Again, to reiterate a point made above, it is not the form that is ultimately important, but the relationships between forms. Therefore, despite diverse manifestations and adaptions, capitalism still nevertheless has a definable set of principles that produces a distinctive political form incumbent with its own rules and norms that applies to the organization of authority, obligation, and obedience that in turn colour public affairs, international conflict, and most importantly social relations.

One useful way to detect the corroding influence of capital on social relations is to observe social inequality. To clarify lest there be some confusion: Social inequality is not group disparity. Structural inequalities do more than distribute wealth upward to the ruling class.[8] And they do more than impose massive hardships and high hurdles on the truly disadvantaged. They curtail abilities and deprive persons of basic needs. They also generate forms of differential power, meaning that the ruling class can undertake collective violence at will thereby inducing high levels of social uncertainty and anxiety, which is dealt, almost exclusively, with a punishment regime. There is a hidden structure to violence: The technocratic language of industrial trade policy can destroy a society as effectively as bombs. Both have precision in mind when created. Both from regular use have legitimated and normalized the consequences of radical uncertainty that are to be borne almost always by persons themselves. As such: social inequality consolidates the ruling class, and shatters everyone else.

Following a series of landmarks studies of post-war America, C. Wright Mills concluded that decisive state power was in the hands of the military, economic and political elites. These groups were interconnected in a social structure where capital gave power. This power tended to concentrate; the more secretive, the more effective. In contrast to liberal pluralist explanations, this rule was not an anomaly, but business as usual (Mills 1948, 1951, 1956). Concurring, Ralph

Miliband declared, 'More than ever before men now live in the shadow of the state' (1969, 1). Therefore, this line of inquiry argued, the unbridled power of the capitalist state was a real threat to its citizens. However, contrary to Mills and Miliband, one prevailing belief during the late twentieth century was that the state was soon to be a redundant unit of analysis in political governance and international affairs. This was because multinational corporations had transcended the regulatory capacity of any one particular state, while persons sensing state decline were reinvesting in cities to open political space to achieve their desired quality and way of life.

Nevertheless, even excluding the post-9/11 unveiling of the security state it was an error to presume, like the hyper-globalists, that the state had ceased to be a viable political actor, or like the hyper-localists that the retreat to cities was an adequate political tactic. The state did not disappear in the 1990s; in fact, it was present through acts of war, genocide, and economic reconstructing. Moreover, despite the libertarian rhetoric of 'rolling back the state' there has been instead an enormous centralization of power. Whereas modern democracies sought parliamentary or congressional systems, late modern democracies are executive democracies; faith is placed in the executive to provide service delivery and to guarantee civil society. But it also means that the state commands the allocation of resources, and keeping in mind where the recession bailout money went, this underscores the fact that Mills and Miliband were correct: the state has been captured by capitalists. Centralization has also allowed executive branches to justify the accrual of instruments of rule that can be used against dissidents and rivals. Indeed, historically states have been relentless in using force to accrue resources.

Consistent with a long traditional in political theory, I consider the state to be an institution that collectivizes violence. As Theda Skocpol writes, 'any state first and fundamentally extracts resources from society and deploys these to create and support coercive and administrative organizations' (1979, 29). Elsewhere Skocpol notes how a state's system of rule has an extra-national dimension while attempting to maintain a domestic order. She writes, 'states necessarily stand at the intersections between domestic sociopolitical orders and transnational relations within which they must manoeuvre for survival and advantage in relation to other states' (1985, 8). Preserving rule requires that the state undertake the 'organization of armed forces, taxation, policing, the control of food supply, and the formation of technical personnel' (Tilly, 1975, 6). Obviously, these resources do not appear overnight. So it is important to note that states develop over time, and maintain a path dependency until circumstances or social pressure create a new institutional order. This attention to continuity and change means that is best to study state institutions in light of their long causal antecedents, paying particular attention to how the state processes social demands into policy as well as the contention over and in institutions by various interests, entrenched or otherwise.

Beyond these observations, the literature on the state tends to split. One group comprises of post-colonial and Marxian historians who demonstrate how subaltern groups and workers resist, appropriate or help construct the state, highlighting how national identities were constituted in part through imperial interests. Involved in this project is an extended analysis of how the state acquires its reality in the daily experience, oppression, and division of the working classes, and how they are put to work on imperial projects. Alternatively, orthodox comparative political sociologists are generally more concerned with how state rule is accomplished; as Skocpol summarises it, 'how states formulate and pursue their own goals' (1985, 9). Tied together, this literature offers a complimentary analysis of state formation, identity, and capitalism. As my interest in this book rests with how the US state's military apparatus secures value and relates to rule, I tend to draw upon the second set of literature, but I try to keep an eye on who happens to be the subject of state violence.

Of late, social scientists tend towards a nebulous definition of the modern state. Emblematic thereof is Schmitter, who defines the state as 'an amorphous complex of agencies with ill-defined boundaries performing a variety of not very distinctive functions' (Schmitter 1985, 33, as cited by Hay 1999, 153). This is generally at odds with conventional Marxian takes that seek to establish that the form and function of the capitalist state, serve the requirements of the capitalist mode of production, and aids the reproduction of capitalist relations. Nevertheless, beyond the general claim that the state is a nodal point in capital relations, there is some disagreement about its precise mechanics. Colin Hay groups these mechanics under the labels 'the state as the repressive arm of the bourgeoisie', 'the state as an instrument of the ruling class' and 'the state as a factor of cohesion within the social formation' (Hay, 1999). While any one of these labels may describe any particular capital-state relationship, applying more in some cases and less in others, each in their own ways gets bogged down when dealing with questions of bureaucratic agency (see Jessop 1990 for full details).

One way to avoid this gridlock is to follow Bob Jessop in understanding the state as 'a specific institutional ensemble with multiple boundaries, no institutional fixity and no pre-given formal or substantive unity' (Jessop 1990, 267). Jessop's model views the state as strategically selective, with structures and operations that while 'more open to some types of political strategy than others,' (Jessop 1990, 260) are not beholden to them. For Jessop, there is no guarantee that the state will act as the bourgeoisie's repressive agents, further the interests of the ruling class, nor constitute a particular kind of society. Hay sums up this contingent approach as 'there can be no general or fully determinate theory of the capitalist state, only theoretically informed accounts of capitalist states in their institutional, historical and strategic specificity' (1999, 171).

I am sympathetic to Jessop's argument about state actions in a capitalist society being contingent, indeterminate, and without guarantee, at least with regard to the intentions of various capitalists themselves. The state's intervention into social life is uneven. Indeed, political aspirations, cadre deployments, and local uses of the state apparatus to settle struggles make it appear as if state power and action can be wholly idiosyncratic and without an overall inherent purpose. But while conceding that the state is not a monolithic enterprise—different agencies may advance different practices and visions of state functioning—it nevertheless remains important to attend to the nature of the state to understand what produces differentials in state functioning and public authority.

In line with the call to be attentive to 'historical specificity' I place significant emphasis on the state's effort to preserve and reproduce the social structure by being strategically selective and situationally responsive. I call this intention the *security state*, the security kernel to which the 'amorphous complex of agencies' attaches to, these themselves having 'no institutional fixity' because they are situationally responsive strategic selections. In this respect, I think the question of bureaucratic agency and relative autonomy can be addressed by distinguishing between the securocrats of the security state, who have a narrow agenda to maintain their power, and bureaucrats staffing the amorphous complex of agencies, whose actions, even if they conflict, are roughly permissible provided they do not thwart the securocrats' goals. This distinction offers one possible way of reconciling 'complexity' and 'coherence' positions staked out in the various ongoing debates between state-as-society and state-in-society proponents.

There is another point worth raising: discussion of the state as an 'actor' is so taken for granted that it is worth remembering that states do not and cannot act. Therefore, mentions of state actions or the *security state* are but shorthand for the various people who staff and administer the organization. Granted there is much politics and jockeying, inside and between political parties, the federal government, the civil service, and the security forces. Brevity and focus exclude an extended treatment of this politics, however suffice to say that the Byzantine complex that presently exists seeks to maintain rule and forestall revolt. Another important point is that members of the security forces and securocrats have a central role in shaping government policy, and in each of their respective ways work toward the 'national interest'. In this way, special attention must be given to how rulers acquire their means of rule and the resources required for coercion and constraint.

Informed by Marxian analysis, this statist modality seeks to retain the view that modes of material production and political domination (overt or otherwise) are important items to study, it does not restrict itself solely to the internal affairs of national entities, but necessarily addresses the international system to account for disparate outcomes, like uneven development. Herein this mixture of material pressures and the drive to accumulate value pattern the formation and development of political and economic relations. One good way to see the connection between these items is to examine the 'economic taproot' of international affairs (Hobson 1965, 71). This means the expansionist tendency of capital via imperial action conducted by the state. 'Imperialism', John Gallagher and Ronald Robinson remind us 'is a sufficient political function of this process of integrating new regions into the expanding economy' (1953, 5), and can be accomplished in many different ways, not necessarily via direct occupation or annexation.

To reiterate a theme in my earlier remarks, empire is *not just* accumulation, nor necessarily authoritarian and draconian rule. On the contrary, it is a kind of polity. As Charles Maier remarks,

> Empire is a form of political organization in which the social elements that rule in the dominate state…create a network of allied elites in regions abroad who accept subordination in international affairs in return for the security of their position in their own administrative unit. (2006, 7)

Maier adds that empires tend to be differentiated in numerous ways, but that the political organization seeks to stabilize these differences by 'reconciling some rituals and forms of equality with the preservation of vast inequality. The empire is large enough that zones of violence and zones of pacification can usually be kept apart' (2006, 23). Further, empires are scalar:

> They replicate their hierarchical structures and their divisions at all spatial levels, macro and micro—at the level of the community and the workplace as well as the continent. Hospitals, offices and factories, shopping malls and markets, stadiums, airports and bus terminals, housing (from gated communities to urban projects), and so on all recapitulate the social structure of the whole. (Maier 2006, 10)

I take this to mean specific accumulation processes are linked to the US social structure, inequality and stratification, as well as public institutions. Imperialism also reveals itself in the systematic cooperation between capitalist states; this reflects the prevailing balance of power in the international system. Here agreements are but a means to maximize returns upon extraction at any given time, and should new methods emerge, or should the balance of power shift, so strategic selections would change. In effect, peace is less about armistice; rather, it is the stability of world order along an American imperative. This understanding of interstate cooperation as tentative, contingent, and without guarantee neatly aligns Jessop's understanding of the state.

There are few other points about imperialism worth mentioning. To begin with, the apparent absence of colonial settlement or formal viceroys does not indicate the suspension of imperial relations between the United States and the other parts of the planet.[9] Rather, the important thing is to examine the extent to which other countries cater towards the US agenda, these being shorthand for the general interests of the US ruling class.

Furthermore, an exclusive examination of formal organizations like the International Monetary Fund (IMF) or World Bank, or trade agreements like the WTO can overlook the informal set of pressures and influences that seek to extort force on other states to do the bidding, however begrudgingly, along terms established by the US. In other words, there are pressures to compel participation in these organizations and treaties to act in accordance with 'numberless indefeasible chartered freedoms'. So much like how 'free labour' refers to detachment and destruction of feudal constraints such that human labour power could be commodified and exchanged on a market,[10] 'free trade' refers to the process by which the autonomy of particular territories is compromised because they are coerced to participate in market exchanges. The stronger party sets the tone of these relations, and that strength may not necessarily be directly evident in the organizations or treaties themselves. Effectively, a constellation of security apparatuses supports the prerogatives of capital accumulation.[11]

1.1 Radical Political Economy as an Organizing Intellectual Framework

In 1999, when Dan Schiller wrote that 'the arrival of digital capitalism has involved radical social, as well as technological, changes' he was well aware of the historical forces that animate our current condition. From his vantage, 'this change does not alleviate, and indeed may increase, the volatility of the market system' (2000, xiv, 206). In 2017, I think Schiller was correct, and that we are now seeing state security forces being further integrated into everyday life to police the by-products of this market volatility. And so to echo him, I seek to demonstrate how inequality and domination are the leading features of digital capitalism.

To guide the analysis in the coming chapters, methodologically I am indebted to radical political economy. Unapologetically historical in orientation, this approach traces the plurality of trajectories open to state development, but is characterized by identifying economics as a prime mover of human affairs. This economic foundation of different institutions and their change over time is then employed to look at the forces exercised over social life. This understanding of economics neatly aligns with Jessop's remarks about the state being tentative, contingent, and without guarantee. In the interest of brevity, I shall not offer a pre-emptive defence of this method. Rather, I hope to show the benefits of this approach by being able to broadly account for outcomes of security and rule, extraction and extortion, exploitation and dispossession. The configuration and ratios between these items highlight how this occurs as rulers co-opt and make alliances with different classes and subjects, whilst concurrently seeking to create and shape certain kinds of subjects. This orientation is analytical, historical, and dialectic.

Guided by the radical political economy tradition, and moulded by events like the Gulf War and the Great Recession, I seek to synthesize much contemporary research on US security state rule whilst simultaneously contributing to a broader understanding of the dynamics of global capitalism and political power in the early twenty-first century, as well as their intersections with cultural and social developments. Examining the US security state's encroachment on civil liberties and the political scramble for positions within the digital mode of production I demonstrate how this dynamic structurally contributes to the widening social inequality currently being experienced in the US.

This exercise requires strong support, and so I turn to various branches of Marxian communication research to account for the inevitable variation caused by politics while not losing sight of the general direction of political development. This kind of project is a social history concerned with understanding the development of structures of oppression and economies of bondage. It includes and synthesizes more narrow sectarian concerns to plot them within a broader understanding of the totality of history, rather than a fetish for its parts. In that respect, there is an analytical utility to grand narratives rationally tested by known historical evidence and functional first material causes to envisage how structures and patterns unfold over time. The conceptual technique is intellectually productive for adequately understanding the origins, transformation, and prospects for social development.

Sadly, grand narratives are epistemologically unfashionable. To explain why it is important to know that in the early 1970s American social scientists, in line with domestic upheaval in social, economic, and political beliefs and institutions, found that the excessive abstraction of explications produced by functionalist sociology were nearly entirely devoid of contextual historical processes. Functionalism's implicit assumption that social systems have reached stability in the composition of institutions made it inherently difficult to deal with social change, and so was ill equipped to understand and explain the most basic features of American life in the post-Vietnam War era such as mass protest, racial inequality, urban poverty, and maladaptive political structures.

Following the collapse of structural-functionalism, American social scientists sought to import social theory from Europe and India and as well cultivating revivals of pragmatism, feminism, and communitarianism to enlarge conceptual, methodological, and political discussion. These new sources, new entrants in general, led to calls for interdisciplinary hoping that cross collaboration would help comprehend the rapid changes to social organization and civil life. Much ink was used addressing these kinds of problems within specific disciplines and produced many handbooks and sourcebooks, theoretical manifestos and programs. Boundary policing and disciplinary politics about inclusion and exclusion, canon wars, methods all played out at the level of individual appointments, search committees, and journal acceptance letters. With so much going on, it seemed hubris to claim a conceptual grasp of the whole.

Presently there seems to be a relative conceptual entente characterized by efforts to offer a diagnosis of contemporary social conditions. To be sure, much like the aforementioned American social scientists, there is some recognition that the intellectual resources at our disposal are insufficient to deal with post-recession social inequalities, looming environmental catastrophe, and systematic oppression of the poor, women, and racialized others. This inadequacy comes, in part, from the lack of intellectual synthesis and a prevailing organizing intellectual framework.

Throughout these developments, the radical political economy tradition has continued, albeit as a minor literature within the broader social sciences. Notwithstanding this relatively smaller position, most importantly, within Communication Studies it has maintained due attention to states, conflict, and imperial actions (cf. Schiller 1969 as the kernel for this research tradition). This is either through research on propaganda (Herman and Chomsky 2002), efforts to understand the general regulatory permissibility facilitating capital concentration on the American continent or abroad (Smythe, 1981, Mosco and Schiller 2001), the development of Arpanet (Feenberg 2009), the close connections between Silicon Valley, entertainment and militarism (Dyer-Witheford and de Peuter 2009, Jin 2013), or the encoded surveillance in emerging labour regimes (Cohen 2011, Neff 2012, Huws 2014). Presently, the interest in value theory and digital economies harkens back to early attempts to delineate the politics and mechanics of industrialism to assess what kinds of structural modifications might occur in the present moment as capitalism attempts to consolidate in the wake of the Great Recession (Wasko 2014, Fuchs, 2016a).

Like Christian Fuchs, I think Marxian political economics offers the best scaffolding for an intellectual agenda that seeks to understand how the various parts of society constitute a whole way of life (Fuchs and Winseck 2011, 267). Scholars within the radical political economy tradition have done much to investigate the close connections between the state, its security forces, and capital. Of course, disagreements abound as intermural debates unfold, but these debates underscore an intellectual agenda proudly 'connected to the struggle for a just society' (Fuchs and Winseck 2011, 268, cf. Greaves 2015). Elsewhere, Richard Maxwell writes that Herbert Schiller's 'ideas helped foster a distinct and robust discourse within critical media studies' which showed 'the centrality of communication in the imperial "American Century"' (2003, 1). His focus is on the North American element of international political economy where he gave central attention to the historical development of states, markets, and conflict, social and military alike. Like Schiller in *Mass Communication and American Empire*, I think there is tremendous benefit to subject foreign policy and state security actions to a methodology predicated upon 'the structural analysis of the largest governmental and corporate producers/users of information, as well as historical analysis documenting a conscious annexation of this resource by US commercial and imperial forces around the world' (Maxwell, 2003, 30).

However, unlike Schiller, I spend comparably less time examining the global resistance and challenges to these aforementioned forces. This is not because I think this resistance is unimportant, or simply because circumstances are different, but rather because in my view the best challenge to American Empire comes from the inside, from internal social movements like the Movement for Black Lives. Non-exclusionary movements like this one demonstrate how a reconstructed Marxism attentive to the legacies of bonded labour in the western hemisphere does offer a way out of the intellectual cul-de-sac of fixed difference versus false universalism. They also move past the obsessions with narrow identities, seeking instead to attend to how the multiplicity of durable forms of oppression and exploitation intersect and operate to reproduce social inequalities. Moreover, these groups are not just offer an inward gaze, but are deeply concerned with American imperial actions worldwide, and so seek to build transnational alliances, to take but one example, support Palestinians by seeking to reduce American martial support for Israel.

So while this book is not an intellectual history of the radical political economy tradition, it does use their concepts to produce an analysis of the US social structure, the coercive elements of global capitalism, and the particular role of digital technologies as coercive in themselves, as well as sites of coercion. To this end, I endorse Fuchs and Nick Dyer-Witheford when they write that 'Marxian analyses are crucial for understanding the contemporary role of the Internet and the media in society' (2012, 793). This kind of project is vital given digital technologies have enabled the militarization in all aspects of social life, even areas that were once previously beyond the reach of state violence. This creates a certain pattern of rule, both abroad and domestic. It is this pattern that I shall attempt to describe in the chapters ahead.

1.2 The Need to Jettison Idealism

Despite the aforementioned literature, one acute problem in Communication Studies more broadly is the neglect of the radical tradition and commodification, let alone the coercive components of that process. Dan Schiller laments that this tradition is the 'sideshow' in the discipline (2011, 265). This sentiment is not meant to lionize the radical, but rather to suggest that there now exists a general historiographic amnesia of the very intellectual tradition that nurtured and gave the discipline distinction. Researchers know historical facts, but are not historically minded. This amnesia is a methodological limitation that curtails empirical inquiry as well as ignores the politicized contexts in which academic questions and concepts emerge.

However, more than neglect, the absence of genuine historical sensitivity reflects a twenty-first-century idealism. I do not mean that this is a feature of this or that current of this or that theory. Nor do I mean it emanates from this particular geographic region, or that sociological stratum of researchers. I mean that this is generally the disposition of the discipline as a whole and its overall trajectory, and I mean this in metaphysical, historical, and ethical senses: conceiving of reality as confined to perceptions, then discussing, rationalising and evaluating an agent's actions in these terms is limited and partial. Granted, ideas are properties of finite embodied minds, but they are also products of historically developing social relations like widespread commodity production. A disciplinary anthropology self-confined to conveying an agent's ontology or aesthetics preferences tells us less than what we ought to know about the historical specificity of those beliefs, and the reason—often elusive to the agents themselves—why those particular beliefs exist at all.

One can see idealism manifest in the revisionist prioritising of agency or the fetish of partial sectarian standpoints and the subjective sentimental judgements which arise therefrom. It is also present in studies completely undertaken without reference to material change, or when researchers emphasize 'nuance' but miss the explicitly entrenched interests of capital. When scholars guided by this idealistic tendency confront material analysis, they often dismiss it as reductive and ethically lapsed for it is inconsistent with an agent's textured self-description. Nevertheless, a good grasp of historically grounded political economy is imperative to understand the structures that shape and situate a person's lived experience, the very forces that give self-description texture in the first place. If anything, historical materialism properly executed is anathema to reduction precisely because of the emphasis on the various particular elements that constitute totality.

This would otherwise be an academic quarrel if not for the fact that the neglecting material change invites politics to become exclusively linguistic in character. Discourse is what is fought over, such as whether one presents the appropriate sentiments or uses the permitted descriptions. This discourse is meant to be corrective to structural injustice, but ironically, politics ultimately comes to favour those skilled in the use of language by demanding an understanding of linguistic and social codes that the truly disadvantaged cannot possibly have already learnt outside of elite higher education, itself subject to numerous class barriers. Inadvertently, this politics polices the expression of lived experiences. So if language exclusively sets the terms of engagement and material evaluation is foreclosed, then there is a great distance between what is thought to be true, and what is true. Idealists can thus posture as radicals without ever expending any effort to first examine material causes that give rise to exploitation, inequalities, and oppression. As with all forms of idealism, this allows the beneficiaries of the social structure to escape criticism by being rhetorically nimble. In effect, idealism actually disrupts efforts to dismantle alienating socioeconomic conditions, and so it weakens scholarship as well as providing a poor substitute for political practice concerned with changing social relationships to the means of production. This means Bryan Palmer's adage—'Critical theory is no substitute for historical materialism; language is not life' (1990, xiv)—applies as much now, as it did at the height of the 'history wars'.

One must not infer from this brief critique of communicative idealism that I dismiss agency to follow an agenda. It is quite the contrary. Persons and their universal emancipation are ultimately the prime Marxian concern—it is the desire for humans to reach their de-alienated species-being: as the adage goes, 'from each according to their ability, to each according to their need'. Alternatively, in a contemporary register: living according to the utility-sufficiency principle persons can fulfil their capacity and flourish. This is what matters. And it is only through class struggle from below, that is coordinated actions of persons using what situated agency they have, that emancipation is possible allowing persons to 'hunt in the morning, fish in the afternoon.' Still, there is much that persons do not know, only partially aware of, mistaken about, or guided by ideological priors. This is because we live in a social structure where the imperative is to 'accumulate, accumulate!' Techniques are thus required to compensation accordingly, and this is the role of Marxian theory. 'Theory', Palmer argues,

> is the *only* way to enhance a history of lived experience, extending understanding of the past in ways that can address human activity with an appreciation of the confinements that were not necessarily perceived and fully comprehended by men and women caught within them. (1990, 94)

To make the point another way: The lived experiences and various beliefs of communication researchers influences their studies and approaches. Researchers are continually shaped by the interaction of identities and class. In my case, this work is informed by growing up in the Global South when the Berlin Wall fell. These events facilitated the end of South African Apartheid. Being from South Africa, there was an ever-present awareness of how natural resources extraction and international trade, client states and interventions, state security forces and military raids, race and class shaped biographies and social issues. Yet, until theory is used to pry open the relationships between apparently discrete areas, it is hard to understand a 'whole way of life' and the long-tail ramifications of structural injustices as various parts work together to reproduce a stratified social order. Seeking some understanding of the totality of interconnected processes requires paying close attention to 'definite social production relations.' Ultimately, it is this desire for enhancement that animates the grand narrative of several features of a historically specific social structure. But doing so first and foremost requires jettisoning reoccurring idealism.

1.3 The Labour Regimes of Digital Capitalism

One way for Communication Studies to do justice to its radical and material heritage would be to pay more attention to the coercive aspects of labour regimes that are created by a capitalist ruling class located in the United

States but which have global ramifications. Nowhere is this more visible than in 'digital capitalism'. Digital capitalism is predicated upon thin margins on vast volumes of trades to produce revenue, but also huge inequality and poor employment thereby pointing to impending conflicts over the struggle of social reproduction. As I will explain, this is because digital communication, with its low transaction costs, is both an enabler and site of global capital accumulation efforts. This mode of accumulation gathered momentum when national capitalism declined towards the end of the twentieth century as the infrastructure of money became decentralized and global, transforming not only economic sectors but whole economies. This is the key to understanding twenty-first-century labour regime changes and I will revisit the topic towards the end of Chapter 2, as well as in Chapter 5.

To deploy Mills' terms it is clear that digital entrepreneurs are the 'new men of power'. Bezos, Gates, Huffington, Omidyar, Thiel, and Zuckerberg are the leading edge of a billionaire class who have increased their wealth from less than $1 trillion in 2000 to over $7 trillion in 2015. Granted, they have different market strategies and products, but each pursues the same basic goal: they seek to induce disruptions and efficiencies with little regard for anything other than profit. Developing online platform services that profit from uncompensated digital work, this ruling class is an unaccountable centre of power notorious for absconding tax obligations, and who employ relatively few people in their companies. Structurally, the result is a rapid transfer of wealth from the many to the few.

In the meantime, it is important to note that in the digital mode of production even seemingly minor technical changes can have significant social ramifications. Consider that the pending impact of automated vehicles extends beyond job losses for professional freight drivers or satellite support sectors like independent mechanics, auto parts retail, car washes, and dealerships but also includes administrative positions in government licensing departments and insurance companies. Still, the same technology can be used for warehouses and storage facilities, further reducing the requirement for labour. This example illustrates how the digital mode of production does not level the playing field, but rather introduces and even amplifies existing social inequalities. The resultant concentration of wealth is less because of any one particular development, and more because intellectual property governs and facilitates the qualified production, distribution and exchange of commodities. In this sense, this property regime is a key site of social struggle. It has several distinct forms:

To begin, the digital market itself is a de facto rent economy; digital rights management ensures that product tampering or modification voids use, and that resale rights are limited.[12] In this sense, the relationship between the producer and the consumer is inverted; instead of production serving the interests of consumption, the interests of the consumer are subsidiary to the producer. The power dynamic in this kind of economy is central to the social costs of digital capitalism.

While on the topic of costs, digital capitalists try to carry as few as possible. For example, in the early 1990s, tax havens accounts held 'more than 20 percent of US foreign direct investment and nearly a third of the foreign profits of U.S. firms' (Hines and Rice, 1994). Now the digital economy has put this into overdrive. As Katherine Rushton reports,

> Amazon's UK operation generated £4.2bn of sales last year [2012], but it used a subsidiary in Luxembourg to help it reduce its corporation tax bill in the country to just £2.4m in 2012. According to documents filed at Companies House, the company received £2.5m in government handouts over the same period. (Rushton 2013)

Amazon replied, saying that [it] 'pays all applicable taxes in every jurisdiction that it operates within.' (see Rushton 2013). Globally, Google has a tax rate of 6.6 per cent (Mossman 2016), and their own fillings show how they 'avoided about $2 billion in worldwide income taxes in 2011 by shifting $9.8 billion in revenues into a Bermuda shell company, almost double the total from three years before' (Drucker 2012). These tax havens are no more than the commercialisation of the sovereignty of fairly fragile or welcoming minnow states; in short deliberate attempts to withhold money from redistributive exercises.

The Panama Papers describe the mechanisms and means the global ruling class use to safeguard their wealth. Given the deliberately complex arrangements, Gabriel Zucman (2015) nevertheless proposes a conservative estimate that 8 per cent of the world's financial wealth, or about $7.6 trillion in 2014, is hoarded in tax havens. This figure will likely increase as emerging economies in the Global South are looted with impunity and as the 0.01 per cent aggressively seek to conceal their wealth. As it pertains to the US Ruling Class, American companies report most of their profits in international subsidiaries that are located in low tax jurisdictions, irrespective of where the goods and services are produced. The money is periodically repatriated under tax amnesties but without significant penalty. In turn, governments overlook tax havens precisely because they are protecting corporate profitability.

A third broad source of problems is a digital divide between labour and capital. Marked by differences in marketable skills and technical competency, this divide has profound implications for class (de)composition and the labour regime. Supporting Christian Fuchs's (2014) observations above, Enda Brophy (2011, 2015) notes how emerging market economies attempt to develop technical service centres, but find themselves betrothed to the risks of capital flight. Here foreign direct investments and capital mobility create and maintain a labouring class that is just technically competent enough to do menial digital work, but hindered from developing technical expertise where they could become producers, and then competitors themselves.

The cumulative effect of ownership for accumulation requires ever-increased efficiencies of production. Initially, this process attempts to make embodied labour—that is the labour time required to make a commodity—the same as counterfactual labour, which is the labour time required necessary to make a commodity. In effect, persons are treated as if they are machines, able to be ever more efficient. However, when increased demands for profits require efficiencies beyond what the person's counterfactual labour might be able to offer there is little other option but to automate the labour process. Two options are possible: either people are left unemployed and underpaid, or subject to a labour market which has yet to account for the intervention of mechanization. This has disastrous impacts for the relative wellbeing of a society. In short, the excess desires for accumulation breaks social goods and introduces new social forms, many of which have undesirable social consequences.

Turning attention away from inequalities and towards the organization of workplaces themselves, the digital component of digital capitalism facilitates the decentralization of the workplace. This means that work occurs at several locations. While some workers may find decentralization conducive to their immediate interests, over the long run it favours the employer by far. To be clear, decentralization is not democratization. A central workplace is an amenable condition to foster labour organization thereby providing unions with an opportunity to strike and disrupt production. By contrast, decentralization means that chances of successful contention begin to diminish. Instead, encounters between organized labour and capital are replaced by individuated direct dealings, with utility and compensation determined on a case-by-case basis. Increasingly workers compete with each other because they are well aware that they are interchangeable. Again, some workers might find due reward for their ability and contribution appealing, but overall this favours the few as opposed to the many.

Contrary to narratives suggesting otherwise, digital workplaces seek to deskill their employees as a way to break the labour costs of highly-skilled employees. Deskilling has other benefits too. For one, this process favours the employer as it lessens the training cost for employees, limits the employee from starting up their own firm, but also allows worker turnover, all the while using the divided labour process to thwart workers from recognising a shared struggle. The ruling class and their agents have then spent considerable time promoting the narrative that automation, not politics, is the cause of job losses in the manufacturing sector.

In an economy with rampant deskilling, high divisions of labour, and ready supply of cheap labour, workers have few opportunities to differentiate themselves. Thus, the unique grounds for an individual worker's wage and salary bargaining are structurally undermined. In these circumstances, workers have two broad options. First, they could acquire additional skills, but often at their own expense or financed with debt. For workers undertaking affective labour, these skills are often intangible and are normally distinctive to personalities. Courses teaching affective skills have proliferated even as it is difficult to establish solid criteria because of the intangible nature of affect. Soon a dilemma arises, for as primary skill sets become narrow and sufficiently common, these intangibles become methods of distinction and inform hiring decisions.

Where labour docility and corporate sycophancy are desired attributes, hiring can be made on the basis of affective servitude, and the willingness of workers to embody the corporate 'brand', which is nothing less than the entire subordination of a person to the goals and purpose of the company as a whole, as opposed to simply being a place to work. Further, it is now an accepted norm that companies will search for a person's online profiles to assess whether they would be a suitable employee – in some cases even demanding passwords to online accounts.

Skilled workers in research and development or executive management are well paid, but they are only a fraction of Silicon Valley's workforce. Most employees are underpaid. Consider that Apple employs about 50,000 people in the US, but two-thirds of them work in retail and earn approximately $25,000, significantly less than the mean national income at near $40,000. Workers who possess skills that are in demand have some geographic mobility, either through international operations, or by deciding to work for other companies. Knowing this, a skilled worker can be enticed to stay with the company, often through stock options. However, as the case of Enron best illustrates, the downside is that the stock options are tied to the company's performance, and given the fictitious nature of this value, it can evaporate due to corruption and mismanagement by majority shareholders and senior executives.

Capitalists favour decentralization and deskilling for an additional reason: short-term contracting and a rotating labour force leave little local labour memory, and employees must heed demands to increase their productive capacities, or they are not retained for the next project. The pretence is that workers are entrepreneurial subcontractors who collaborate with firms. Nevertheless, this more resembles sharecropping insofar that there is an illusion that workers are freely choosing their life course (and sometimes they are insofar that the system allows them to do so) but these persons are still beholden to a system which has shifted the risk from capital to workers. There is also the asymmetrical information of the process that capital withholds from workers. Together, this is a designed recalibration of the burden of risk: workers carry what used to be done by capital. Simply put, decentralization has radically shifted the balance of power to employers to the extent that capitalists can push portions of risk onto the labour force and population as a whole. One major problem is that people now live in precarious circumstances characterized by highly individuated work in workplaces with little room to confront employers.

Unfortunately, most digital work itself lacks meaning, social purpose, genuine agency or discretionary judgement. The intensity to maintain productivity gains means that contemporary workplaces are mentally taxing and emotionally draining. Productivity gains mean that there could be shorter workdays, but capital seeks to maximize the exploitation of labour. Additionally, longer work hours are a means of rule, dissipating a person's energy, paired with an economic culture calculated and built upon consumptive practices meant to shore up emotions, status, and boredom (Graeber 2013).

Even the unemployed are often busy undertaking unpaid work simply for the honour thereof. Although it can be for the social good, like voluntary community service, some work is undertaken at corporations or public institutions. These kinds of jobs range from internships to research associateships at medical units and are often undertaken to hide unemployment, maintain skills or access to institutional resources, accrue professional networks, as well as maintain a personal identity and a belief of social contribution. While these may be good reasons to do the work, their circumstances are precious and marginal. Moreover, as these jobs are funded out of pocket by the unpaid worker, they are in fact subsidizing the employer for what Erik Bahre (2014) describes as 'the honour of exploitation'. This means that unpaid workers draw upon state or civic welfare, family or intergenerational wealth, or personal debt to subsidize corporations or institution. This is the near ultimate reserve army of labour; at capital's disposal and off the books.

Within professions, unpaid internships are used as class filters. Effectively, as Sarah Kendzior puts it, they transform 'personal wealth into professional credentials' (2013) all the while undermining wages. This aids differential life chances as these credentials beget other opportunities. In this framework, the rich use divide and rule tactics to create a near global labour market wherein wages are in a race to the bottom. At the bottom, forces within the state are making life harder for the unemployed by withdrawing social services or putting in place humiliating means testing (cf. de Peuter, Cohen, and Brophy 2015).

Altogether, these developments point to a totalising predicament where many people will lose their source of income then have to compete in a labour market where their skills are redundant, and in which the number of jobs are shrinking. With looming machine learning, there is little to indicate that this will change. So it is morally callous to simply tell people to work harder or longer hours, or to insist that they undertake low-wage easy-entry work, in part because this kind of work is currently hard to come by as it is. Along similar lines, as not everyone can perform difficult, high skill, high demand jobs it seems contrary to human flourishing to enrol people in meaningless make-work projects as it wastes valuable human potential and time that a person could use to enrich their life. In short, persons are exploited for their surplus until they are surplus.

A fourth point worth considering is the entanglement of the international division of labour. To better illustrate this divide, consider Apple, a company that at the end of 2016 had nearly $240 billion in savings: it clearly represents issues surrounding material and immaterial labour in digital capitalism. Marisol Sandoval writes,

> For many years Apple's products have been known as the preferred digital production technologies for the knowledge work of designers, journalists, artists and new media workers. iPhone, iPod and Co are symbols for technological progress that enables unprecedented levels of co-creation and sharing of knowledge, images and affects as well as interaction, communication, co-operation etc. At the same time during the past years Apple has become an infamous example for the existence of hard manual labour under miserable conditions along the supply chain of consumer electronics. (Sandoval 2013, 319)

Elsewhere, when describing the materiality of digital labour, Trebor Scholz says,

> It's worth remembering that whether a worker toils in an Amazon warehouse or works for crowdSPRING, her body will get tired and hungry. She'll have to take care of car payments, medical bills for her children, and student debts, not to mention saving for retirement. Digital work makes the body of the worker invisible but no less real or expendable. (Scholz cited by Carrigan 2017)

These bodies—as well as the international division of labour—are often an afterthought. Unfortunately, this is why people tend to overlook that 'the global information economy is built in part on the backs of tens of millions Chinese industrial workers' (Zhao and Duffy 2008, 229). These bodies are important components in global supply chains. Meanwhile, the management of these goods 'overlap with specific time conflicts with are inherent in worker exploitation and the associated strategies of class rule' (Hope 2016). Thus, the coordination of space and time is crucial to understand the labour regimes of digital capitalism. But the nature of digital work is the disaggregation of workflows and permits the general neglect of how labours and infrastructures combine to create these supply chains.

Nevertheless, there is a coming crisis as the Chinese working class aspires to a fairer share of profits. 'The labour force in China, the base of global electronics supply chains', Vincent Mosco writes,

> has grown restive in recent years, prompting tighter workplace controls and a redeployment of electronic manufacturing sites. It is unlikely these measures will do anything more than delay the inevitable choice between substantially raising the living standards, including the wages, working conditions and political freedom of China's workforce, or face escalating mass civil unrest. (Mosco 2016, 526, cf Sealey 2010)

Accordingly, one contributing factor in China's 'historic claims' over the South China Sea is to use nationalist sentiments to help quell and offset brewing civil unrest.

1.4 The State of Data

Gina Neff and Dawn Nafus note that 'when data mediates so many things, control over the meanings of data is a type of power' (2016, 186). With this remark in mind, I turn to briefly give attention to the digital mode of production, which Vincent Mosco illustrates by using the case of cloud computing. This mode 'involves the storage, processing, and distribution of data, applications and services for individuals and people' (Mosco, 2014, 17, also see Mosco 2016, 517). It also 'deepens and extends opportunities to eliminate jobs and restructure the workforce' (Mosco, 2014, 166), by 'increase[ing] the economic efficiency of networks by allowing them to be shared more thoroughly and effectively among many users' (Schiller, 2000, xv).

Set side by side with the decentralized and on-demand workforce, cloud computing enables aspects of 'leaner production'. Co-currently, the miniaturization and relative cheap cost of sensors means that they can be installed almost anywhere to detect almost anything, allowing distributed networks to collect a range of data. And so social life is increasingly excessively mediated through data or platforms that harness data. To be sure, as the average internet user spends nearly three hours per day on social media networks; they create consumer data for behavioural analysis. Mosco writes that 'cloud computing and big data are vital for building and managing the global supply chains necessary to sustain the complex networks of transnational capital' (Mosco 2016, 526), and if the previous section is correct, then the entangled labour regimes do not offer much hope to increase human flourishing: what freedom there will be is workers free from the ownership of property.

Despite my assessment, scholars like Viktor Mayer-Schönberger and Kenneth Cukier make the promissory proclamation that 'The world of big data, is poised to shake up everything from businesses and the sciences to healthcare, government, education, economics, the humanities, and every other aspect of society' (2013, 11) Similarly, Erik McAfee and Andrew Brynjolfsson laud this this development as a near unparalleled 'management revolution' offering more opportunities for competitive advantage and improved forecasting (2012). This practice is only going to become more common as it is now cheaper to store data than delete it.

These 'celebrants' suggest that the comprehensive scope of big data will overcome the problems of limited samples, incomplete data, and other kinds of sampling errors showing that was once thought to be idiosyncratic behaviour is a product of deeper, hidden variables. Implicit in this endeavour is the assumption that with enough sophisticated statistical tools and a large enough collection of data, signals of interest can be weeded it out from the noise in large and poorly understood social systems thereby overcoming the limits of intuitive lay accounts of causal relations thus correcting for perceptive bias.

Notwithstanding the possibilities, the big data hubris has several methodological oversights. As boyd and Crawford (2012) note, it changes not only the scale and scope of research, but also the 'objects of knowledge'. To use a mundane example, as most data analysis involves cleaning there is always a moment for subjective decision making about categorization. Furthermore, irrespective of size, big data is hardly random or representative. So big datasets are not necessarily good datasets. As Alice Marwick writes, 'Big Data is made up of "little data,"' here, 'Each piece of information, by itself, may be inconsequential. But the aggregation of this information creates a larger picture that may be more than the sum of its parts.' (2013, 2, 5) Moreover, the proprietary nature of big datasets means that there is no general epistemic community to check methodology and results.

This means one needs to understand the conditions of production of data, and this includes the potential methodological compromises or compounded sampling errors of datasets that are laced together. These limitations curtail possible statistical interpretations. So as boyd and Crawford note 'claims to objectivity and accuracy are misleading'. Irrespective of size and scale, datasets have limitations to the kinds of queries that can be run, and so have partial conclusions.

Compounding these methodological errors, Zeynep Tufekci notes that web-platforms have sampling and selection issues. These arise 'when big data sources are too few,' she writes, 'and when structural biases of these too few sources cannot be adequately explored' (2014a, 1). The design characteristics of these platforms matter, as those that design the system, design which questions to ask, and so in turn get to dictate the shape of the findings. Jaron Lanier elaborates:

> Facebook suggests not only a moral imperative to place certain information in its network, but the broad applicability of one template to compare people. In this it is distinct from Google, which encourages semistructured online activity that Google will be best at organizing after the fact. Twitter suggests that meaning will emerge from fleeting flashes of thought contextualized by who sent the thought rather than the content of the thought. In this it is distinct from Wikipedia, which suggests that flashes of thought be inserted meaningfully into a shared semantic structure. Wikipedia proposes that knowledge can be divorced from point of view. In this, it is distinct from the *Huffington Post*, were opinions fluoresce. (Lanier 2013: 188–9).

Notwithstanding the different appearances of the design of these platforms, common to all of them is a process of 'datafication'. This process is the induction of previously quantified items, and storing them for later examination or sale. Here, 'Google's augmented-reality glasses datafy the gaze. Twitter datafies stray thoughts. LinkedIn datafies professional networks.' The problem with a datafication design is that it cannot capture historical elements, meaning that researchers have a one-dimensional understanding of the present.

The value of data lies in making connections and seeing patterns in mined and aggregated data, about the relationships whatever they might be, whether as boyd and Crawford write 'about an individual, about individuals in relation to others, about groups of people, or simply about the structure of information itself.' This is the attempt to quantify and score all aspects of human performance. But in trying to measure the things that can be measured, so presuming all important job information is quantitative and not qualitative. As the adage goes, just because something is easy to measure does not mean it is important while counting the countable because they are countable is hardly an improvement. Therefore, there are epistemological category mistakes and this renders conceptually flawed interpretations of actions.

Besides epistemic errors, it is important to note that big data has class effects. To elaborate, the observational and predictive analysis of big data sets will give some an advantage to certain kinds of opportunities. What will emerge is a kind of information inequality. Thus, the principle of equality of opportunity is eroded if it is not paired with equal access information. To this extent, the enclosure and commodification of data will likely follow a similar tale to that of land; the need to do so arises from the crisis and limitations of the prevailing mode of production, and this instituted change supported by the state through law and coercion.

There is a prima facie case that new digital technologies of governance and control continue the objectives of Taylorism's scientific management by seeking to retain a monopoly of knowledge over the work process to raise productivity and reduce overheads. This management revolution is rhetorically positioned as for employee self-improvement. However, more nefariously, by employing predictive statistical analysis of performance-outcome and user-generated data the field of 'worker analytics' seeks to extend managerial control to statically capture and assess. Dedicated analytics teams are attempting to use predictive analytics to assist companies 'grow smarter'. These processes illustrate the respective efforts to optimize the exploitation of labour. This fine micro-analysis of workplace behaviour means that workers are vulnerable to dehumanization as their 'time-on-tasks' are repeatedly logged (see Huws 2016).

The hubris of a relentlessly empirical data-driven approach to the labour market, supposedly means the transformation of nearly every aspect of hiring, performance assessment, and management. Efficacy is meaningless if this practice is ethically fraught and unduly intrusive. Even so, there is a legitimate concern that this kind of approach will lead to systematic bias against whole groups of people by increasing the divergent life courses between classes, making upward social mobility even more difficult and so solidifying social stratification. Without a person's consent, their digital footprints are being sought to quantify and measure that person's employability, and hence their ability to reproduce themselves in capitalism. The proposed benefits of cost savings and increased efficiency are questionable returns for mass surveillance or when automation mistreats human interactions as problems in need of technical solutions. This is especially true given the relationships between corporate surveillance of consumers and workers, and the US government's domestic surveillance of citizens, a topic which I will address at length in Chapter 3 and Chapter 4. Altogether, these errors set up the ruling class for a gilded life.

While these developments are worrying in and of themselves, the larger purpose of this analysis is for capitalist firms to identify areas where they can automate their administrative and clerical labour, either replacing the labour regime, or using the threats of these technological interventions to suppress wages (Mosco 2016, 522). This is a continuation of the general tend to assess the labour process to see what machinery can be substituted for employees. Where once manufacturing jobs evaporated, so too is there the looming prospect of 'knowledge workers' jobs evaporating.

These cases point to some of the perennial problems of labour, which are reduced labour demand, efforts to induce labour docility, and the creation of a reserve army of labour, and an international division. Any potential labour renaissance has to work around these realities. Nevertheless, labour movements are fragmented and union membership is in decline while it is rare that emerging areas of the economy are unionized. Meanwhile, collective labour is largely defensive, seeking to hold onto provisions largely at the expense of future employees who will likely not be extended the same provisions.

Weak labour rights are unsurprising, for in a market society capital is given the lion's share of policy concern and consideration. It has also allowed capital to reinterpret labour law to shift as much of the cost of labour training onto the public purse and personal debt, all the while claiming that the profit margins are too tight for regulatory tinkering. This rhetoric is doing little more than ensuring that electorates do not push for suitable administrative oversight. This way capital can maintain control over the production process. Beyond the need of a reserve workforce, capital has always fantasised about all other labour being self-supported and ready-to-hand.

Central to these labour regimes is the state. The capitalist state maintains the rule of law and so enforces private property rights. A high functioning state is necessarily symbiotic to markets, providing the basic public goods and power supply that enable profit-seeking activity. As a contemporary example, the products that digital entrepreneurs peddle are only possible because universities or the US military supported the initial research. The utility of cellular devices that connect to the internet or rely upon GPS comes directly from US state investment, through either TCP/IP which was a DARPA project, or TRANSIT, a satellite navigation system created for the US Navy. All of the fundamental research of private commercialized digital technologies—the ones currently driving the US economy—has been paid for by the public sector. This happened via grants to universities, but also through defence procurement. To elaborate, often under the pretext of increasing security, one of the main roles of the Pentagon has been to use tax revenue to subsidize the ongoing development of advanced digital technologies until these become profitable. Using the public sector to carry the enormous costs, the ruling class has been able to sustain research into improved manufacturing of items like transistors, supercomputers, aircraft, satellites, fibre optics, all of which are then are transferred to the private sector where profits can be extracted. This is but another way in which the security state protects the interests of the ruling class.

Granted, Silicon Valley and the security state do not always neatly align, as the iPhone encryption case after the 2015 San Bernardino attack demonstrates, but such cases are anomalies. For the most part there is a tight convergence between these two clusters of interests. The convergence is evident when agencies of the security state purchase data storage services from Amazon Web Services (AWS), or when Eric Schmidt, the former chief executive officer of Google, was invited to head a newly formed Pentagon advisory board aimed at bringing Silicon Valley innovation and best practices to the US military. This development creates 'a dangerous direct connection between anti-democratic forces in the United States' (Mosco, 2016, 519).

Still, the basic facts of the organization of cloud computing specifically and the digital mode of production more generally predispose persons to surveillance. As data moves from being under personal control to being vested with remote parties it is susceptible to surveillance and analysis. This is because the nature of capitalist firms is to maximize profit-seeking ventures, even if they come at the expense of ethical norms like privacy; it is simply a part of their everyday business practices (see Mosco 2014). When there are objections to this general organization of digital production, it tends to concentrate upon cybercrime where hackers have compromised the security of these facilities in one form or another and customers have been compromised. But in an ironic twist, digital firms deflect and use these events to increase state controls over information, thus justifying the growth of the security state's investigative powers in the area. All in all, people do not know the full extent of how their audience power is commodified and how vulnerable they are to subjugation

What political resistance there is to this social structure is itself vulnerable to digital coercion because activists' 'digital repertoire of contention' and organizing is predicated upon using tools owned by the 'new men of power' or surveilled by the security state. This is particularly acute for the 'The New Civil Rights Struggles' currently underway in North America; struggles which are inflected by matters of identity and class, as well as responses to the intrusion and shaping of conceptions security and freedom through algorithmic regulation, whether by corporate entities or by the state.

Movements like #OccupyWallStreet, #BlackLivesMatter, and #StopSOPA, as well as the national security whistleblowers like Chelsea Manning and Edward Snowden, make the headlines, but they are a fraction of a great many organizations labouring against structural injustice. Despite their differences, a shared feature of these organized struggles is how their demands for a radically reformative politics is fundamentally incompatible with actually existing capitalism. A product of increasing social inequality broadly construed, these new civil rights struggles are advancing the outlines of political agenda part reformative and part revolutionary and attempts to contend stratifications solidifying in the early part of the twenty-first century. The social and political theory behind this is orientated towards the repressive dimensions of political and economic power of the capitalist state and its security auxiliaries.

Contrary to prevailing ideology, the practices and processes I have described above are persistent problems of capitalism: it makes people surplus to production without granting them the dividends of that production. As Jean and John Comaroff write,

> Capitalism flourishes as democracy is displaced by autocracy or technocracy; where industrial manufacture opens up ever more cost-efficient sites for itself; where highly flexible, extraordinarily inventive informal economies—of the kind now expanding everywhere—have long thrived; and where those performing outsourced services for the north develop cutting edge enterprises of their own, both legitimate and illicit; where new idioms of work, time, and governance take root, thus to alter planetary practices. (2012)

One cannot be neutral about capital. Nor can one be neutral about the states and security forces that maintain its imperial character. And so this is not the time for idealism.

CHAPTER 2

Extraction, Expansion and Economies of Bondage

As Barry Posen remarks, the US has 'command of the commons—command of the sea, space, and air' (2003, 7). Explaining how this came to be, this chapter provides an historical account of the relationships between the US state and capital. This is done as a prelude for a discussion of late twentieth-, early twenty-first-century military digital technological development that follows in the next chapter. In presenting this review, I want to emphasize not only the politics of labour and class formation, but also the international economy in which these reside, particularly the economy of bondage in the western hemisphere. I consider these mechanisms that facilitate dispossession. To assist in making this argument, I apply selected aspects of Marxian political economy to the American colonies and the polities that proceed them, and tackle their contradictions, both material and ideological.

An exercise of this type, spanning more than three centuries, involving multiple social and cultural influences, geographic regions, and drawing on ideas and perspectives from several disciplines, will inevitably be highly selective and thematic. So even while I do this, it is necessary to underscore that the American colonial and federal experience is not regionally homogenous. In *The Agrarian Origins of American Capitalism,* Allan Kulikoff makes this point well, saying that, 'this process was complex, multifaceted, differentiated, contested. It took centuries, not decades, to complete' (1992, 1). So this chapter hardly substitutes for a fuller and robust history of the US. Rather the intent is to overview the historical forces that create a path for uneven development in the US itself.

To be sure, sympathetic chroniclers of capitalism tend to emphasize industrialization and wage labour as a way to claim praise for the innovative yielding of mass produced goods and modern infrastructure that dramatically changed

---

How to cite this book chapter:
Timcke, S. 2017 *Capital, State, Empire: The New American Way of Digital Warfare.*
  Pp. 25–53. London: University of Westminster Press. DOI: https://doi.org/10.16997/
  book6.c. License: CC-BY-NC-ND 4.0

social life over the last 150 years or so. However, this selective retelling neglects that capitalism's wealth accumulation precedes the industrial revolution and comes with bloody hands. Capitalism, Marx notes, is intimately entwined with predatory violence. The famous passage here is,

> The discovery of gold and silver in America, the extirpation, enslavement and entombment in mines of the aboriginal population, the beginning of the conquest and looting of the East Indies, the turning of Africa into a warren for the commercial hunting of blackskins signalised the rosy dawn of the era of capitalist production. (Marx 1977, 915)

Marx is well aware of how slavery and colonialism play decisive roles in the creation of world trade and are necessary conditions for large-scale machine industry. These concerns pepper almost all of his work and can especially be seen in his attention to imperial scale administration of dispossession and expropriation, extortion and exploitation that occurs in the Americas, East and South East Asia, and Africa during the nineteenth century. Even government intervention in rural Europe indicates the extent to which the pursuit of free trade by the emerging bourgeoisie in powerful European states was predicated upon unequal exchange and unfree labour. The brutal oppression and repression of peasants, serfs, and slaves demonstrates how coercion ties together the countryside and the colonial hinterland as sites of extracting surplus value; how 'free trade' is an exploitative reign underpinned by military capability and force. And precisely because this component of capitalism is downplayed, it is vital to ensure that constraint is given due attention. But, before doing so I want to briefly review orthodox explanation for oppression and repression offered by select non-Marxist traditions. I hope that this comparison will provide a base with which to highlight the superiority of more radical approaches.

2.1 European State Formation

The theory of state formation roughly attends to the process by which a state accumulates power and grows in economic productivity using a system of rule that has coercive, administrative, and fiscal dimensions. This system of rule builds political and institutional capacities through the consolidation and expansion of bureaucracy to extend command and control capacities. Rulers use these capacities to eliminate, neutralize or disarm rivals. Here less efficient polities capitulate and succumb to those which are more efficient. In this framework, war-making leads to state consolidation, integration, and pruning of political polities, eventually converging on a basic type of polity, but whose variation hinges upon differential mixtures of coercion and capital.[13] Randall Collins provides an excellent summary of this process:

The state originates as a military organization, and expands by military conquests (e.g. Prussia) or alliances (e.g. Dutch); military costs are the biggest item in the state budget; the 'military revolution' in size and expense of troops, weapons and logistics leads to creation of administrative apparatus (bureaucracy) to extract revenues. From here on several historical pathways can be followed: resistance by aristocrats and populace to revenue burdens and administrative encroachment can lead to state breakdown and revolution, or alternatively to authoritarian restoration, or to state disintegration; what happens to states which take the latter pathways is usually a fatal geopolitical weakness that ends the independent history of that state. In the long run, the states which survive are those which successfully expand their tax extraction and administrative organization; and this penetrates into society, breaking down patrimonial households, inscribing individuals as citizen-subjects of the state, and thereby creating mobilizing conditions for modern mass politics, and for state welfare administration. (Collins 2004, 5)

Herein, the distribution of income is shaped by the way rulers extract their resources and the kinds of alliances they form with different strata of producers. However, as weapons and military planning become more complex and expensive so the production of violence will lead to the professionalization of war making. Specialization factors into the creation of a strong centralized state, as the state only has to negotiate with those who are able to contribute substantially to their coffers; the distribution of income becomes skewed as rulers ally with the richest fraction of the population; perhaps imposing a lower extraction rate for example. Thus, a highly extractive fiscal system and social inequality will prevail. Distribution becomes more unequal the smaller the number of rulers relative to a population. The ruling elite controls capital-extraction in its territory through monopolizing the means of coercion while offering protection and security to its subject-populations. On occasion, there have been organizational and technological changes that have broadened the political base of government; democratizing them, reducing inequality and the uneven distribution of income and power. In this respect, equality is the result of a particular uniform distribution of resources in relation to a specific technology of production.

Complementing the aforementioned relationship, Charles Tilly notes that around 1400 CE, European political elites used loans from merchants to hire mercenaries and expand their territory. But by the 1800s mercenary armies were no longer cost effective, their loyalty could not be guaranteed, nor could they field the same number of troops as a state with a professional army. Similarly, the strategic contribution of the cannon rearranged the state's internal distribution of power, removing it from feudal lords—leading to their demise—and concentrating it in the sovereign. City-states could only resist the power of cannon once they built wide earth-based walls that could deflect and absorb the impact of cannon shot. This particular distribution of power devastatingly combined authoritarianism, economic stagnation, and inequality into a social form.

What apparently broke this distribution of power was the industrial production of relatively cheap guns and the creation of conscripted armies. Absolutist regimes, well aware of what would happen to their power, tried to stave off nationally conscripted armies, but the military advantages offered by universal conscription allowed new technological developments to be deployed to match the changes in the scale of warfare. A concurrent development was that the cost of warfare increased, and thus more financial resources were required. To collect and administer this capital extraction, rulers had to develop administrative capacities to manage logistical support for the centralized means of coercion and finance: taxes had to levied; debts collected; investments managed and security forces paid (see Finer 1997, 98, Tilly 1990, 189–90, Tilly 1975, 73–74, Giddens 1985, 111–116). The finance to support these administrations came from taxing the wealthy, and exploiting the labour power of subject-populations. In return, some of these classes were granted limited political rights of representation, and the state had to invest in some services to keep its legitimacy; the state had to acquiesce to particular classes' political contention to retain their rule.

From approximately 1900, warfare became relatively more expensive. States therefore required additional revenue, soldiers, and labour power to conduct warfare. One option was to extract resources in the form of taxation and labour from their subject-populations. This development provided an opportunity for the working class to contend for political representation. In many cases, these contentions were successful. Thus, the advent of modern industrial war is linked with the extension of political rights (cf Levi 1997, Scheve and Stasavage 2010). But wider political representation meant that populations were more reluctant to engage in protracted wars, and this constrained the state's external violence.

From the study of state formation, Tilly classifies states according to revenue/extraction and coercion/violence spectrum. He identifies three main means of rule: coercion intensive, capital intensive and capitalized coercion (Tilly 1990, 30). Coercion intensive sees rulers use coercion to extract rents as resources are not under their direct control. Capital-intensive rule occurs when rulers have direct control of resources and can exchange them to fund war-preparation. Capitalized coercion arises when wealth is relatively evenly distributed throughout the society. In response, rulers tax subject populations or conscript their labour power. Tilly suggests that coercion-intensive and capital-intensive states tend not to need to rely upon the consent of the governed. Rulers simply need to control agents who will do their bidding. By contrast, because wealth is diffused through the population a capitalized coercion state must strike a bargain with its subjects. In return, a state enters a contract committing to obligations with subjects, and setting standards for compliance and, thus acquiring legitimacy.

The expansion of administrative apparatuses has a consequence for state politics. It prompts civilians to make claims upon these administrations and rulers. Tilly calls this 'the central paradox of European state formation' describing the process as 'the pursuit of war and military capacity…as a sort of by-product, led to a civilianisation of government and domestic politics' (Tilly 1990, 206). I understand him to mean that as rulers come to rely upon using civilian life as resources for war, so civilian populations become better positioned to bargain with rulers. Simultaneously since the administrative class could also petition rulers to provide more resources to them, they made claims themselves under the bargain of withdrawal of services. This increased the extent to which civilians decreased the asymmetrical power ratio between the state, themselves, and other functionary groups. This is known as the 'civilianization of politics' through the changing civilian constituency of politics.

The civilianization of politics represents an opportunity for civilians to constrain rulers. As civilians enter into arrangements wherein they bargain compliance, this, at once, gives them advantage in the political bargaining process. This is because as rulers demand funding for their military, so civilians can withhold these funds. As Tilly writes, 'Under these circumstances, the most a ruler can hope for is grudging consent.' Grudging consent 'depends critically on how rulers acquire the means to rule.' While resources vary over time 'the principle remains the same: Effective rule depends on the continuous production of crucial resources. If the resources dry up, rulers lose the means of enforcing whatever decisions they make and state capacity collapses.' Non-democratic regimes differ from democratic ones insofar that they gather resources through coercion as opposed to extraction. Subsequently, there is some space in democratic societies to set limits on extractive activates. Citizen-Subjects have 'substantial power to accept or reject their demands' by exercising their 'voice'. Tilly proposes that there is 'political value [in] grudging consent' because 'it means that citizens and their representatives remain properly wary about the harm that rulers may do' (all Tilly 2009, 1).

For Tilly, democracy is the 'outcomes of continuous negotiations between rulers and ruled over how resources for governance are acquired and subsequently how they are used' (2009, 3). He argues that a sustainable democracy is unlikely without a state extracting resources from a set population, for if the state does not need to extract resources, then the voice of citizens has no bearing upon how governance is conducted. Tilly writes that, 'In mature democracies, most negotiation between leaders and citizens centres on government's performance—how resources are used' (2009, 3). He proposes that it is the ruler's desire to seek control that leads them to bargain with the population. Resistance to unjustified extraction is the path towards democracy, resistance to extraction requires that rulers bargain with populations, thus promoting democratization. How rulers acquire rule provides the conditions under which the civilianization of politics may be possible. Still, by taking advantage of tensions between rulers and the ruled, there is scope to balance compliance and grudging consent such that citizens get service delivery, and the state maintains nominal control. Democratization turns on how citizens can collect to resist the excessive extraction of the state, and 'develop the breadth, equality, binding and protection of their voices' in a manner to express when the state is out of bounds (2009, 7).

While Tilly offers a rich account of the formation of modern states, he nonetheless has several shortcomings. The first set concerns a lack of sustained examination of the changes in production and their effects. For example, the rise of the factory system allowed for the mass production of armies through quickly redeploying the industrial apparatuses. The second point that he overlooks is the introduction of legal regimes that dispossess peasants and workers of their land and labour. This mode of legitimation even required citizens to be drafted to mass produce armies, thus sanctioning the use of their lives for the accumulation drives that underpin the initiation of warfare. Simplified, mass labour and mass production allow mass armies.

To illustrate some of Tilly's oversight, consider the role of Classical Political Economists in the formation of English capitalism. Adjacent to their formal economic theorems, they nevertheless advocated for policies that contradicted their stated laissez faire principles, insisting that non-market forces were needed to accelerate capitalism in rural areas. Similarly, their preoccupation with urbanization, converting peasants and other small rural producers into workers reveals how the Classical Political Economists were unwilling to let market forces shape the economy. Under the pretence of an efficient division of labour, this conversion was coercive for it saw the preoccupation for internal organization of firms and factories imposed on all aspects of life including the relationship between individual firms and households. As a result, the separation of agriculture and industry meant that people were pressed to reproduce themselves through the market.

Rigging the economy in favour of the landed gentry, then later the bourgeoisie, this state interventionalism took many forms, most notoriously in Games Laws and enclosure. Both were brutal, albeit useful instruments to separate people from long standing rights and depriving them of traditional means of support and sustenance. Intervention also appears in efforts to restrict the viability of traditional occupations. All these imposed hardships were directed to coerce people from the countryside to urban areas to undertake wage labour; it was effectively a way to keep people from being able to reproduce themselves outside a wage labour system and was paired with laws to limit resistance thereof. Once in cities, the newly urbanized were subjected to many moral and disciplinary campaigns to make them suitable for wage labour. In parallel, the legal system criminalized vagrancy, permitted debtor's prisons, and legitimated dispossession. Eventually, lacking any real alternatives, there was little choice but for people to work for subsistence wages. In describing these practices, Marx said 'The expropriation of the direct producers was accomplished by means of the most merciless barbarianism, and under the stimulus of the most infamous, the most sordid, the most petty and the most odious of passions' (1977, 928).

Even today, too often there is a general failure to appreciate the coercive bedrock of labour contracts. The presumption that through volition, economic forces will achieve naturally optimal arrangement neglects the class struggle, both 'from above' and 'from below' involved in shaping the very conception of what a 'naturally optimal arrangement' looks like and to whose interests it serves. This is because it cloaks dispossession.

In contrast to the Classical Political Economists, Karl Polanyi sought to bring attention to the actual historical experience wherein people were separated from their means of production. Famously, in *The Great Transformation* Karl Polanyi writes, '*laissez faire* was planned' (1957, 141). Part of this institutionalism that emerged in nineteenth-century Britain involved Classical Political Economists promoting the forced reconstruction of society along a 'self-regulating market economy', the result of which was colonialism, world wars and severe economic depressions. The general orientation was that the market had become the prime institution in society, subjugating other kinds of social institutions and interactions, and ideologically justified through a 'stark utopia' (1957, 3). This transformation was a qualitative change from traditional society to a market system, politically induced through the 'fictitious commodification' of 'land, labor and money', (1957, 252) using 'written records and elaborate administration' to track exchanges (1957, 48).

When reproduction almost always hinges upon the market it 'subordinate[s] the substance of society itself to the laws of the market.' This involves the institutionalization of 'scarcity' which had to be taught (1957, 216). A market society tends to ever expand the range of commodification, and is not exclusively economic, but rather a particular institutionalized kind of economy, one that rests upon power differentials and the ability to use force, that has specific social relations that spring from the commodification of property and production. In summary, not every economy is a capitalist market; not every exchange is a market exchange. Subsequently, this calls attention to understanding the institutionalization of the market system.

When human life is overly exposed to market fluctuations, well-being and survival are market-conditioned. In these conditions, suspending this kind of exchange would threaten the society itself. Polanyi had a notable hostility towards liberalism because he regarded its promotion of individualism as a misguided philosophical anthropology that neglects that humans are social creatures. He forcefully argues that the market society, rather than being the epitome of human nature, corrodes it. Accordingly, petitioning and demanding institutional security against the market system is thus rational self-preservation. Collective organizing to form a resistance movement to the market society is a matter of life or death.[14] But it spawned a concurrent resistance movement that is best encapsulated by the conceptual phrase, the 'double movement'.

While state formation literature could take a more sustained treatment of military-capital relationships, the general findings are not surprising to those familiar with Marx, who conceived of the state as a relationship between the police and management orientated internally, and militarily and diplomatic efforts orientated externally, and these processes themselves mediated by alliances and political manoeuvres with particular classes.

2.2 American State Formation

European Liberal democratization and the development of capitalism was a prolonged process with many complex and deep variables. Still, without getting too caught up in the debates seeking to pinpoint how, why, and when capitalism developed, it would nevertheless be a mistake to overlook how the profits from the slave trade factored into early industrial capital accrual. Consider, for instance, that in *The Price of Emancipation*, Nicholas Draper shows how emancipation in British colonies in August 1834 led to more than 40,000 property compensation awards totalling £20 million, currently worth around £17 billion. Similarly, Walter Johnson writes, 'the payments constituted about 40 percent of total government expenditures that year' (2013, 1). Most of this fiscal transfer went to the gentry and the ruling class, thereby demonstrating the value of slavery to the British Empire's economy, and how it provided part of the financial input for the growth of English Capitalism. This hardly an exclusive feature of English Capitalism; as C. L. R. James said, 'Negro slavery seemed the very basis of American Capitalism' (1938, 29). For this reason, Matt Karp in *This Vast Southern Empire* (2016) highlights the role of British emancipation in prompting segments of American Capitalists to advocate for an expansionist foreign policy to maintain an economy of bondage based on property rights. With these anchoring remarks in mind, in this section I cover the role of coercion, labour power, and class in American economic and political development.

For present purposes, this begins with Spanish expeditions in the early sixteenth century. With brevity in mind de Solis, de Mendoza, de Ayolas and Cortes' colonial practice in the Americas involved capturing indigenous leaders and then expropriating their wealth whereupon they established themselves as rulers taking control of existing methods of taxation, tribute and forced labour. Bartolome de las Casas' *A Short Account of the Destruction of the Indies* provides a substantial account of cruelty, dispossession and exploitation:

> To realize their long-term purpose of seizing all the available gold, the Spaniards employed their usual strategy of apportioning among themselves (or en-commending, as they have it) the towns and their inhabitants…and then, as ever, treating them as common slaves. (de las Casas cited by Acemoglu and Robinson 2012, 14)

As an example of this practice de las Casas describes how a king agreed to fill a house with gold in exchange for this freedom. The king sent his subjects to acquire gold but it was insufficient for the Spaniards. For this, under a legal pretence, they laid formal charges against the king for breaking the contract. Finding him guilty, he was sentenced to torture for 'not honoring the bargain'. De las Casas said,

> They tortured him with the strappado, put burning tallow on his belly, pinned both his legs to poles with iron hoops and his neck with another and then, with two men holding his hands, proceeded to burn the soles of his feet. From time to time, the commander would look in and repeat that they would torture him to death slowly unless he produced more gold, and this is what they did, the King eventually succumbing to the agonies they inflicted on him. (de las Casas cited by Acemoglu and Robinson 2012, 14)

De las Casas' testimony did little to alter colonial practice; instead these methods were refined. For instance, in 1569 Philip II sent Francisco De Toledo to oversee colonial extraction. As Viceroy of Peru, De Toledo instituted the forced removal of indigenous populations to towns, the co-option of Inca traditions of forced labour for mining. Other 'reforms' included the introduction of head taxes—a fixed sum payable in silver—and mandated the indigenous population to carry goods for the Spanish elite. These techniques were, Daron Acemoglu and James Robinson write,

> designed to force indigenous people's living standards down to a subsistence level and thus extract all income in excess of this for Spaniards. This was achieved by expropriating their land, forcing them to work, offering low wages for labor services, imposing high taxes, and charging high prices for goods that were not even voluntarily bought. Though these institutions generated a lot of wealth for the Spanish Crown and made the conquistadors and their descendants very rich, they also turned Latin America into the most unequal continent in the world and sapped much of its economic potential. (Acemoglu and Robinson 2012, 19)

In combination with expansion through dynastic alliance making it the leading European power in the period, this wealth funded Spain's European ambitions. This expansion compelled several conflicts, such as an eighty-year war with the

Netherlands, war with the French for Italian provinces, an undeclared war with England with the famous Spanish Armada, and later the Thirty Years' War, a devastating major European conflict. Spanish debt rose from 1.2 million ducats to 6 million between the 1530s and 1600, while dispossession in the Americas yielded a growth from 200,000 ducats to 2.2 million in the same period (Fukuyama, 2012, 359). But as Hans Koning notes,

> For all the gold and silver stolen and shipped to Spain did not make the Spanish people richer. It gave their kings an edge in the balance of power for a time, a chance to hire more mercenary solders for their wars. They ended up losing those wars anyways, and all that was left was a deadly inflation, a starving population, the rich richer, the poor poorer, and a ruined peasant class. (Koning as cited by Zinn 2003, 18)

The relative decline of Spanish hegemony provided an opportunity for the Dutch and the English to break the Iberian trade monopoly in the Atlantic and Pacific. The primary institutional instruments of this exercise were chartered companies, the Dutch East India Company, Dutch West India Company and the English East India Company respectfully. However, while some Dutch territorial footholds were established along Atlantic Africa and the Americas, often these were captured, like New Amsterdam by the English in 1644, or locals rebelled, like Brazil in 1654 (Wolf 2010, 129–130).

England was initially in the shadow of the Dutch and Spanish. As a late entrant into the colonialization of the New World, and thus missing out on the gold and silver mines and labour in South America, the English had to direct their efforts towards North America. Early English colonies at Roanoke and Jamestown could not replicate the models of violence that the Spanish used. This was because relative to South America, the population was significantly less dense in North America, and therefore fewer people to compel into forced labour. Nor was there much of a forced labour tradition in North American indigenous populations that could be grafted onto colonial rule. In addition, despite better weaponry, the colonists were outnumbered and emaciated. Still, Howard Zinn is correct to note that Jamestown was established 'inside the territory of an Indian confederacy' (2003, 13) which meant that English aggression and expansion caused skirmishes and raids that escalated into massacres on both sides. As Daron Acemoglu and James Robinson summarise, 'the underlying circumstances were just too different' (2012, 22).

As the Virginia Company could not undertake forced exploitation, nor was there gold and silver to acquire, the only remaining option was to import labour to work the land—corn for subsistence, tobacco for export—and impose 'a work regime of draconian severity for English settlers' (Acemoglu and Robinson 2012, 23). There was a redirection from exploiting the indigenous people to exploiting the colonists, but given the open frontier and options of living with the indigenous population, this was difficult to enforce at less than subsistence food rations. A new strategy was employed in 1618. It involved allowing settlers to acquire 50 acres of land and in 1619 the establishment of a General Assembly. Acemoglu and Robinson conclude, 'the only option for an economically viable colony was to create institutions that gave the colonists incentives to invest and to work hard' (2012, 26).

While this kind of explanation is fashionable in contemporary development economics, Acemoglu and Robinson's analysis skirts actually existing historical material conditions. First, their explanation ignores how the land grants occurred because English colonial governors declared that Indians had natural but not civic rights to land and so could be dispossessed. Conveniently, this meant Indians had no legal standing in colonial courts. Second, it ignores the extent to which English weapons were superior to those of Indian origin. The last error is overlooking the role of imported slave labour, which began in 1619. (By then, at least a million slaves had been imported from Africa to Portuguese and Spanish colonies in South America and the Caribbean). As Zinn remarks, 'everything in the experience of the first white settlers acted as a pressure for the enslavement of blacks' (2003, 23).

These errors are apparent when one examines labour regime change. For example, in *Tobacco and Slaves*, Alan Kulikoff's (1986) study of the seventeenth-century Chesapeake region, he analyses the transition from indentured servants of English origin to slave labour of African origin. The change in this labour regime turns upon the decline in the price of tobacco between 1620 and 1680. Mostly this decline was offset by improvements in productivity, yields, and imported slave labour, meaning that the cultivation of tobacco nevertheless remained profitable. Indeed, the indentured English servants who completed their contracts—under harsh conditions it must be said—were able to acquire land and servants themselves. These freedmen were able to become relatively rich, eventually forming their own hierarchy and family dynasties which they converted into political office and influence. The political influence of these dynasties rose so that the English consolidated their American colonies to ward off Dutch and increasingly French competition in the region.

From about 1680 onwards, tobacco profits had declined to the point where it was difficult to cover production costs. This meant fewer opportunities for newly freedmen to become landholders; the by-product of which was regional class stratification as classes simply reproduced themselves. Only when tobacco prices rose in the 1740s did prosperity return, but this was hardly comparable to the tobacco boom in the seventeenth century. Similarly, around 1700 the development of a naturally increasing population allowed for generational replacement for whites, and around 1720-1730 for blacks. A growing slave population was revolutionary and created a material basis for the development of a ruling class as the rich could invest in slaves who in turn would produce vast quantities of tobacco. As Zinn remarks, 'Slavery grew as the plantation system grew' (2003, 31).

Importing African slaves brought with it an associated set of problems: they were reluctant workers, and so owners sought coercive activities and mistreated them. While an inefficient labouring class, slaves nonetheless reduced production costs. Owners spent a considerable amount of time trying to make slaves effective and efficient, as well as creating a ruling class ideology. This was the basis of their class formation; it revolved around controlling the means of production and reproducing their capital stock. But it also involved constant fear of slave rebellions, resistance, and insurrection, particularly when aided and abetted by sympathetic whites.

Slavery was a popular method of acquiring labour power, and by the mid-eighteenth century about half of the households in the Chesapeake region owned slaves, and it was likely that the slaveowners' children would inherit slaves too. This inheritance meant that there was growing class differences between rich gentry and poor yeomen planters. The rebounding of the tobacco commodity price in the 1740s limited, but did not eliminate, social conflict between the two classes. Slavery also reduced class tensions for it cultivated a racist ideology that helped consolidate the planters as a united group even though there were two distinct class relationships. As to profitability, shortly after the American Revolution, James Madison reportedly boasted that on an upkeep cost of about $13, he would make about $260 per slave per year.

Nevertheless, there remains the question of why the colonists did not enslave the indigenous population. The absence of a forced labour tradition is not a sufficient explanation. In explaining this, some scholars suggest that African slaves were apparently more suited to intensive labour (See Wolf 2010, 203 for details). However, this explanation does not seem satisfactory, for even if one accepts the racist premise, it does not account for the costs of importing slaves. Another kind of explanation points to the proximity of the indigenous population, proposing that slavery would have increased native rebellions, but this skirts the fact that rebellions and revolts already occurred. Eric Wolf points out a more hideous calculation: that the English 'subcontracted war' and displacement to various indigenous groups, using one group to displace another in preparation for English settlement and expansion. The indigenous population were also useful assets, allies and clients for the English, Dutch, and French as they fought one another. Slavery would hinder that process. Lastly, native America groups signed treaties to return runaway slaves in exchange for guns, which then later could be used in the inter-colonial conflicts (See Wolf 2010, 203).

Throughout this political development, it is important to note how American crops were a component of a global commodity chain that brought profits to Europe. Indeed, C. L. R. James in *The Black Jacobins* cites the French socialist, Jean Jaurès's observation that 'the fortunes created at Bordeaux, at Nantes, by the slave trade gave the bourgeoisie the pride which needed liberty and contributed to human emancipation' (1989, 47). It is this historical contradiction that James set his sights on arguing about the economic importance of Caribbean colonies to early French industrial growth. Developing this line of inquiry Eric Williams' *Capitalism and Slavery* argues that the capital accumulation achieved via slavery helped British agriculture, the growth and development of banking institutions, insurance, and the initial industrial infrastructure. More recently, Sven Beckert shows how 'the growth of cotton manufacturing soon made it the center of the British economy,' becoming 'the driving commodity behind the Industrial Revolution…there was of course inventiveness and innovation in other industries, but cotton was the only one with a global scope' (2014). Accordingly, the abolition of it in the British Empire might have taken the guise of a moral cause, but it had more to do with economic rationalizations—and indeed one might add once British naval power underwrote global trade, abolition was meant to preserve British power through denying this cheap source of labour power to other European states.

The Dutch's presence having receded and the expulsion of the French following the French and Indian Wars gave Britain hegemonic control of North America. But it also meant that the British tightened control over the colonies, partly to extract colonial wealth to fund the war effort, doing so by implementing revenue generating administration like the Stamp Act of 1765. This occurred against a backdrop where American colonial trade had become vital to the British economy, growing from about £500,000 in 1700 to nearly £3 million in 1770. But these two developments meant that the British need for the American colonies was not reciprocated. With the removal of the French, there was an opportunity to act on this asymmetry.

2.3 Intra-Ruling Class Struggle and Bargained Settlement

By 1760, stable local political and social elite had formed, with imperial loyalists and nationalist factions. Nationalists wanted to redirect much of the rebellious energy towards English imperial agents, whereas the imperial loyalists wanted to suppress it. From a material vantage, the American Revolution was a fraction of the local elite seeking to capture and consolidate power from the British as well as thwart local rebellions from slave and underclass alike. The goal was to install themselves as the ruling class and thus oversee land and labour on their terms.

In the revolutionary movement, the key political battles were in the Northern Colonial cities. Artisans were relatively easy to co-opt to the cause, as they were interested in protectionism, and resented British competition. The propertyless population presented a different kind of problem, as following the French and Indian Wars many were unemployed and starving, thus prone to mob violence and property damage. Practically, this necessitated finding a means by which to bring these various classes together. Mostly it was accomplished by attributing the cause of grievances to the British, arguing that poverty was the result of imperial wars. Wary of a turn on local elites, this rhetoric deliberately skirted how unlimited property accrual caused poverty. Polemic pamphlets like Thomas Paine's *Common Sense* forged this movement, although local elites were cautious of the direct democratic impulse in the population. As a remedy, they sought to constrain it by designing a strong central government so as to project unity and common interest.

Waging the Revolutionary War proved difficult for the Colonists for several reasons. First, because in the Southern Colonies militias were required to maintain control over slaves, where depending on the region comprised anywhere between a quarter and half of the population in places. Wealthy Northerners, who owned these slaves, were less inclined to use these resources lest they lost their investments. At the time, approximately 10 per cent of the population owned about half of the wealth in the country, and owned a seventh of the population as slaves. Similarly, poorer southern colonists resisted revolutionary mobilization, because 'they saw themselves under the rule of a political elite, win or lose against the British' (Zinn 2003, 75).

Initially the militias drew from those that had property, but they had to supplement their numbers by commissioning the poor, some of whom joined hoping that military service would bring income but also yield upward social mobility. Despite the nationalist elite's stake in the successful outcome of the war, the poor did the majority of the fighting. When and where drafts took place, there were provisions where the rich could pay to get out of their service, or could provide a substitute.

The militias provided an additional benefit as a means of converting neutral or reluctant colonists into believing in the grander cause, and to paper over the continuing simmering class tensions that arose when, for instance, the wealthy hoarded commodities. Still, as Zinn remarks, 'when the sacrifices of war became more bitter, the privileges and safety of the rich became harder to accept' (2003, 74). Altogether, these conditions led to several mutinies. In response, some colonies made constitutional concessions, such as lowering property qualification franchise thresholds, but this was only to the extent that the prevailing rule remained.

A second set of difficulties emerged in the early part of the war when losses at Bunker Hill and Brooklyn Heights among others revealed the colonists lack of military power, let alone decisive power. Due to guns being unaffordable—costing at least several months wages—less than a fifth of eligible colonial citizens owned firearms. Even when the Revolution began, the Continental Army were under-armed, and this continued until Yorktown, where thousands of weapons were captured. So while the colonists did have a few minor wins, it was only when the French joined the war, providing a naval blockade limiting British supplies and reinforcements, that the colonists were able to gain momentum.

Ultimately, the nationalist's victory can be attributed to geopolitical struggles, and not the strength of the revolutionary force itself.

After the war, the prevailing nationalists redistributed land confiscated from loyalists. They mostly allocated it to themselves, making a very wealthy ruling class. That said, they did use land allocation as a tool of support, particularly with smaller farmers, as well as reducing the number of tenant farmers, who had been a political nuisance in the years before the Revolutionary War. Nevertheless, despite these land allocations, the class structure itself remained unaltered: Northern merchants easily moved into houses confiscated from the Loyalist elite. Edmund Morgan's analysis is that 'the fact that lower ranks were involved in the contest should not obscure the fact that the contest itself was generally a struggle for office and power between members of an upper class: the new against the established' (1978, 178). The aforementioned rhetoric, military service, and land redistribution were techniques to disguise social inequality and rally support for an otherwise oppressive class structure. This is not to indicate that there were no interclass conflicts in the new ruling class, but rather there was broad agreement that they had installed desirable circumstances for themselves. Through informal means if possible and formal means when necessary, the ruling classes' interests were steadily upheld.

The nation state was a popular symbol of support that could create consensus and consolidate rule for capitalists. As Zinn writes,

> the manufactures needed protective tariffs; the moneylenders wanted to stop the use of paper money to pay off debts; the land speculators wanted protection as they invaded Indian lands; slaveholders needed federal security against slave revolts and runaways; bondholders wanted a government able to raise money by nationwide taxation, to pay off those bonds (2003, 83).

This is a theme in American history, the mobilization of lower class energy for upper class politicians to advance their narrow goals, wherein the ruling class does recognize and attend to grievances only to the extent that recognising and addressing them is an effective tactic of rule, which then legitimated and upheld the belief that the political representatives were attending to social problems.

Within American cities like Boston, New York and Philadelphia, a working-class consciousness was forming. Most of it was aspirational in character as artisans sought democratization, with specific demands including a more direct, open, and inclusive process of decision making, equitable taxes, price controls, although there were some direct attacks on wealth and the right to acquire unlimited property. This is particularly acute when one examines the class rebellions that occurred from 1740 onwards. Zinn's synthesis of evidence shows that these rural rebellions were 'long lasting, social movements, highly organized...aimed at a handful of rich landlords, but with the landlords far away, they often had to direct their anger against farmers who had leased the disputed land from owners' (2003, 59). In response, mild legislative reforms were enacted, but so were penalties for contention. Again, this is indicative of another theme in American politics, where distance, social or geographic, means that protest and anger is misdirected, thus hindering the chance of broader solidarity emerging.

The Revolutionary War had terrible consequences for Indians. With the British defeated, the Americans directed their attention towards the dispossession of Indian lands. This process was often accompanied by genocidal violence, which was a continuation of the tacit policy implemented by the British. Similarly, encroachment and displacement were practices that continued. Wealthy Northerners encouraged poor Americans to push westwards into Indian Territory, hoping that their settlement would take the brunt of the Indian's reprisals. This expansion reveals a contradiction where Americans fought an anti-imperial war while simultaneously undertaking imperialist actions themselves.

By contrast, the war had mixed results for blacks. Many free blacks had fought for the British so the colonial victory meant they fled to other parts of the empire. In Northern states the practice of slavery declined, albeit slowly, from 30,000 slaves in 1810 to 1,000 in 1840. The free blacks in the North began to petition for political rights and access to public programs; some were granted, others denied. In the South however, slavery expanded as cash crop plantations grew. Cotton production figures bear this out; whereas in 1790 there were a thousand tons of cotton produced, by 1860 this had increased to a millions tons. The number of slaves quadrupled, from 500,000 to 4 million in the same period.

The outcome of the Revolutionary war cemented a foundation where blacks were either slaves or occupied a lower social status, Indians were subject to genocide, women were subordinate, the Southern property-less population remained poor, and the Northern urban working class received minimal dividends, while merchants joined the ruling land holding class. The control that the ruling class exercised on the social structure meant that formal elections were insufficient to take on entrenched interests and the social inequality it reproduced. Indeed, the purpose of the federal government was to enforce a kind of law and order that favoured those with large property holdings. Ensuing this paramountcy involved co-opting small property owners to build a broad base of support so that coercion could be kept at a minimum.

The next major political development, at least with respect to the shape of the social structure, was an inter-class struggle to define which kind of capitalism would prevail in the US. The tension in the lead up to the American Civil War was less between the working poor in the industrial North and smallhold farmers in the agrarian South than it was between expansionist Northern capitalists who sought free labour and tariffs and Southern landowners who believed these changes would undermine their prosperity. Even so, these two groups were financially interdependent upon one another. For example, Beckert shows how 'the growth of cotton manufacturing soon made it the center of the British economy,' becoming 'the driving commodity behind the Industrial Revolution…there was of course inventiveness and innovation in other industries, but cotton was the only one with a global scope' (2014). Most importantly, however, in this system slaves were not only the means of production, but functioned as financial collateral for expansion of the cotton industry, but also industrialism. The role of mortgaged bodies accounts for why slavery persisted even as the Northern workers were a more productive labouring class. Interdependency rests on revisionist historiography often initiated and undertaken by scholars like Cedric Robinson among others, who stress the deep interconnection between slavery and industrialism, that these modes of production are not only compatible, but complimentary in actually existing capitalism. Robinson calls this 'racial capitalism,' drawing attention to bonded labour and the racialized positions of those recently dispossessed through exaggerated differences that permitted targeted violence to ensure subjugation.

As an industrial scale conflict, the Civil War leaned on labour power: the working class for the Union, and slaves for the Confederacy. This is evident in the Emancipation Proclamation, issued in January 1863. Silent on slaves in the Northern-affiliated states and so contrary to idealistic revisionism, the proclamation sought to undercut the labour power of the South. (It was the subsequent Thirteenth Amendment that declared an end to slavery). Later, W. E. B. Du Bois noted how 'slaves had enormous power in their hands. Simply by stopping work they could threaten the Confederacy with starvation.' (2013, 109) And indeed this was the consequence of about 500,000, or about 1 in 5 slaves, fleeing plantations. Many joined the Union forces, swelling the ranks of the black component to 200,000 troops. Together, these developments were decisive to the Union war effort.

As like the Revolutionary War, again the wealthy like J. P. Morgan, John D. Rockefeller, Andrew Carnegie, and James Mellon could purchase military exemption. Accordingly, the disproportionate burden placed on poor white soldiers led them to resent fighting for black emancipation and capitalism, and so led to several revolts in Northern cities in 1863. Similarly, in the South, where about two thirds of the population did not own slaves, lived on subsistence wages and in squalor, there was marked social inequality with the richest families owning about half of the regional wealth. As and when Southern soldiers realized they were fighting for the rich, this weakened their morale thereby compromising their combat effectiveness.

In the immediate post-war era, overseen by occupying forces, Southern Blacks were able to elect Black representatives to state legislatures and Congress, integrate schools and became politically active. Black women, like Sojourner Truth, were active and asserted that they too required rights, otherwise they would be subordinated like slaves had been before. But while there were formal improvements in status and legal racial equality, material relations did not radically alter. For example, while some confederate land was expropriated and sold at auction most of this was beyond the reach of former slaves. Rather these auctions were a wealth transfer to Northern investors and speculators. Additionally, blacks were effectively made serfs through various 'black codes' mechanisms. These enforced unfree labour conditions reproduced black subordination.

Furthermore, Southern white oligarchy organized hate by creating the Ku Klux Klan and similar terror organizations. The function of these groups was to reduce Blacks to their pre-Civil War status. Lynching and raids, beatings and burnings were widespread and commonplace. Courts refused to support the goals of black civil rights and even permitted segregation (cf Plessy v. Ferguson, 1896). Given these conditions, some blacks went north to escape violence and poverty. Still, the North itself was not absent racism: several states had differential property qualification thresholds for franchise between blacks and whites that existed up to the Civil War, while many denied Blacks the right to vote altogether. Eventually by 1900, segregation policies and practices were legal in many Southern states. Racism functioned to similar effects in the North.

The post-war reconstruction saw a coalition of Northern Industrialists and Southern businessmen-planters emerge, of whom many were worried that the 1873 depression would lead the existing riots of farmers and working class escalating to threaten the existing economic order they headed. As Du Bois wrote 'in America in 1876 a new capitalism and a new kind of enslavement of labour'. Solidified by the 1877 compromise, this new capitalism swapped the withdrawal of occupying Union troops and political autonomy in the South for support of the Northern political agenda and land speculation. Further, as Alabama, Tennessee and Georgia had coal and iron deposits railroads were built to extract these resources. And depending on who was to be enriched, the land on which the railways were to be built was bought above or below market rates. As such, the purpose of the 1877 compromise was to manage inter-ruling class conflicts peacefully, while managing and undermining working class rebellion, while adopting policies that ensured the stability of the social structure, and thus policy changes, if any, could be anticipated, and would not create major deviations.

Between rural displacement and immigration, urbanization led to overcrowding in American cities. Compounded by economic crisis from industrialization, high food prices, slums and disease there was simmering discontent, and the white working class lashed out at blacks, and immigrants, in part, because the use of black and immigrant labour drove down the cost of labour, but also fragmented the working class. Though these conditions did spawn a radical labour movement which directly attacked the idea of private property, courts declared trade unions to be illegal restraints on trade, although these judgements were protested. And while throughout the Reconstruction Era, presidential power authorized the military to use violence to break up national strikes and marches on Washington, 1877's nationwide strikes from railway labourers signalled the extent to which the ruling class needed this compromise. Labour did organize and won victories through protracted strike action, but overall, these concessions ensured that the order itself was preserved. It also underscored for labour that they were not sufficiently powerful to defeat a capitalist state, particularly when divided by race, gender, and language. As such, the 1877 compromise indicated capital's advancement would come through the intense exploitation of white, black, Chinese, immigrant, or female labour, each rewarded and oppressed differently to create terraced segregation in the class structure. So besides women, Indians, and immigrants, the white working class were also not fully benefiting from reconstruction.

Concurrently with these politics, the Reconstruction Era saw steam and electricity displace human labour, the creation of a rail network, and telephones and typewriters increasing the speed of business. Mechanization in the agricultural sector displaced farmers to cities. Technical improvements meant the deeper coal deposits could be extracted. Businesses merged to try to impose monopolies, price cartels were established. There was an active redistribution of wealth to the rich, facilitated by state legislators and federal power. Indeed, the railway industry captured Interstate Commerce Commission, inverted its original purpose of consumer protection. This gave the impression of government supervision, but in practice it was nominal. Similarly, the Fourteenth Amendment, established to protect blacks, was interpreted to provide protection for corporations. Furthermore, the post-1877 compromise was the creation of a 'steel navy', which entailed buying steel from Carnegie at artificially inflated prices. As these examples show, corruption at all levels of government, intense exploitation of labour, and dispossession facilitated the creation of fortunes.

Reconstruction saw many working class rebellions, national strikes, industrial sabotage, and tenant struggles. The labour movement, with vital female involvement, won concessions in the late 1880s for shorter working hours and higher wages, establishing new norms for the workplace. Labour candidates did win in city mayoral elections. Guided by socialist principles, this labour insurrection was more organized in the 1880s and 1890s than the spontaneous ones in 1877. But labour fights were vicious, and the police killed members of the radical labour movement at regular intervals. Outside of urban areas and between 1860 and 1910, the US Army systematically waged war on the Indians on the Great Plains as a prelude to the railways expropriating land for their purposes. The Indians resisted this advance as well as they could given the preceding centuries of genocide. While hegemonic, capitalism's power was not total nor without resistance.

2.4 Consolidation and Collapse, Contention and Cooperation

At the beginning of the twentieth century, the consolidation of industry and the introduction of new machines by large capital investment meant that bankers controlled the American economy. But repeated financial collapses and crises meant that the rate of profit tended to fall, so capitalists sought to improve productivity through instituting Taylorist principles in the workplace, which as Harry Braverman indicated, was to make labourers interchangeable, particularly suited to immigrant labour, further divesting the division of labour in production of any trace of unique humanity. Pressures for increased productivity came at the expense of workplace safety standards. In 1904, 27,000 workers were killed on the job, continuing from the previous century's trends. In 1914, the Commission on Industrial Relations found that 35,000 workers were killed, and 700,000 injured. There was no compensation for families for these accidents.

Due to racism and union leadership, especially in the American Federation of Labour—who represented 80 per cent of unionized workers—blacks were excluded from the same labour organizing efforts, which was particularly hard as they earned about a third less than white counterparts. Leaders of the AFL were co-opted by the ruling class, and used force to coerce its own members. Du Bois in 1915 said 'the net result of all this has been to convince the American Negro that his greatest enemy is not the employer who robs him, but his fellow white working-man.' Still other union activity from radicals, like Eugen Debs and Mother Jones and others in and around the Industrial Workers of the World, kept socialist politics going, aiming beyond higher wages to seize the means of production.

Still, the 1893 depression underscored for the ruling class the overseas markets for US goods would relieve the problems of under-consumption and prevent another economic crisis that would fuel class war 'from below'. So once the North American continent was under American rule, capital needed to expand elsewhere. The 1898 Spanish-American War was just such an exercise. The event provided an opportunity to take territory from a European power and establish an economy suited to the US ruling class's interests, either as an export market for goods, or as a place to trade goods like fruit and tobacco at lower costs. Through a combination of annexation and peace treaties, the US acquired Wake Island, Puerto Rico, Hawaii, and Guam, as well as the Philippines. With Cuba, the Plait Amendment forced Cubans to subordinate their sovereignty to American military and economic interests, and so is a good example of formal indirect rule. American Prosperity depended on extracting wealth from foreign markets, and as Woodrow Wilson said, it could be accomplished either by 'righteous conquest' or by being 'battered down'. The result would be the same, 'an open door to the world.' (Wilson, various, cited by Zinn, 2003, 339)

The Spanish-American War also made the US ruling class acutely aware that capital's expansionist commodification exercises had to be securitized. As Alfred Mahan argued, these newly acquired territories had to be supported by a military infrastructure to connect markets and control the conditions of trade. So extraction, exploitation and dispossession required not only the predominance of economic strength, the co-opting of local authorities, but coercion to ensure that these practices continued on American terms. So much like how the state security forces had been used to subordinate the American working class, thereby catering to the interests of domestic free trade, so too was the same logic applied to foreign trade.

The advanced capitalist countries in Europe were feeling similar pressures. The decline of British hegemony stoked competition for control of territory between advanced capitalist states, causing a resource acquisition race in peripheral regions. Du Bois was very perceptive when he observed that the First World War was over Africa. Much like how the British had to colonize North America because it was what remained, so too was the war about late industrial powers seeking sites of extraction for their own colonial system; Africa offered much in terms of raw resources, cheap labour, and unexplored regions. Du Bois also noted how colonial expansion, dispossession and exploitation was a means of preserving rule and quelling social unrest by appeasing the working class. Improved standards of living came from exploiting and repressing 'the darker nations of the world-Asia and Africa, South and Central America, the West Indies, and the islands of the South Seas'. This surgically removed the radical spirit of a working-class consciousness.

Formally, Woodrow Wilson sought to keep the US neutral, but there was commercial advantage in selling military supplies to the British. Indeed, it was imperative to do so given a recession in 1914 as growing industrial unemployment posed a political problem. From 1915 to early 1917, the US sold goods worth $2 billion to the Allies. This industrial policy bound war and prosperity together, but it also signalled a draconian approach to radical labour organizing. For instance, the Espionage Act (1917) was employed to quell dissent, while the radical newspapers and magazines were barred from using mail services. Furthermore, the state undertook mass arrests of union leadership under the pretence that radical labour was undermining the war effort. Irrespective of whether this was true, the greater function was to remove sustained organized opposition to the ruling class.

A similar pattern occurred in the Second World War. Initially the US sought to profit off the conflict by selling weapons to the Allies and Soviets; their involvement in the conflict occurred primarily because their economic interests were threatened. In line with this explanation, and as the Atlantic Charter illustrates, American involvement in the conflict occurred because the US saw it as an opportunity to exercise some control and influence over the postwar international order. Indeed, this was an economic necessity as the Second

World War saw the rapid decline of British hegemony and the rapid rise of the USSR, a state itself concerned with imperial ambitions. Lastly, both wars were an opportunity to repress class struggle 'from below'.

Returning to the pre-war period, one major development was that women won the right to vote in 1920, but were divided along the existing party lines. Concurrently the decade saw unemployment decrease and general wages increase. Nevertheless, these positives papered over deeper systemic problems, like for example, prosperity concentrated at the top echelons of society or mass opinion controlled by large-scale publishing houses. With Andrew Mellon as the Secretary of the Treasury under Harding, Coolidge, and Hoover, the top income tax bracket fell from 73 per cent in 1920 to 25 per cent in 1928, with capitalist newspapers cheerleading these politics.

Triggered by the stock market crash of 1929, The Great Depression revealed the problems in the social structure, which included extremely high levels of social inequality and economic misinformation. However, the biggest contributing factor was capitalism itself with its monistic drive for profit at the expense of all other things. Mass unemployment followed as industries cut back on production, farms turned to dust, and tenants evicted. Government inaction contributed to Franklin D. Roosevelt winning the 1932 election. His administration enacted the New Deal and other legislative reforms to reorganize capitalism to induce stability thereby removing the conditions for spontaneous rebellions and general strikes by the working class and avert a revolution. Although an incomplete appraisal of this development, Paul Krugman nevertheless offers a good starting point for this particular discussion. In *The Conscience of a Liberal*, he contends that Capitalists have waged a prolonged and deep campaign to re-capture the state and to reclaim the economic wealth that had been 'taken from them' by Roosevelt's New Deal. At the time, the centrality of the market had produced a 'vast inequality in wealth and power, in which a nominally democratic political system failed to represent the economic interests of the majority.' The public policy interventions offered by the New Deal and subsequently the Great Society programs attempted to overturn this wealth distribution. For the most part, it was successful. Krugman writes that the richest 0.1 per cent 'owned more than 20 percent of the nation's wealth in 1929 but only around 10 percent in the mid-1950s;' and he calls this 'the Great Compression of income inequality' (2007).

Notably, the New Deal 'invigorated the economy' through assisting the working class. Redistribution combined with war production created a 'great boom in wages' that 'lifted tens of millions of Americans...from urban slums and rural poverty to a life of home ownership and unprecedented comfort.' So high was material prosperity that Peter Gomes wrote of 'an era of unprecedented economic growth and prosperity, where more people have more faith in the chairman of the Federal Reserve Bank than in the president of the United States' (2000, xvi). Roosevelt Era Progressives were also in the business of fending off socialism by removing the conditions that made their cause appealing. So appealing was this that in 1910 Victor Berger was the first Socialist Party member elected to Congressional office, and where soon after the Socialist Party were able to make an inroad into municipal government, having 73 major elected officials in 1911. Capitalism remained intact after the New Deal; the rich still maintained the commanding heights. What appears to be the increase of democratization, through for example, reforms to decentralize power at the municipal and state level was but a way to install a slate of big business surrogates that were able to impose a consensus.

The Progressive Period was one of begrudging reform, to quiet protest not making structural changes. Capital sought to co-opt labour and thus dissipate the revolutionary energy in order to maintain the long-term stability of the social structure. This involved providing workers with compensation and accident insurance, better occupational health and safety, often through state legislation, although the Supreme Court said these kinds of laws were an unconstitutional deprivation of corporate property without due process. This reveals a fracture in the ruling class between those who wanted to maximize immediate yields and reformists, who sought long-term stability even if it meant giving up short-term profits. Emblematic of the reformist position was Harry Truman's Baylor speech where he tried (unsuccessfully) to argue for the creation of the International Trade Organization (ITO), which while removing US domestic economic protections and tariffs, would yield greater access to new markets, facilitating capital accumulation. This cleavage represents the prevailing split in the ruling class, the kind that developed in the twentieth century, and their intermural disputes over the perverse calculus measuring the tolerance for exploitation and extraction.

Despite the failure to create the International Trade Organization, the reformists were able to somewhat quell the blunter and more brutal edges of capital labour relations. Nevertheless, as C. Wright Mills' *New Men of Power* (1948), *White Collar* (1951), and *The Power Elite* (1956) collectively show, Postwar American society was organized around elitism, political apathy, technocracy, and oligarchy. In these books Mills describes the social structure of the United States, where organized labour leadership traded the advancement of their self-interest for representing their declining members against industrial transformations, an expanding professional class sought to secure their social and occupational status by embracing consumerism, and an overlapping elite where democratic mechanisms barely blunted their desires and position.

As Tilly might argue American mass prosperity in the post-war period was a result of social contention based primarily on the payback from labour power for wartime military service. Even then, mass prosperity was white, male, and geographically concentrated in major American centres. People outside of that bracket did not really receive the dividends of growth, all of which underscores how capital co-opted this segment of society to reproduce the social structure.

Still, due to protracted struggle, Civil Rights legislation was introduced to counter structural racial prejudice, and involved removing barriers for blacks to higher education, forced desegregation of schools and universities. Further helped by The Higher Education Act of 1965—a needs-based federal financial aid—Black enrolments increased, and these students took the energy and power of the Civil Rights Movement into the classroom. Beside counter-cultural forces and radicalism by students who did not have to work and had lots of free time to organize, there was a dynamism on US campuses.

2.5 Neoliberalism and the Great Recession

Dissatisfied with the repercussions of the New Deal and the Great Society, and concerned with their relative decline of power, the libertarian faction of the US ruling class rallied, investing in the post-Eisenhower Republican Party. Rationally exploiting sentiments in American politics, they sought to appear anti-establishment, and built a broader coalition to mobilize religious and cultural commitments to their advantage, albeit with internment success in the immediate post-war era. Still, they sought to frame the Civil Rights, feminist and counter-cultural movements as threats to the established social structure. Indicative of this view is Samuel Huntington. Commissioned by the Trilateral Commission for a report, his assessment was that 'the 1960s witnessed a dramatic renewal of the democratic spirit in American.' Huntington characterized 'the predominant treads of that decade involved the challenging of the authority of established political, social, and economic institutions' including 'a pervasive criticism of those who possessed or were even thought to possess excessive power or wealth.' (1975, 59–60). As Huntington portrays it, social services mandated by items like civil rights increased 'governmental debt from $336 billion in 1960 to $557 billion in 1971' creating 'inflationary tendencies'. Similarly, unionization of governmental employees was a problem as governmental officials were tasked to 'avoid imposing higher taxes to pay for the higher wages' (Huntington 1975, 103). Huntington leaves out how many of these governmental employees were black, for they were aided by justifiable affirmative action that was absent from the private sector. The main problem, however was an 'excess of democracy'; the solution was rule via expertise (1975, 113). He concludes his assessment with a revealing fatal conceit:

> The vulnerability of democratic government in the United States thus comes not primarily from external threats, though such threats are real, nor from internal subversion from the left or the right, although both possibilities could exist, but rather from the internal dynamics of democracy itself in a highly educated, mobilized, and participant society. (Huntington 1975, 115).

These remarks reveal the extent to which the ruling class see an informed and active democratic citizenry as a threat to their social positions. Thus, from their vantage point it is in their interest to weaken the education system more generally through underfunding and to cultivate political apathy wherever possible.

The libertarian wing had the best opportunity in the early 1970s. The cumulative effect of military defeat in Vietnam, economic stagnation, Nixon's decoupling the dollar from the gold standard, as well as the oil crisis in response to the 1973 Yom Kippur War along with several other factors, underscored the need for the ruling class to reassert its control over the social structure. Waging a long campaign—Jane Mayer's *Dark Money* (2016) provides a case study of the Koch family, one node in this general turn—and test-running economic policies in Latin America (see Peck 2010, Harvey 2007), Reagan's election was the defining moment for the reactionaries. This was because supply side economics gained presidential affirmation. Krugman writes that supply side economics 'claimed without evidence that tax cuts would pay for themselves', but without much support from 'professional economic research'. In their implementation, this economic thought has wrought considerable damage and harm, mostly by diminishing the prospects for Americans for economic progress. By contrast, 'if gains in productivity had been evenly shared across the work force, the typical worker's income would be about 35 percent higher now [2007] than it was in the early seventies'. Increasing social inequality is a telling indicator of class struggle 'from above'.

Emblematic of the tone of the era, Charles Peters's *A Neoliberal's Manifesto* (1982) described a movement that 'no longer automatically favours unions and big government or oppose the military and big business.' Presented as a revolutionary project that rejected the politics of economic redistribution, this movement implemented a kind of public policy where the first impulse was always to let social issues be addressed by market driven solutions, by for instance the privatization of public goods. Herein neoliberalism can be understood as a method of statecraft, one that certainly advances and caters to the interests of the US capitalist ruling class, but perhaps most importantly redirects public contention from specific and known rulers to abstract and impersonal markets (see Krippner, 2011).

Throughout, these general developments severely weakened organized labour's position and jobs were outsourced to other parts of the world. The ramification was to suppress uneducated wage labour. If the working class hoped that the election of Bill Clinton was to reverse these actions, they were sorely disappointed as his administration declared the 'end of big government'. Throughout this period, the productivity of graduates greatly increased, the result of which was that middle-class prosperity without a degree evaporated as social inequality accelerated. As wages for uneducated labour declined, entry into the higher echelons of the workforce was predicated upon receiving a university degree—the cost of which is more than the mean yearly income—university enrolments increased throughout the 1990s and 2000s. Good portions of these admissions were by blacks and Hispanics, who, because of structural injustice, were more likely to require Pell Grants. The point is that debt bondage dramatically increased, thereby conditioning citizens to adopt an instrumental rationality in order to escape potential bankruptcy. This ideology has little scope—or time—for contemplative dissent. Accordingly, it well serves the ruling class.

Turning to the efficacy of the campaign, Krugman cites figures that show that in the 1920s, the top decile of income earners hoarded 43.6 of total income, with the top one per cent hoarding 17.3 per cent. In 2010, after forty years of prolonged political manoeuvre, the top decile hoarded 44.3 per cent, while the top one per cent hoarded 17.4 per cent. In this fashion, it is a kind of rent seeking and the arbitrary inequality comparable to that of the *ancien régime*. In this respect, the reactionary movement is a revolutionary force, for it does not intend to conserve or protect any particular institutions or values aside from those that serve wealth.

These issues were leveraged to justify constructing a right-leaning economy. The purported economic goal of this project was to insulate wealth from redistributive exercises, thereafter using re-regulatory efforts to implement a 'trickle-up' economic arrangement that divert the yield of economic growth and advantages to designated population groups. Here, re-regulatory denotes not the removal of stale policy and laws, but rather the attempt to change the regulatory framework to make it more favourable to the ruling class. Deregulation is simply a rhetorical move that seeks to diminish concerns over the rise of a new regulatory apparatus. In part this was to lift restrictions on capital, but also to promote the capacity for flexible accumulation, that being the easier entry and exit of capital to assist in attaining higher returns on investments. Essentially, technocrat state officials and other agents of the ruling class used macroeconomic policy sought to increase rates of return on financial assets, but in doing so eroded the bargaining power of the American working class.

Explanations for the success of the reactionary movement either tend to prioritize economic issues over social conservatism, or stress the role played by evangelicals in electoral politics, or point to the manipulation of widespread racism. While there is something to these explanations, partisan advocates thereof primarily err by mischaracterising the central ideological axis upon which the conservative imagination rotates. This rotation concerns the belief that domination and hierarchy is just. The willingness to dominate others unites social and economic conservatives, as well as racists. It is accepted because domination is a required characteristic to ensure accumulation continues unabated. To bring several aforementioned observations together: education is prohibitively expensive, and so in addition to existing class barriers and filters already safeguarding access thereunto, debt bondage is a technique of indirect rule, the aim of which was to hollow out radicalism thereby inducing supplication of the professional class, whose support is vital given the marginalization of general labour. The backlash from general labour remained mystified, and re-directed to minorities to aid in dividing those who otherwise share an interest in emancipation.

Libertarians' concerted push back has changed the American intellectual landscape, particularly liberal thought. In their political retreat from New Deal and Great Society social programs liberals have conceded, perhaps even capitulated to, the general political terrain to the libertarian agenda. Exemplary of this trend is the career of John Rawls. A *Theory of Justice* (1971) is primarily concerned with economic questions: the legitimacy of allocation, the moral imperative of redistribution, and welfare are all efforts that require attention to the consequences of property relations, the control of production, and assumptions informing distribution. Drawing upon Keynes, who argued that a private property-based market tended to be unstable due to high unemployment, Rawls and fellow liberals came to doubt that it was an adequate foundation for a stable, free society. Instead, their prevailing belief was that private property crippled the working classes, rendered them bonded to the economic system, created inequalities further alienating people from their liberty and thereby hindered persons from selecting their own ends.

However, in the face of criticism, some legitimate, much less so, Rawls's critics pulled American political philosophy towards the management of apparently intractable differences in culture, language, and religion. Administrative concerns displaced critical elements. Co-currently, difference increasingly referred to identity, not social inequalities, while the encumbered debates over the priority of the right over the good obscured the right to goods. For wealthy cultural elites—left neoliberals—issues in personal aesthetics became problems to study, the result of which was to convert private belief and practice into matters of public politics, all the while ensuring that class became at best a subsidiary concern in the high strata of US intellectual politics. In short, the emancipatory necessity of understanding objective social relations was replaced by the reactionary urgency to mobilize subjective concerns.

Still, this is not to give post-war twentieth-century American liberal thought a pass. One major problem with robust welfare state liberalism is that is often preserves the class forces that seek to stop it from existing. From the vantage of radical critique, not only does the liberal state provide insufficient freedom, it is unstable and unable to maintain the affordances it does offer. Even then, it is too susceptible to the pull of capitalist ideology. Here. By this, I mean that by being receptive to the ideas that preserve incumbent interest, liberalism offers a radical diagnosis but incremental change.

Incrementalism is present in Ben Bernanke and Mark Carney's respective recession assessments. In May 2013 they gave speeches conceding that the presumed 'end of monetary policy history', a focus on macroeconomic stability above all else, contributed to the financial instability that caused the Great

Recession (Bernanke, 2013, Carney, 2013).[15] Employment, output, the exchange rate, credit and assert prices were, for example, considered only in relation to this bearing and filled under 'constrained discretion'. The downside was that generally legislators, policy-makers, and central bank technocrats failed to link liquid capital flows and financial imbalances in many advanced economies.

Initially the 2008 crisis was treated as a limited event. Most explanations and analysis concentrated on micro factors such as rogue financial actors, shadow banking enterprises, or the nature of markets themselves.[16] But when 'Echoes of the Great Depression', were observed, Carney writes, this:

> motivated a swift and aggressive response. Major central banks provided hundreds of billions of dollars in extraordinary liquidity through a combination of repo facilities, standing facilities, securities lending and reciprocal swap agreements. (2013, 9)

These measures sought 'to provide the stimulus to support activity and price stability. The links between price and financial stability were increasingly evident.' The collapse necessitated that,

> In the fall of 2008, in response to the rapidly deteriorating conditions in global financial markets, a weakening U.S. economy, and an abrupt drop in commodity prices, G-10 central banks, including the Bank of Canada, conducted an exceptional, coordinated interest rate cut of 50 basis points. (Carney 2013, 8)

The need for coordinated action like the move away from inflation targeting to financial stability and expanding the role of central banks highlights how interconnected the economic system is. Now central bankers have been tasked to play a supervisory role, 'it conceptualizes and carries out both its regulatory and supervisory role and its responsibility to foster stability.' Carney describes this as the need to 'complete the contract' with a public at large (2013, 18).

When attempting to stabilize the post-Recession economy the US and Canadian central banks focused on monitoring and evaluation exercises with regulatory policy and practices to detect the financial vulnerabilities that exist in deeply connected and systematically important financial systems. These central banks also sought to understand how shadow banking, asset markets, and the non-financial sector contributed to the collapse. Overall, Bernanke and Carney agreed that better research and hypothetical stress tests could lead to better management when these circumstances reoccur.

Notwithstanding these aspirations, the US Reserve Bank has to work with indirect legislative frameworks such as the Dodd-Frank Act, which are statuary designed to fail. For instance, the United States Government Accountability Office suggests that Financial Stability Oversight Council mission is 'inherently challenging'. This is because:

Although the Dodd-Frank Act created FSOC to provide for a more comprehensive view of threats to U.S. financial stability, it left most of the fragmented and complex arrangement of independent Federal and State regulators that existed prior to the Dodd-Frank Act in place and generally preserved their statutory responsibilities. As a result, FSOC's effectiveness hinges to a large extent on collaboration among its many members, almost all of whom come from state and federal agencies with their own specific statutory missions. (US Government Accountability Office 2012, 8)

Perhaps for this reason, Carney observes that 'Globally, central banks are now being simultaneously accused of being ineffective and too powerful' (2013, 3). Accordingly, Bernanke and Carney suggest the need for a reconceptualization of the practice of the reserve banks. Still, inflation targeting maintains rentier income at the expense of employment policies. This is not so much irrational exuberance as structural entrenchment.

Given the technical cloaking of these issues, Dean Barker is correct to note, 'the public and even experienced progressive political figures are not well informed about the key policies responsible for this upward redistribution, even though they are not exactly secrets.' (2011, 1). So these ameliorative, preventative, predictive, and re-conceptual approaches outlined above are likely to be ineffective at averting capitalist economic crises as they lack a broader historical understanding of capitalism itself and the indirect and invisible coercive mechanisms that support the reproduction of its expansionist tendencies. 'It may be', Ellen Meiksins Wood said twenty years ago, 'that we are seeing the first real effects of capitalism as a comprehensive system. We are seeing the consequences of capitalism as a system not only without effective rivals but also with no real escape routes. Capitalism is living alone with its own internal contradictions' (1997, 558). Ominous and unsettling, Wood's words speak to the wider setting of US militarization, a topic I directly discuss in the next chapter.

CHAPTER 3

Calculation, Computation, and Conflict

During the First World War, massive artillery barrages caused the majority of causalities on the Western Front; indeed, many more soldiers were killed by falling debris than small arms fire (cf. Middlebrook 1971).[17] This was partly due to the stable fronts that in turn compelled a change in military doctrine, and so whereas artillery had once primarily supported infantry manoeuvres, in stalemate warfare they became paramount elements in controlling battles. One American observer wrote that,

> the artillery has now reached such a position of importance that successful attack or defense is impossible without it…Infantry officers do not hesitate to say that infantry should not leave its trenches until the artillery preparation has really smashed all targets…also, the infantry can advance only so far as their artillery can escort them with fire. (cited by Grotelueschen 2001, 5)

As the Allied adage went, 'artillery conquers, infantry occupies'.

This new doctrine quickly depleted Britain's stock of shells and caused political scandal in 1915. In response, David Lloyd George was appointed as the Minster of Munitions, but nevertheless the Asquith administration fell in 1916, replaced by one headed by Lloyd George himself (see Adams 1978). One task of his government was to better plan the strategic production and distribution of these shells. Britain would go on to produce nearly 260 million shells through the course of the war, underscoring the importance of artillery dominance.[18] Once having arrived at the Western Front via rail lines the shells were distributed to gun crews and a different kind of calculability took over. Tactically the first gun in the battery would fire; forward observers would report the landing and gun crews would recalibrate; the process was repeated until the guns zeroed in on the target. To increase effectiveness, engineers and signal

---

How to cite this book chapter:
Timcke, S. 2017 *Capital, State, Empire: The New American Way of Digital Warfare.*
  Pp. 55–76. London: University of Westminster Press. DOI: https://doi.org/10.16997/book6.d. License: CC-BY-NC-ND 4.0

corps installed telegraph or telephone lines for forward observers, but these lines were often cut off by enemy artillery fire and would need to be repaired or replaced – a task made hazardous by enemy snipers and rifle fire.

When the communication infrastructure was intact, the staff at the artillery headquarters had to calculate targeting using variables like distance, elevation, charge, weather, height differences, and the distances between enemy and friendly troops. Ordinarily it took anywhere from 15 minutes to 1 hour to coordinate artillery strikes: after the initial call for artillery from the front line commander the signal went to the staff headquarters to calculate the trajectory and who then relayed the information to artillery commanders. If any branch of the established command was out of contact, it was difficult to get artillery fire approved. Delayed and poor communication or incomplete geographic and weather information could risk friendly fire incidents. Similarly, because of the slow turnaround times front line commanders could not seize opportunities as they might occupy ground set to be bombarded by their own side. So poor communication of calculations reduced operational effectiveness.

After the war, there were several country specific approaches to this problem. Common was the allocation of mortars to infantry units for line of sight operations, where teams could make accuracy corrections themselves, lessening their reliance on divisional command. The German and Soviet armies also developed short-range line of sight guns to support infantry units. Germany combined precision airpower with armour, and trained their officers to operate without divisional oversight to radically exploit battlefield opportunities. France expanded their staff and added long-range cannons to divisional artillery units, but this proved unable to respond to rapid moving fronts in 1940. Conversely, the British standardized their artillery and added mechanical calculation machines to allow artillery staff to calculate ballistics faster. The British also sought to decentralize artillery command by providing radios to forward observers to shorten the command structure.

While the US was a late entrant into the war, the American Expeditionary Force's (AEF) frustration with trench warfare left a strong impression within the US military. Whereas the AEF observed, adopted and incorporated elements of European artillery doctrine, their officers, especially General John Pershing, believed that this mode of warfare was 'based upon the cautious advance of infantry with prescribed objectives, where obstacles had been destroyed and resistance largely broken by artillery.' This over-reliance on artillery produced a conservative infantry subject to 'psychological effects' that lacked the ability to create a decisive offensive. Drawing upon established American military thought and practice in Mexico and the Indian Wars under Manifest Destiny, and the conditions on the Western Front, Pershing advocated for aggressive infantry manoeuvres assisted by artillery to rout, pursue, and destroy enemies. He called this 'open warfare', the purpose of which was 'to bring about a decision the [enemy] army must be driven from the trenches and the fighting carried out into the open' and 'an aggressive offensive based on self-reliant infantry.' (Pershing as cited by Grotelueschen 2001, chapter 1).

Upon review of their combat performance, the US undertook several research and development programs to make military power more effective. One initiative was to continue to develop armour, but as these weapons had to manoeuvre under battlefield conditions there were limits to the calibre of guns that could be mounted on chassis. Another initiative installed automated analogue computation equipment on battleships so that the rates of accurate fire could be increased (see Mindell 2002, chapter 2), however the operational conditions of land warfare differed from those at sea, so this solution was not easily transferable. One notable difference to other military reconfigurations was that the US miniaturized radios to the point that they could be carried and operated by a single person. Radios were deployed at the company level, so field officers and NCOs could order artillery support, making them more self-reliant. To make this system more effective, the US pre-calculated ballistics data for any given scenario. This effort involved a small army of mathematicians and technical staff aided by the ENIAC computer. Additionally, throughout the 1930s the US Department of Defense (DoD) undertook a programme to land survey parts of Europe to make extremely detailed and accurate maps. Altogether, this meant that US artillery was able to respond quickly to calls for support than other military peers.

This brief overview of the development of early twentieth-century artillery warfare is indicative of several key initial developments in computational warfare in late capitalism: the general characteristics are the increase in scope and scale of coordinated calculability between the strategic and tactical level. Building upon these insights, in this chapter I advance a working conjecture that the development and expansion of detection and the tracking media facilitates the social reorganization of coercive power that can in turn increase social stratification.

3.1 Cold War Social Science

The marriage of radio, surveying, and calculability was very successful for the US military in the Second World War. In the post-war period, the US sought to replicate the success of this kind of mapping and calculability of populations in the ramp up to the Cold War. To counter a rising USSR, the US required constant technological and intellectual innovation to compete and foster economic growth. One method to achieve this objective was to use universities as the foundational research and development arm for blue-sky military and corporate imperatives. The US government and subsidized industry investments in academia sought to create a stock of exploitable ideas as components for strategic competitive advantage. Perceiving the character of this problem requires setting aside the objectified private agendas of various stakeholders, and instead seeing higher education as part of public and economic policy about knowledge production to support imperial rule.

Roger Meiners (1995) points out 'By 1950 over $150 million a year was being spent by at least fourteen federal agencies, [while] over two-thirds of all budgeted university research came from federal money.' Meiners continues,

> Much of the initial funding for social sciences research came through the Department of Defense. The Office of Naval Research sponsored research in the fields of human relations, manpower, psychophysiology, and personnel and training. The Air Force, through the RAND Corporation and the Human Resources Research Institute, sponsored studies on topics such as group motivation and morale, role conflict, leadership, and social structure in the military community.

The initial post-war boom in veteran students aided this research agenda as over one million extra students enrolled in 1947. Meiners (1995) notes that in 1946, total university enrolment stood at 2.6 million students, double that from 1938, while from 1956 to 1966, federal spending increased by near $3 billion (Brock 2010). Using the Servicemen's Readjustment Act of 1944, the US subsidized about 2.2 million military personnel though higher education, many of who would not have been able to attend otherwise (Olson, 1973). Costing around $5.5 billion, this seemingly egalitarian public policy was designed to create a staff for the Cold War industrial enterprise.

Within this broader transformation of American social science, one notable initiative was the US funding of the Bureau of Applied Social Research (BASR) at Columbia University. For example, Elihu Katz and Paul Lazersfeld attempted to understand the behavioural influence of mediated messages in mass print and broadcast communication to better influence target populations, irrespective of whether those populations were domestic or abroad (see Pooley 2008). Presuming quantitative survey methods to be more rigorous than other kinds of social inquiry, Katz and Lazersfeld began refining public opinion research programs, and importing techniques from actuarial statistics to test difference messages to detect whether the composition of content registered different efforts or not.

In a similar vein, Daniel Lerner's *The Passing of Traditional Society* underscored the belief held by many US media researchers in the early Cold War that mass media could induce social transformations. Informed by his wartime occupation as a propaganda analyst in the Psychological Warfare Division (Shah 2011), Lerner's book was the product of an another notable BASR project, which had been funded by the US State Department to assess the effectiveness of Voice of America in influencing public opinion in the Middle East. Lerner advances a psychosocial theory of modernization wherein groups moved 'from farms to flats, from fields to factories' (1958 47). Urbanization would be a catalyst for the development of modern institutions, paramount of which was a market system. When combined with high rates of literacy and contemporary media consumption, Lerner proposed that this would create 'empathy', an effect where behavior becomes associated with Western beliefs and values. This geopolitical theory, while being less rooted in European colonial assumptions about racial attributes than pre-war social theorists, still nevertheless maintains sufficient residual trace elements of racial superiority of the American variety, albeit coded in the language of cultural adaptability.

3.2 The Strategic Return to Centres of Calculation

While telling about the goals of the US, Katz and Lazersfeld's as well as Lerner's programs do not match the scale of the US Army's Human Terrain System (HTS). Initialled in 2006 and costing $725 million until discontinued in 2014, HTS was the most expensive social science programme ever undertaken. (Most of these funds went to two defence contractors, BAE Systems and CGI Federal). Conceived at the US Army's Training and Doctrine Command (TRADOC), then headed by General David Petraeus, the programme embedded social scientists in combat brigades both to ensure better sociocultural understanding of the populations under occupation as well as to address institutional racism in the US Army.[19] Together this social scientific 'soft power' was meant to aid counter-insurgency operations. Numbering more than 500 personal at one stage, five person HTS teams were embedded collecting data, gathering information and undertaking psychological operations (See Nigh 2012, *Human Terrain Team Handbook* 2008). To outsiders these teams presented less lethal options to manage occupation, and fitted into the population centric counter-insurgency doctrine TRADOC was developing.[20] Eventually 30 Human Terrain Teams were deployed in Iraq and Afghanistan, however many personnel had inadequate language skills or lacked local cultural knowledge. Moreover, the programme was beset by accusations of institutional racism, ignoring sexual harassment, and of participating in interrogations (Varder Brook 2013). These problems might have been tolerated had the programme been an operational success, but brigade commanders found the HTS teams ineffective (Clinton et al. 2010).

Post-surge, as the US Army reduced troops in Iraq and Afghanistan, the HTS programme sought to retain relevancy by repurposing themselves to be able to gather information about local populations in areas where the US Army anticipated conducting operations. But this redirection was not met with much enthusiasm as the US Army faced budget cuts and so the programme ceased being funded. Roberto Gonzalez (2015) argues that another contributing factor was HTS's close connection with Petraeus, who lost power after he was dismissed as the Director of the CIA following the Petraeus-Broadwell scandal. Still, the decline of counter-insurgency operations and Petraeus's scandal are secondary reasons for the cancelation. Rather cancellation represents, as Gonzalez writes, 'the broad shift in Pentagon priorities, away from cultural intelligence and towards geospatial intelligence' (2015). Notwithstanding the long association between anthropology and the intelligence community documented by David Price (2008, 2016), as one critical geographer writes, 'It's algorithms, not anthropology, that are the real social science scandal in late-modern war' (Belcher 2013, 63). These priorities return intelligence collection to the strategic centre of calculation and to the various agencies of the state. The proceeding sections are case studies of drone warfare and mass surveillance and are used to analyse the ramifications of covert computation.

3.3 Automated Lethal Robotics

All branches of the US military are researching or seeking to develop robotic instruments of war. The US Navy is attempting to build armed submarines and helicopters such as the Fire Scout. At the time of writing, the US Marines are testing Gladiators, small tracked vehicles armed with machine guns that are intended to operate in front of advancing troops, while the Army uses Packbots to assist in bomb detection and detonation. Using funds provided by the Defense Advanced Research Projects Agency (DARPA), several companies are iteratively making hominoid-esque robots like Boston Dynamics' Atlas. Biomimicry extends to pack animals such as the BigDog and drones that look like birds (McDuffee 2013). Suffice to say that even if the military budget were to shrink, these kinds of robotic systems are deemed crucial pieces of future military capacity, force, and planning. To examine this trend, I use the case of drones. Here I follow Derek Gregory (2011) and understand these technologies as part of a 'scopic regime', by which he means to draw attention to the specific techno-culture manner of employing sensors and optics to display and coordinate warfare.

First used for tactical reconnaissance, drones have become a near indispensable battlefield technology with offensive capabilities. From 2002, when a couple of strikes targeted Salim Sinan al-Harethi and Nek Mohammad—with an estimated High Value Target to Total Deaths ratio (HVT:TD) of 1:5—the offensive use of drones escalated from 2005 onwards. Eventually, between 2009 and 2010, there were 161 strikes, killing 1,029 persons with a HVT:TD ratio of 1:147, suggesting indiscriminate targeting (Hudson, Owens, and Flannes 2011). And still, Gen former director of the NSA and CIA, General Michael Hayden, has said that 'Our tolerance for collateral damage is far too low.'

The most recent phase of the drone program is characterized by an increase in attack frequency, sanctioning targets of opportunity, and likely larger payloads exacerbating civilian deaths. From 2011, the Obama administration announced plans to begin an aggressive new drone-warfare campaign in Yemen directed against al-Qaeda in the Arabian Peninsula, Somalia (Mazzetti 2011), as well as providing drone support to foreign nations such as Uganda and Burundi in addition to anti-piracy operations in the Indian Ocean (Turse 2011). Due to the multiple areas of operation, state secrecy, and absent reports, it is difficult to estimate the number of casualties drones have created.

Drone warfare has been marked by so-called 'signature strikes'. Daniel Klaidman describes signature strikes as 'targeting of groups of men who bear certain signatures, or defining characteristics associated with terrorist activity, but whose identities aren't known', (2012) and Greg Miller describes them as 'surgical, often lethal, and narrowly tailored to fit clearly defined U.S. interests.' This is particularly distressing when the US military is testing software that will program drones to automatically hunt, identify and engage targets without a human pulling the trigger. (Finn 2011). Combined with revelations about NSA mass surveillance there is little to inspire confidence that future signature strikes will not automatically scrape big data gathered through data mining.

The Obama administration overruled the use of signature strikes, preferring instead Terrorist Attack Disruption Strikes (TADS). However, as Miller reports, TADS are aimed at 'wiping out a layer of lower-ranking operatives through strikes that can be justified because of threats they pose to the mix of U.S. Embassy workers, military trainers, intelligence operatives and contractors scattered across Yemen.' But by that definition, it seems that TADS and signature strikes are practically one and the same (Miller 2012). And if anything, one can infer from Miller's report that the US has inserted trainers, operatives and contractors into Yemen in an effort to erode the threat presented by AQAP (al-Qaeda in the Arabian Peninsula) (but itself likely inducing blowback).

The American public is told that extrajudicial casualties from drones are primarily militants but these claims remain unsubstantiated and under investigated even as strikes have become routine (Sokol 2010). The Brookings Institute estimates that 10 civilians are killed for every militant. It seems the official line is similar to that provided in the Vietnam War; 'anybody dead was considered a VC.' This method is used in areas as widespread as from Northern Mali on the Islamic Maghreb and the Philippines's Abu Sayyaf and Jemaah Islamiyah (Oumar 2012, Ahmed, 2012). The lack of judicial oversight, superseding legal constraints, extra-judicial killings, massive collateral damage, secret 'kill lists', and the uncertainty caused by the lack of transparency and accountability leaves little information for a proper public debate. The Obama administration claims they follow strict internal reviews to prevent abuses, but there is no way to verify these claims. What has happened is the installation of an undemocratic and illiberal self-regulating centralized authority yielding lethal force. Therefore, the intellectually responsible position is to be suspect of this politically centralized bombing.

The US state claims that greater transparency, while desirable, must be weighed against revealing the sources and methods of the intelligence community, and the 'requirement of non-acknowledgement'. The former reason seeks to preserve a tactical edge over enemies, but this does not explain why representatives or the judiciary cannot provide oversight. The later reason indicates cooperation with other countries whereupon operational involvement is unacknowledged, and official credit of tactical successes are taken by the host country. Here the Yemen, Philippines, and Mali governments insist they carry out strikes to preserve their sovereignty, even while lacking the capability to do so (Booth and Black 2010). However, by not acknowledging external involvement, this is withholding crucial information from their citizens.

Given the states in which they are used, drones destabilize already frail political systems by inflaming social volatility and isolating populations from political elites and governance structures that are seen as powerless to stop this terror (Crilly 2011). In Pakistan, for instance, the CIA wants the drone campaign to continue unabated, whereas the State Department argues that the drones risk destabilizing a nuclear power (Entous, Gorman, and Rosenberg 2011). As it has been conducted, drone warfare seems strategically misguided, lacks decisiveness and incurs significant political and diplomatic costs. Target populations live in constant terror of being attacked. And non-combatants' deaths and feelings of asymmetrical vulnerability, even if they are not ideologically sympathetic to local combatants, create incentives for the target population to retaliate against convenient targets. Altogether, drone warfare, rather than bringing stability has simply compounded violence and instability. But it appears as if this cost is acceptable because it gives an under-informed public the impression that potential conflicts and attacks are being averted.

In 2011, the United States operated approximately 60 drone bases planet wide (Turse 2011, Whitlock and Miller 2011), and the Obama administration planned for more bases in Japan, South Korea, and Niger. Similarly, in the first half of 2013, the US Navy on separate occasions successfully launched and landed an automated X-47B drone from an aircraft carrier and its software is being tested for inflight refuelling. These developments can increase surveillance and reconnaissance capabilities, but to see them as isolated or minor events is to miss the point that they are a key part of a constantly expanding project of global surveillance, one that involves a complex labour process. To elaborate upon the last point, Gregory cites figures that 185 persons required to support one Predator drone flight (2011, 194). So military labour power is still required to man 'unmanned' weapons systems.

Despite requiring good operating conditions (Turse 2012), and being easy to target necessitating deployment to safer operating areas, proponents promote drone warfare as more precise and discriminating, hence more militarily effective and even ethically obligatory (cf. Strawer 2012). They cite additional benefits such as payload variability for weapons and surveillance, as well as their long range and extended flight times all at a relatively low production and operating cost, compared to manned aircraft (basic models cost $4.5 million). Proponents further suggest that the moral questioning of this mode of warfare is factually incorrect, confused, or misguided. For instance, Peter Beaumont does not distinguish between which weapon has caused injury and death (Beaumont, 2012). He argues that the central question is whether a weapon system is used in line with prevailing international conventions and norms:

> In conflict, within the existing framework of international humanitarian law, whether an attack is justifiable and legal is defined both by the nature of the target and proper consideration of whether there will be civilian casualties and whether they are avoidable. (2012)

Therefore, Beaumont concludes, 'the notion of drone warfare [is] not more horrible than a Tomahawk cruise missile fired from a distant ship or a bomb dropped indiscriminately on a village by a high-flying F-22 or MiG.' By inference, what matters is the existence of a targeted killing programme, not the instrument. Moreover, an excessive focus on the instruments blurs the key issue, which is the willingness to use deadly force to further imperial aspirations. The right question to ask of drone warfare, Beaumont thinks, is whether

> as a military tool, drone warfare is actually effective; whether its use is justified when set against the political fallout that the drone campaign has produced and whether drones have actually reduced the threat posed by militants.

This subjective utilitarian view of military tools is not an engagement with morality and ethics, but simply a political calculation regarding technology use where drones are just another tool to apply lethal force. In this respect, Joseph Singh, a researcher at the Center for a New American Security sees no qualitative difference between drones and piloted aircraft in terms of the application of lethal force. He writes, 'any state otherwise deterred from using force abroad will not significantly increase its power projection on account of acquiring drones' (Singh 2012). Other commentators present the false choice between national insecurity and assassinations as if there were no better ways to achieve security and peace. Another kind of discussion that takes place is the presumption that Drones are a moral imperative. 'You can far more easily limit collateral damage with a drone', former Secretary of Defense Robert Gates declared in 2013, 'than you can with a bomb, even a precision-guided munition, off an airplane.' (Gates cited by Wolf and Zenko, 2016) But this is a falsehood. Using the publicly available data, Amelia Mae Wolf and Micah Zenko (2016) compared airstrikes and drone strikes, finding that 'drone strikes in non-battlefield settings — Pakistan, Yemen, and Somalia — result in 35 times more civilian fatalities than airstrikes by manned weapons systems in conventional battlefields, such as Iraq, Syria, and Afghanistan.' The ground truth reveals the equivocation of these bulk moral arguments.

Opponents of drone warfare, like Michael Ignatieff, suggest that drone proliferation has changed the nature of warfare (2012). In a passage worth citing at length, he writes

> In his essay 'Reflections on War and Death' French philosopher Jean-Jacques Rousseau "asks the reader what he would do if without leaving Paris he could kill, with great profit to himself, an old mandarin in Peking by a mere act of his will. Rousseau implies that he would not give much for the life of the dignitary." Imagine if great numbers could so exercise their will. What violence would be unleashed, how many prostrate bodies around the globe who never knew what hit them? (Igantieff 2012)

The passage remarks that the ease of killing without consequence lowers the threshold for public acquiescence to conflict. Reduced-risk operations lessen political aversion to commission attacks in official and unofficial conflict areas. This enables conditions where strikes become more frequent and militaries less prudent in their use of force relative to the industrial mode of war. This, in turn, contributes to and exacerbates existing conditions (such as political repression and famine in the case of Yemen, sectarian turf wars in the case of Pakistan, or a failed state in the case of Somalia) thereby producing more enemies. The deception is that 'these new technologies promise harm without consequence', but Ignatieff says, 'there is no such thing.' Gregory provides a harrowing aphorism 'The death of distance enables death from a distance' (2012, 192). Proponents of drone warfare miss the point that distance—physically and psychologically—is an ethical matter.

In the final analysis, it appears as if foreign drone strikes serve two functions. The first is to engender domestic political satisfaction amongst an otherwise blasé public; the second is that the greater part of the Middle East is a laboratory for operational testing in advance of future conflicts. Not to put too fine a point on it, the military adventurism in the Middle East is, in part, a technological proving ground for the other aspects of the New American Way of War. The apparent ease of operational deployment means that missions can be run with minimal accountability; hence, military force is more aggressive and less discriminating. This is important to consider given that military technological pathways are prone to becoming locked in by the market in one way or another. There is little to suggest that effects from the efforts to robotize the battlefield will be any different.

The current research agenda for drone includes automated lethality and the capacity to operate from aircraft carriers as the development of X-47B Unmanned Combat Air System demonstrates. To date, there has not been sufficient attention to the kind of battlespaces, the kinds of weapon systems that could (and will be) deployed, nor the vanishing boundary between domestic surveillance and battlefield technology deployments by combat systems like the X-47B. Absent too is a discussion of the extent to which the domestic deployment of drones as surveillance systems in combination with the de facto handheld computing devices acting as tracking devices, and how this might erode liberties of all kinds. Another key area to see this domestic and foreign line being erased is in the aforementioned cyber warfare.

To end this section, it is worth bearing in mind that while my discussion of automated robotics warfare has focused on drones, their use on the ground is as significant. The US Army (2017) has a Robotic and Autonomous Systems Strategy that describes how 'Unmanned Ground Systems' can complement existing military labour by improving soldiers' situational awareness and improve firepower. The mid-term goals of are to 'Increase situational awareness with advanced, smaller RAS and swarming; Lighten the load with exoskeleton capabilities; Improve sustainment with fully automated convoy operations; Improve maneuver with unmanned combat vehicles and advanced payloads' (2017, 7). That most of these robotics are conceptually to attuned to operate with 'increased congestion in dense urban environments' (2017, 1), it is telling about the US militaries thoughts about the nature of future combat operations and kill chains.

3.4 Extrajudicial Drone Strikes

Vincent Mosco describes drone warfare as 'a global system combing electronic surveillance and algorithmic decision making'. (2017, 2) As he correctly notes, the development of automated lethality and the deployment of drones cannot be disentangled from extrajudicial signature strikes in non-declared war zones that often result in significant civilian casualties. To begin, while periodically frowned upon, US Presidential sanctioned assassination was a common tactic throughout the twentieth century—Eisenhower on Lumumba, Kennedy on Castro, and Johnson in Vietnam—it has now come out of the shadows and been used to gain political capital and electoral clout. To justify this development, the Obama administration has written legal opinions, but which it claims must be necessarily secretive. What details have been made available are limited; President Obama has attempted to reassure citizens that drone targets must pose 'a continuing and imminent threat to the American people'. The White House maintains that 'lethal force must only be used to prevent or stop attacks against U.S. persons, and even then, only when capture is not feasible and no other reasonable alternatives exist to address the threat effectively' (White House, 2013). This carefully worded criterion does not differentiate between an American citizen and an enemy combatant. When questioned by Senator Rand Paul whether the president could authorize a targeted attack against a US citizen in the United States, Attorney General Holder replied that there could be:

an extraordinary circumstance in which it would be necessary and appropriate under the Constitution and applicable laws of the United States for the president to authorize the military to use lethal force within the territory of the United States.

This reasoning implies that domestic drone strikes on American citizens are permissible in certain conditions. Moreover, it is indicative of the state mentality which has sought to expand mass surveillance through legal contortion which little resemble International norms for governance, transparency, and accountability and which likely make John Yoo proud. Peter Van Buren puts it brilliantly:

> Prior to [al-Awlaki's] killing, attorneys for his father tried to persuade a U.S. District Court to issue an injunction preventing the government from killing him in Yemen. A judge dismissed the case, ruling that the father did not have "standing" to sue and that government officials themselves were immune from lawsuits for actions carried out as part of their official duties.
>
> This was the first time a father had sought to sue the U.S. government to prevent it from killing a son without trial. The judge did call the suit "unique and extraordinary," but ultimately passed on getting involved. He wrote instead that it was up to the elected branches of government, not the courts, to determine if the United States has the authority to extrajudicially murder its own citizens.
>
> The extrajudicial killing of an American citizen seemed to [the judge] to be nothing but a political question to be argued out in Congress and the White House, not something intimately woven into the founding documents of our nation. (Van Buren 2014)

Equally worrying, is then Attorney General Eric Holder's 2012 interpretation of the Fifth Amendment, where he said,

> that a careful and thorough executive branch review of the facts in a case amounts to 'due process' and that the Constitution's Fifth Amendment protection against depriving a citizen of his or her life without due process of law does not mandate a 'judicial process.'

Effectively, the standards for due process—which supposedly curb the abuses and excesses of the state—are determined by the state itself, without judicial oversight. As we shall see in the following section, these actions cannot be disconnected from Holder's extensive use of the Espionage Act to prosecute whistleblowers (see Carr 2012), nor his prosecutors from seizing records from journalists (see Bronner, Savage, and Shane 2013).

3.5 The Order of the Internet of Things

The US's attempt to weaponize communication has long been a part of postwar politics and has shaped the rule that the state imposes order. During the Cold War, for example, J. Edgar Hoover's Federal Bureau of Investigation (FBI) deployed counter-intelligence programs to disrupt civil rights activists and the peace movement. Agents collected information on targeted individuals (up to half a million citizens) to discredit them. Pressured by the outrage following revelations about the scope and centralization of this intelligence gathering, the House and Senate Intelligence Committees became permanent features of Congress, and in 1976, Attorney General Edward Levi established guidelines to limit federal investigative powers. But this oversight and curtailing of power was less motivated by the revelations themselves, but rather because Hoover's FBI turned their powers inwards to the ruling class, transgressing the order of things.

The limitation on investigative power was temporary, and beginning in Reagan's first term many suspended techniques were reauthorized in one form or another. This continued irrespective of which party controlled the various branches of power. For example, during the Clinton administration, the Communications Assistance for Law Enforcement Act (1994) required telecommunications companies to make their designs accessible via backdoors to law enforcement surveillance. Following the Oklahoma City Bombing the Antiterrorism and Effective Death Penalty Act (1996) expanded this program authorising targeted surveillance based not upon investigating acts, but their associations. The response to 9/11 near completely remove all barriers to full-scale total state organized data collection and created a funding boom as the newly established Department of Homeland Security sought to coordinate and install a digital surveillance apparatus. The Patriot Act (2001) allowed state agencies to visit public events and collect information on persons and organizations, even those that did not appear to have criminal intent.

The basic contours of the mature state security institution begun to be revealed in a few years after 9/11. In October 2004, *New York Times* investigative reporters James Risen and Eric Lichtblau discovered the NSA's domestic warrantless surveillance programme. When asked for comment, the Bush administration pressured the *New York Times* to hold the story, claiming national security. Bill Keller, then executive editor, decided again publishing. It was only after learning that Risen planned to publish the article in a book—*State of War*—that the newspaper published the story in December 2005. From Risen's reports, the decision involved deliberations that included Arthur Sulzberger Jnr talking with President Bush in the Oval Office. Subsequently, Risen and Lichtblau's reporting was awarded a Pulitzer Prize, but the expansion of the security state continued unabated. I now turn to provide a brief overview of that development.

While the NSA has a long history of information gathering, after 9/11 the agency greatly expanded by building facilities in Georgia, Texas, Alaska,

Washington, and Utah, in addition to directing more resources to overseas stations. The agency's goal is to pre-emptively monitor and identify any individual's 'communications fingerprints'. Currently with a budget of $10.8 billion per year and 35,000 workers, the NSA is a security leviathan. It undertakes mass surveillance for the White House, Pentagon, FBI and CIA, but also the Departments of State, Energy, Homeland Security, Commerce, and the United States Trade Representative. But despite extensive service for these departments, there is a near total invisibility of these activities to the public, and is the inverse of the NSA's extensive efforts and ambitions 'to answer questions about threatening activities that others mean to keep hidden' (NSA 2007).

The department's intelligence programs include Social Network Analysis Collaboration Knowledge Services, which attempt to register social organization hierarchies; Dishfire collects and stores text messages; Tracfin records credit card transactions; Orlandocard installs skyware on personal devices. These programs illustrate how surveillance has moved beyond the mandate for a military advantage to encompass a survey of the general population, home or abroad. Public records and third party record compliance from banks, social media sites, and GPS location information can augment these profiles (Risen and Poitras 2013a). Concern about these activities is downplayed as just 'metadata'; still, even if just metadata, it is still very revealing as basic data analysis can be used to infer a person's associates, build behavioural patterns, or predict actions. Indeed, General Michael Hayden, former director of the NSA and CIA, has said, 'We kill people based on metadata' (cited by Cole, 2014, 1). This does not bode well given automated lethality discussed above. As such, US mass surveillance has established new norms that other states do and will follow, in effect making all traffic, private and public, on the internet fair game. Intrusive surveillance of this sort directly creates conditions where citizens can easily be subjugated—the Snowden files show this is not an abstract threat.

An internal NSA strategy policy document (2012) reveals that the agency views its mission as 'dramatically increas[ing] mastery of the global network' and acquiring communication data the agency deems of strategic value from 'anyone, anytime, anywhere'. Former NSA Director General Keith Alexander's motto 'collect it all' best captures this directive (Greenwald 2014, 95). To do so the agency has petitioned for legal and policy accommodations and adaptions, undertaken liberal interpretation of existing laws, or disregarded them altogether to pursue their objective. They have even spied on the standardization bodies that set particular encryption specification. This aggressive surveillance has been rebuked by Judges in the Foreign Intelligence Surveillance Court (FICA), even while the court has authorized these programs. This is a secret legal process, so citizens are unaware of the extent to which they were subject to surveillance and their rights compromised. Nevertheless, all these actions are justified by appealing to the demands of the information age:

The interpretation and guidelines for applying our authorities, and in some cases the authorities themselves, have not kept pace with the complexity of the technology and target environments, or the operational expectations levied on the N.S.A.'s mission. (NSA 2012)

Still, the NSA has bragged about operating in 'the golden age of Sigint' (NSA 2012, 2). Similar to the Pentagon's Human Terrain System—a militarized anthropology whose ostensible purpose consists of a computerized system of statistical demographic information on occupied populations with the aim of providing actionable military intelligence—so too do NSA projects seek to profile populations. One project, Mainway, in August 2011 was collecting data from nearly 2 billion phone records per day. From what little is publically known, this project used Section 702 of the 2008 FISA Amendments act to force American service providers to give data on Americans' calls to foreign nations. The 2013 NSA budget requested funds to increase data collection capacities to record 20 billion events per day as well as a system that can integrate different data streams within the hour to create bulk data, then to share that data for more effective analysis (Risen and Poitras 2013a). Little else is known because FICA proceedings and rulings are classified.

To build upon this point, under current law, aspects of the NSA's data-mining practice is legally binding (cf. Smith *v.* Maryland 1979 and Patriot Act 2001) and is understood by the NSA to apply 'without regard to the nationality or location of the communicants' (as reported by Risen and Poitras 2013a). But prima facie this scope presents a serious attack on free speech and liberty. As Josh Levy crisply observes, 'The chilling of free speech isn't just a consequence of surveillance. It's also a motive' (Levy 2013). The constant threat of direct monitoring with privacy being de facto non-existent, and the affective anxiety caused by it, is anathema to liberty. Authoritarians claim these measures are for public safety, but in practice, surveillance is internally directed to preserve the regime, not to ward off external threats. Such social conditions fracture civic life as it is impossible to trust others. In addition, the prospect using evidence acquired without due process, or trumped up evidence, in an attempt to forestall protest. The point is not whether this or that administration will or will not act in this way, but rather that the infrastructure is in place with the implicit latent rationale that it ought to be used; the state establishes an infrastructure that it 'won't control', rather than 'can't control'. These conditions are primed for institutional abuse.

When these items are discussed in public, the US state opportunistically mobilized a rhetoric of national security interests, cyber warfare and preventative security to exploit public fears of terrorism to install ever more monitoring devices to justify mission creep and security drift. Human rights language is also co-opted to justify security. But this is an inversion of what has actually happened, as since launching the Global War on Terror, the US has pushed aside legal safeguards that protected civil liberties, subordinating them to the interests of the state. This has happened without public disclosure, nor robust and informed debate about the desirability and consequences of these goals and methods. This is near obvious when examining the proportionality of policy actions that what is taking place is systematic pervasive surveillance. Arguably, contemporary surveillance is more pervasive than under most authoritarian and totalitarian regimes of the recent past. As Heidi Boghosian, notes 'corporations and our government now conduct surveillance and militaristic counterintelligence operations not just on foreign countries but also on law-abiding U.S. citizens working to improve society', and whole 'lives are subjected to monitoring, infiltration, and disruption once they are seen as a threat to corporate profits and government policies' (2013, 21). Indeed, the NSA has been collecting information in anticipation of discrediting dissidents, but this collection fails to meet the standard of probable cause.

It would be unwise to underplay the danger and significance of this emerging capability to expand the range and kind of harm, and the implications for national and international security (for an extended treatment of this issue see Kello 2013), too much that remains unknown about technological volatility and defence complications that could lead to strategic instability. Emblematically, there is tremendous confusion over Stuxnet, the first publicly disclosed cyber weapon. Due to a lack of information about the weapon itself, there are many unanswered questions about who deployed it, and the extent of sabotage done to the Natanz uranium-enrichment plant and the IR-1 centrifuge control system (Langer 2013). Mass surveillance and Stuxnet has initiated a cyber arms race to build capacities, gather resources, and train staff. But this is a race with no direction and without an understanding of pace.

Despite the NSA's effort to reassure American citizens that its actions are not as nefarious as press reports indicate, and that all data queries relate to foreign intelligence efforts such as counterterrorism, counterproliferation and cybersecurity, time and time again, claims about the NSA's lawfulness and conscientious protection civil liberties are demonstrated to be false. Similarly, its claims of thwarting attacks are drastically overstated. Foreign Intelligence Surveillance Court Judge John Bates in a recent ruling painstakingly catalogued 'pervasive violations' of previous court orders, rampant 'unauthorized electronic surveillance' of US citizens, and a 'history of material misstatements' about how NSA programs worked (Bates as cited by Gosztola 2013). So the agency has a credibility gap.

The danger of massive data gathering exercises takes on another dimension as domestic government agencies begin acquiring drone programs to assist with law enforcement. For instance, the FBI, Homeland Security, and Coast Guard deploy these resources for border patrol and drug interdiction. It would be an error to downplay these concerns as in previous instances the NSA has shared criminal evidence with law enforcement agencies, who in turn then misattribute the source of their information to retroactively manufacture legal chains of evidence to justify arresting a suspect (Menn 2013). This makes a mockery of due process principles.

The NSA also partners with universities. Likewise, consider the Minerva Research Initiative, a DoD research programme that funds university research into population and media dynamics of civil unrest. With an allocated budget of $75 million over 5 years, Minerva's aim is to 'to improve DoD's basic understanding of the social, cultural, behavioral, and political forces that shape regions of the world of strategic importance to the US.' A typical example is a Cornell based project that uses 'digital traces' to model 'the dynamics of social movement mobilisation and contagions' to determine 'the critical mass (tipping point)'. Case studies include 'the 2011 Egyptian revolution, the 2011 Russian Duma elections, the 2012 Nigerian fuel subsidy crisis and the 2013 Gezi park protests in Turkey.' Another project, based at the University of Maryland, aims to understand how climate change influences civil unrest. These projects seek to conduct 'study of emotions in stoking or quelling ideologically driven movements to counteract grassroots movements'. Most notably, in 2012 university-based researchers used Facebook privacy policy to skirt informed consent and conducted an experiment where user's timelines were modified to measure how 'emotional contagion' spreads (Kramera et al. 2014). One of the lead authors, Jeffrey Hancock had previously worked on other Minerva funded projects like Modeling Discourse and Social Dynamics in Authoritarian Regimes.[21]

Social media research is not limited to universities acting on behalf of the security forces; sometimes they conduct this research directly. For example, the Intelligence Advanced Research Project Activity programme examines Twitter to predict civil disorder. General Michael Flynn, the then director of the Defence Intelligence Agency, is on record as indicating that social media has opened up new areas of inquiry. 'The information that we're able to extract form social media', he said, 'it's giving us insights that frankly we never had before' (see Tucker, 2014, 1). Each individual project looks inconspicuous, but much like the development of military hardware at US universities during the Cold War, when seen in totality it is anything but. To one analyst's eyes, 'Minerva is farming out the piece-work of empire in ways that can allow individuals to disassociate their individual contributions from the larger project.'

These cases show how the US continues to weaponize social science, using it as an instrument of imperial rule. This practice has drawn criticism from the American Anthropological Association who argue that the Pentagon lacks 'the kind of infrastructure for evaluating anthropological research' in the case of the HTS. They called for such research to be overseen by the National Science Foundation (NSF). Accordingly, the DoD and the NSF signed a memorandum of understanding to cooperate on Minerva. But, as the AAA writes, this arrangement 'undermines the role of the university as a place for independent discussion and critique of the military'. But it seems the horse has already bolted: the American Psychological Association has sought to protect James Mitchell and Bruce Jesssen, psychologists who assisted the CIA in its torture programme (in addition, members of the American Medical Association were present at torturing).[22] Republican Senator Tom Coburn had various proposals to restrict political science research to areas that provided benefits for national security.[23] These developments wither social science.

The security forces have partnered with ICT companies to use their resources, sometimes via political pressure to provide keys to their encryption, other times via court orders to install backdoors into software. Still it is not just overt; reports indicate that the CIA pays AT&T about $10 million for metadata search series (Savage 2013). As AT&T provides infrastructure for other telecommunications companies, they are able to provide information of those that use the infrastructure, not just their customers. As the CIA is prohibited from domestic surveillance, the contact has 'safeguards' to ensure privacy protection with international calls with one end in the US. AT&T is said to 'mask' several digits of the phone numbers. But given database triangulation, this is hardly a barrier. Besides, as Savage reports, there is still the possibility of inter-agency cooperation where the CIA can refer these numbers to the FBI, which then can subpoena AT&T for uncensored data (Savage 2013). AT&T has a history of extensive cooperation with the state. It facilitated the Bush administration's warrantless wiretapping surveillance program, embedded employees with the FBI and DEA.

Data companies collect and amalgamate online and offline information to understand behaviour. ChoicePoint, owned by Elsevier maintains 17 billion records on businesses and individuals. Or consider that one of the leading companies in this area, Acxiom, processes about 50 trillion data transactions per year, and averages 1,500 pieces of data per consumer. The pieces come from tracked online information combined with public records such as credit reports, criminal records, Social Security numbers, to build a profile of a person making genuine anonymity almost impossible. Reminiscent of Alexander's remarks above, Scott Howe, Axciom's CEO, has said, 'Our digital reach will soon approach nearly every Internet user in the US.'

The scope of this information brokerage rivals that of the NSA, yet this business remains near entirely unregulated, and with little public understanding of this business sector. Data collection happens through consent for direct data in return for services, but also through the passive collection by private entities by unknown, little known or involuntary means. It may seem as if the data-brokers do not endanger human rights, at least relative to governmental surveillance, but this neglects that the US government, federal and local agencies purchase data from these sources. In this respect, government access to customer data blurs the lines between agencies tasked with serving the public and corporate profit seeking. The consequence of aligning consumer marketing and state security is possible inference-based discrimination or police targeting.

There are uncomfortable relationships between corporate surveillance of consumers and workers, and the US government's domestic surveillance of citizens. Telecommunications companies and retailers routinely capture everyday consumer data and hand over to the state. In the wake of the Snowden revelations, as a public relations exercise ICT companies proclaim they are complying with the law, but as the AT&T-CIA case shows, voluntary cooperation does continue. Still, statements indicating legal compliance can be misleading insofar that broadly applicable laws have not been revised in light of technical developments. Where there are revisions, the new statutes often cater towards the ruling class's interests. Consider that companies like Booz Allen Hamilton sponsored legislation like the Digital Accountability and Transparency Act 2014 or the Cybersecurity Information Sharing Act, 2015. While there has been targeted protest on bills like CISPA and SOPA, this activism has not generally sought to situate this legislation as but the latest iteration of a drive to formally entrench the security state. This is worrying, given that US legislators are woefully under-informed about mass surveillance, and so susceptible to manipulation campaigns, it makes it difficult to justify this public policy as having democratic legitimacy.

While the NSA has claimed great success, there is little evidence to support these claims. As Democratic Senators Ron Wyden, Mark Udall, and Martin Heinrich (2013) made clear in a *New York Times* op-ed,

> The usefulness of the bulk collection program has been greatly exaggerated. We have yet to see any proof that it provides real, unique value in protecting national security. In spite of our repeated requests, the N.S.A. has not provided evidence of any instance when the agency used this program to review phone records that could not have been obtained using a regular court order or emergency authorization.

Despite the massive investment of funds and resources, investigations have yet to say whether the NSA's programs have yielded results that have stopped terror activities. Using intensive and extensive surveillance in Afghanistan, there was little tactical success nor enough insight to produce strategic success (Savage and Weisman 2015).

However, even if mass surveillance did meet its ostensible goal, and even if there was public oversight, principally it is right to oppose it. This is because it creates docile, non-threatening and productive subjects. Glenn Greenwald puts it well:

> The danger posed by the state operating a massive secret surveillance system is far more ominous now than at any point in history. While the government, via surveillance, knows more and more about what its citizens are doing, its citizens know less and less about what their government is doing, shielded as it is by a wall of secrecy. (2014 208–209)

Debates about efficacy miss the point that mass surveillance unduly infringes upon a person's dignity. Constant surveillance and monitoring induces people to performing a particular kind of subjectivity, limiting the scope for dissent or plain difference of opinion. The shrugged response of 'nothing to hide, they have nothing to be afraid of' underestimates the extent to which people monitor their actions because they do not want to attract the attention of the state. In other words, they go out of their way to do nothing contentious. But when people face the prospect of authorities holding them accountable for specifically framed records, it is nothing less than a direct attack on their freedom of speech, belief, consciousness: in short their very personhood.

As vast portions of people's lives are mediated it is near impossible to live without constant sharing of data, recording or conducting activities on digital devices. The current Supreme Court ruling on data indicates that authorities must obtain a warrant to search a cellphone, but Fourth Amendment 'expectations of privacy' are forfeited when this information is transmitted. With real-time transmissions, this practically means that there is no expectation of privacy and that the cellphone of every person is turned into a tracking device making them susceptible to dragnet data collection. This underscores the point that mass surveillance and the interception of communications is not selective. It operates by the presumption of guilt, grants no respect for privacy rights nor the need to justify interference, thus nullifying civil liberties. As networked computing is central to economic activity and social life there is no practical distinction between the offline and online world. In this respect, digital liberties are civil liberties and their widespread compromise is unacceptable.

Others acknowledge state monitoring, but downplaying the need for absolute privacy. Indeed, it is seen as a negotiation of selective disclosure in exchange for access to digital services. But this requires a person to be digitally literate about the implications of what they are granting access to, and that opt-outs are available. Still, the worry is about breach of rights, undue pre-emptive data recording that tracks every aspect of a person's life. Given that the value of data lies in its secondary application, it is impossible to specify any one particular risk at this point. That said, one can generally anticipate some: the consequence of near continuous ever present surveillance through ubiquitiously handheld cellular devices, internet browsing, and sensors which have normalized a culture of obedience are anathema to a democratic society and will ultimately prove corrosive for meaningful social relations.

While their disclosures provide a partial overview of NSA's operations, whistleblowers like Edward Snowden and journalists like Risen reveal how the security state, with the assistance of corporations such as AT&T, Facebook, Google, and Verizon, has built an extensive intelligence-gathering infrastructure using programs like PRISM, XKeyscore and other strategic information operations to build dossiers. When whistleblowers speak up or journalists investigate these actions, agents of the state use intimidation tactics or character assassination. As Chelsea Manning, Julian Assange, Edward Snowden, and Barrett Brown can attest, incarceration or exile are also viable options. Consider the treatment of Risen. In *State of War* he details how Operation Merlin, a covert CIA operation undertaken in the Clinton administration to delay the Iran nuclear programme had the opposite effect.[24] Following publication, both the Bush and Obama administrations undertook a protracted effort to pressure Risen to reveal his sources. Using the Espionage Act of 1917, the Justice Department indicted Jeffery Sterling, a former CIA officer. While there was evidence of correspondence between Risen and Sterling, pre-trail filings indicated that the Justice Department believed that to convict Sterling, they required Risen to testify because Sterling revealed classified material in interviews, so Risen was an eyewitness to the felony. After several years, Justice did eventually concede that Risen could avoid testifying about his source, this framing of the case and protracted pressure infers that reporting on classified material is deemed an act of co-conspiracy in espionage by the US.

Without a federal shield law, reporters claim First Amendment protection, but *Bransburg v. Hayes* (1972) is often interpreted to mean that journalists have no special right to testify in a criminal case.[25] Justice Powell did indicate that this privilege,

> should be judged on its facts by the striking of a proper balance between freedom of the press and the obligation of all citizens to give relevant testimony with respect to criminal conduct. The balance of these vital constitutional and societal interests on a case-by-case basis accords with the tried and traditional way of adjudicating such questions.

This is hardly reliable protection, particularly when Eric Holder's Department of Justice prosecuted and imprisoned a number of people for disclosing classified information to the press, even if it was about matters of public interest like warrantless surveillance or CIA torture programs. Indeed, these efforts found the Justice Department had undertaken extensive wiretapping and recording of Associated Press reporters to investigate leaks. Upon this becoming public knowledge, in July 2013 the Justice Department issued new guidelines when dealing with the press in investigations, but this was predicated upon protections only when reporters were undertaking 'ordinary' newsgathering, this itself being undefined and so open to draconian law enforcement. This raises the question of whether the DoD or the Justice Department considers protest movements and social activism—which are normatively vital for a democratic polity—a threat to national security.

To conclude, part of the success of the US security state has been its ability to mobilize privately organized industrial strength, and has directed the dividends to new technological developments cementing state-capital relations in the military industrial complex while periodically intervening into popular culture to create soft power. The state's control of data presents opportunities to limit dissent and marginalize internal rivals, while commodification of data points to the urgent need for sustained digital liberties activism. While one should not discount the role and lobbying done by the emerging cyber-industrial complex, or the politics involved, it is clear that the US has 'weaponized the internet' (Weaver 2013), making it an instrument of control and oppression. Therefore, it is important to underscore the point Zeynep Tufekci (2014b) makes that 'How the internet is run, governed and filtered is a human rights issue.' At stake is the very moral agency of people's lives, and the infringement of a person's right by a state set on reducing citizens to nothing but subjects.

CHAPTER 4

Internal Rule and the Other America

Identity cannot help but be a by-product of inequality and exploitation, of capital's discretion to assert difference and distinction all the while maintained by brute force or systematic racism. 'Racial regimes do possess history, that is, discernible origins and mechanisms of assembly. But racial regimes are unrelentingly hostile to their exhibition. This antipathy exists because a discoverable history is incompatible with a racial regime', Cedric Robinson says, and with its 'claims of naturalism' (1997). Many strategies are used to install this regime, including violence like assassinations and state repression of biracial unions. The black experience in the US is of good example of this process.

Despite the US state's attempts to justify police militarization, this kind of targeted violence undergirds a system of domination – structured often along race and class lines. Whereas the previous chapters addressed strategic calculation and rule, this chapter turns towards domestic issues detailing the status of public institutions in the US and their relationship to the production of patterns of subjugation. The specific cases are certainly not intended to be exhaustive of all the institutional arrangements in the US state, but rather to be indicative and emblematic of them. Continuing the theme of constraint, I examine who bears the brunt of these efforts. In response to the recently highly publicized police shootings of unarmed black people, social movements like #BlackLivesMatter—now part of the Movement for Black Lives—have shown the extent of state sanctioned violence against black and brown bodies, where the torture and loss of black life at the hands of the state is deemed acceptable, and where black people are deprived of their basic human rights and dignity by a 'blue wall of terror'. These movements have also sought to demonstrate how these practices are themselves linked to broader structural injustices, such as the US prison industrial complex, the militarization of inner city communities. So while police brutality is a problem, it is best thought of as an indicator for greater troubles in the social structure of the US. It is in this direction that this chapter will travel.

How to cite this book chapter:
Timcke, S. 2017 *Capital, State, Empire: The New American Way of Digital Warfare.*
Pp. 77–98. London: University of Westminster Press. DOI: https://doi.org/10.16997/book6.e. License: CC-BY-NC-ND 4.0

Throughout this treatment, I want to underscore that I am neither 'speaking for', nor 'speaking of', but rather 'speaking about'. This is because, as Linda Alcoff notes,

> speaking for others is often born of a desire for mastery, to privilege oneself as the one who more correctly understands the truth about another's situation or as one who can champion a just cause and thus achieve glory and praise. And the effect of the practice of speaking for others is often, though not always, erasure and a reinscription of sexual, national, and other kinds of hierarchies (1991, 32).

Furthermore, I am not attempting to define black thought, nor flatten it out, but rather to find some interesting features that relate to recent historical-material developments. Similarly, I want to avoid making selected members of community ventriloquists of black lived experience. In the exercise I am guided by Alcoff's heuristic, will writing about state violence 'enable the empowerment of oppressed peoples?' (1991, 32). I am reluctant to declare 'yes', for two reasons. The first is because doing so strikes me as undue bravado, something Alcoff warns about. The second is informed by the sheer contingency of empowerment, something the state wishes to mitigate in its favour. With this said, overall the goal is to reiterate the salience of structural racism, classism, and sexism in America, all the while demonstrating how the state is responsible for, encourages, and condones this violence.

4.1 The Atrophy of Opposition and the Truly Disadvantaged

Racism is insidious, and is one prop of the American social structure. This is evident in the vast disparities between blacks and other groups in health and wellness (life expectancy, rates of major illnesses, suicide), economic (household income, property ownership, assets, unemployment,) and social indices (educational attainment, incidence of poverty, incarceration). Involved in these disparities is that cities and towns present residential segregation which introduce school segregation. As Douglas Massey and Nancy Denton noted in *American Apartheid*, 'racial residential segregation is the principal structural feature of American society responsible for the perpetuation of urban poverty and represents a primary cause of racial inequality in the United States' (1993, viii). Lastly, there is a scarcity of blacks in the ruling class or in prestigious professional careers.

Nevertheless, scarcity does not mean total absence. There are successful blacks, and indeed Barack Obama, who associates with the black community, won two presidential elections. Moreover, there have been black cabinet officials, mayors and Supreme Court appointments and indeed blacks are important figures in athletics and the entertainment industry. For this reason, in Obama's first term, there was much public discussion about whether the US was on the threshold of entering a stage of post-racial political development. Generally, the apologist argument went that race's role in informing life chances and prospects was declining; for if the US electorate could vote for a black person, so the reasoning went, then there were considerably fewer discriminatory attitudes than, say the late 1950s when the Civil Rights Movement was initiated. In short, the current social structure, while imperfect, was transcending past repressions.

Presented in self-congratulatory terms, and notwithstanding sociological evidence indicating otherwise, the post-racial society thesis invited poor political analysis, the ramifications doing more harm than good. As opposed to situating black people in a historically specific social structure, the thesis cast black people as authoring their failures. This is irrespective of whether this is by lapsed behaviour, poor morals or ethics: The negligent use of personal agency explains the social disparity and the lack of individual upward social mobility, and not structural oppression.

An added grotesque feature of this thesis is that by implication, the state can suspend welfare targeted at racial redress, or establish a sunset clause for affirmative action hiring policies. So, in practice, the thesis is less than noble, because rather than champion and expand upon the few social gains made thus far, it was instead used to challenge and justify dismantling the state's capacity to attend to discrimination. Put simply, the narrow elevation of an elite few does little for the material conditions of many others.

Still, the black community is divided on the merits of the post-racial society thesis. Consider Obama's 2013 Morehouse 'no excuses' commandment speech as emblematic of elite blacks focus on individual drive and ambition:

> We've got no time for excuses—not because the bitter legacies of slavery and segregation have vanished entirely; they haven't. Not because racism and discrimination no longer exist; that's still out there. It's just that in today's hyper-connected, hyper-competitive world, with a billion young people from China and India and Brazil entering the global workforce alongside you, nobody is going to give you anything you haven't earned. And whatever hardships you may experience because of your race, they pale in comparison to the hardships previous generations endured—and overcame. (Coates, 2013)

While Obama does not set aside the problems of race, nor the lack of sufficient redress, but in a sleight of hand, he—indicative here of wealthier blacks—absconds and redirects blame to the poor. Ta-Nehisi Coates argues that Obama's condescending tone is reserved for blacks, which is in poor taste given that that constituency provided him significant political support and thereby well-positioned him to address larger structural issues.

But more important than tone, Obama's remarks reveal a contradiction. Keeanga-Yamahtta Taylor describes this contradiction well when she writes that 'For Black elites, in particular, their success validates the political and economic underpinning of US society while reaffirming the apparent personal defects of those who have not succeeded' (2014, 8). Adolf Reed explains this contradiction by pointing to 'the atrophy of opposition within the black community'. He means that certain kinds of blacks have been pacified, such that 'antagonisms have been so depoliticized that they can surface only in alienated forms' where 'traditional forms of opposition have been made obsolete by a new pattern of social management' (1979). The reason for this is that capitalism adjusted to black radical protest by co-opting blacks into the elite, and involving them in restructuring capitalism. To this extent, this is similar to Derrick Bell's (1995) observation that the American constitution privileges property over justice: His interest convergence theory proposes that racial advances and civil emancipation will only occur to the extent that they align with the interests of the (white) elite. In other words, the neoliberal ruling class incorporated elements of the black community to stall radical protest of the same social structure.

To link this back to the previous point, blacks are not responsible for their own predicaments and plight, so there is no basis to claim that black culture, or parts thereof, is at fault. Such attributions are a racist denial that culture is built upon material conditions. This explanation is used to abscond from examining the reason for the material conditions in the first place. But even if one were to take on those terms, blaming black culture is akin to saying that blacks have not integrated into the broader American society, which itself fails to acknowledge how racism and economic imperatives have worked to keep blacks from integrating.[26] So ultimately, this explanation preserves the American social structure while suggesting that blacks create their own burdens.

This is very different from the structural critiques advanced by the social movements in the 1960s, including the Civil Rights Movement. Even if Reed is correct when he suggests that these struggles for equality failed to produce the solidarity required to carry and advance a broader 'coherent opposition' to the 'administrative apparatus', (1979) these movements nevertheless examined black poverty and disparity using an historical analysis of oppression and exploitation of blacks.

Of course, black elites are still victims of discrimination, implicit and institutional. Indeed, they carry more debt and have less wealth comparatively to whites. However, their economic resources still provide them a better position from which to address racism or at least buffer themselves from racist social structures. The reduction of formal racism, combined with apparent just desert component of the post-racial society thesis, means that lower class blacks are just that much more susceptible to the damages and harms produced by the social structure, and especially so if the state withdraws from welfare provisions or redistribution efforts.

A good portion of the affinity and subscription to the thesis turns on the lived experience of class as it informs different political philosophies, actions and conclusions, and it arises from the experience of different kinds, types, and intensity of racial inequality and discriminatory actions. While an affluent black family living in Bel Air undoubtedly experienced systemic racism it is of a quantitatively different sort than that experienced by a black family from West Philadelphia and the politics and worldview of these two families would reflect that. This can explain why the black community includes theorists as far apart as Cornell West and Thomas Sowell, or jurists Thurgood Marshall and Clarence Thomas. So like all communities, one must resist reifying Black American as a uniform mass, in part because of the pronounced social inequality between blacks as well as different explanations for it.

To explain this divergent black politics, in *The Declining Significance of Race* William Wilson argued that there was a historical transition 'from economic racial oppression experienced by virtually all blacks to economic subordination for the black underclass', the result of which was that 'the Negro class structure has become more differentiated' (1978, 152–3). In *The Truly Disadvantaged* (1987), he built upon this claim arguing that with the extension of civil rights and the Great Society programs under advanced capitalism the urban poor have come to suffer from both race and class subordination, inflected in part by the history of marginality and redundancy where class markers start to emerge in black society. Although the upper incomes of blacks trailed whites, structural changes explain the split in black income where, in the late 1980s, income inequality between blacks was greater than those between whites do.

In accounting for this growing social inequality, Wilson observed a meaningful connection between the declining economic prospects of young urban black men. With brevity in mind, in 1950, about half of young black men were employed as farm labourers in Southern agriculture. However, massive sector-wide mechanization meant that these jobs had near but vanished by 1970. For these reasons, blacks migrated to northern industrial cities where they found employment in the manufacturing sector in vehicle and steel production, partly because these were jobs that, at most, required completing high school. But deindustrialization and off-shoring of production facilities meant that many of these jobs disappeared when the manufacturing sector contracted in the late 1970s and 1980s.

As cities became centres of financial and professional services, there were fewer vocation and employment opportunities for the low-skilled uneducated black men. These new jobs required more education attainment, something their class background made difficult to attain. Concurrently, baby boomers and white women flooded the labour market. So with affirmative action policies, necessary to help redress decades of discrimination, better educated, higher class blacks were better positioned to take advantage of them. As a result, they did relatively well in comparison to poorer blacks and so were thus able to leave the cities like their middle-class white counterparts. Aside from losing vital networks of support and community institutions, the poor were left further behind in ghettos with concentrated poverty thus making it much more difficult to compete for positions. Already precariously positioned, it is easy to see how recessions and unemployment disproportionally affect black men. This produced class-decomposition and the reduction of working class blacks. Altogether, poor urban blacks were severely alienated.

Admirable for giving priority to material developments as opposed to explanations predicated solely upon racist attitudes or helpless dependency, Wilson points out these critical economic structural changes produce the social relations in urban areas. What this means is that it was not that the Great Society social programs failed to reduce poverty so much as it did not anticipate a changing economic base. Wilson concludes that tolerating high unemployment rates does untold damage to the inhabitants of urban ghettos, and this indicates that a fiscal policy that gives priority to rentier income over employment maintains the underclass. Therefore, the alienation of poor urban blacks is result of deindustrialization of production, the financialization of the global process of capital accumulation, and the fiscal withering of welfare programs through intentional resource starvation by those that controlled the state.

Overall, this economic stratification and segregation are indicative of a social structure in which blacks have greater obstacles, fewer life chances, more violence, and indignity; or what Oscar Gandy (2009) calls 'cumulative disadvantage'. Due to class and racial positions, poor blacks' prospects are bleak and they are more susceptible to disasters, natural or economic. Illustrative of this was Hurricane Katrina which 'exposed our nation's amazing tolerance for black pain', argues Jamelle Bouir, it 'was one of the worst disasters in American history: It killed more than 1,800 Americans, displaced tens of thousands more, and destroyed huge swaths of New Orleans' (2015) It was not only a storm that made landfall, but a social disaster (cf. Smith 2006,) thereby becoming a defining element within black political consciousness and indicative of the ruling class's indifference and neglect of poor black residents. The lack of provisions and treatment plans are enduring aspects of black subjugation, which many suspect would not have been the case had it been a white wealthy city. The second example arises from the 2008 recession wherein blacks' wealth was disproportionately tied up in homeownership some of which was the result of discriminatory and corrupt lending practices. Together, these cases set the stage for black pessimism with institutional order, and where radical blacks make 'no excuses' for the ruling class.

4.2 The War on Blacks

Dan Baum, writing in *Harpers*, claims that John Ehrlichman, Nixon's White House Counsel, admitted that the War on Drugs was a cynical political manoeuvre. 'The Nixon campaign in 1968, and the Nixon White House after that, had two enemies: the antiwar left and black people', says Ehrlichman. He continues:

> We knew we couldn't make it illegal to be either against the war or black, but by getting the public to associate the hippies with marijuana and blacks with heroin, and then criminalizing both heavily, we could disrupt those communities. We could arrest their leaders, raid their homes, break up their meetings, and vilify them night after night on the evening news. Did we know we were lying about the drugs? Of course we did. (cited in Baum 2016)

Subsequent administrations, Congress, governors and state legislative houses have used the state crackdown on narcotics and the War on Drugs as a proxy for their particular interests. But irrespective of the particular politics, the outcome was a social structure where mass incarceration of 2.3 million people and governing through crime were key features.

To staff this apparatus, from 1992 to 2010, local and state police personnel increased from 603,000 to 794,000, about two-thirds as many active-duty US military personnel. Local police expenditures have increased from $40 billion in 1982 to over $100 billion in 2012 (Justice Policy Institute, 2012). Including federal spending on law enforcement by the FBI, ATF, and Homeland Security the figure in 2015 was $265 billion (Bureau of Justice Statistics, 2015). FBI statistics show that crime fell 19 per cent between 1987 and 2011. This holds even in cities where police forces have been subject to budget cuts. This funding coincides with an increased use of 'no-knock' laws to conduct police raids, the instances increased from thousands during the 1980s to 40,000 in 2005, to an estimated 80,000 in 2013.

These harrowing figures are not coincidental, but reflect political choices. For example, while Clinton's administration inherited the War on Drugs, he nevertheless oversaw and encouraged the largest ever expansion of the penal system. This was because, in an attempt to counter the Republican 'Southern Strategy' and win back white voters, Clinton era Democrats pursued a political strategy that scapegoated and sacrificed urban black communities through an extensive disciplinary regime that included the withdrawal of welfare and the implementation of punishment. The tough on crime agenda coincided with an economic collapse caused by offshoring manufacturing and deindustrialization that had been particularly hard on urban African Americans and especially so on young black men. This lack of decent work resulted in class decomposition and a sharp rise in inner city crime, which was compounded by drug epidemics, and racially segregated jobless ghettos.

US legislators have also created a draconian and disproportionate punishment system that uses marginalized populations as inputs for the prison-industrial complex. Indicative of systematic over-imprisonment, in his 1994 State of the Union address, Clinton advocated for a federal 'three strikes' law and shortly thereafter signed the Violent Crime Control and Law Enforcement Act (1994) that authorized $16 billion for police and prison system. This imprisonment of blacks leads to social stigma and economic exclusion, thus reduces their life chances and prospects for rehabilitation.

Not only is there a pipeline from schools through the justice system to corporately owned prisons, but while imprisoned inmates are forced to labour on behalf of their incarcerators under the guise of rehabilitation. Working for excessively low wages, this involuntary labour can generate up to $30,000 a year benefiting corporate prisons. Companies, such as Whole Foods, take advantage of prisons that are little better then modern day poor houses. As Chris Hedges notes,

> The bodies of poor, unemployed youths are worth little on the streets but become valuable commodities once they are behind bars... The criminalization of poverty is a lucrative business, and we have replaced the social safety net with a dragnet. (2013, 1)

For-profit-prisons have a stake in incarcerating citizens. This has led to about 2.2 million people imprisoned at any given time, a 500 per cent increase over thirty years. The school to prison pipeline where minors are treated like adults, shuttled from underfunded school to a prison complex is particularly egregious. Studies have shown that police and juries estimate black children to be older than they are, and more readily try them as adults in court. These criminal records ensure that young blacks cannot enter adult life as a normal person, and at a structural level, leads to political incapacitation.

It is often said that Bill Clinton reduced the unemployment rate. However, this is a good example of defining the problem away as prisoners are not counted in US statistics for poverty and unemployment rates. Thus record low unemployment rates among African Americans are tied to record high incarceration rates. In fact, as Michelle Alexander writes, 'when Clinton left office in 2001, the true jobless rate for young, non-college-educated black men (including those behind bars) was 42 percent.' Compounding these problems was Clinton's general redirection of $54 billion from welfare towards the penal system. Amongst other things, this introduced means-testing, reduced the public housing budget, eliminated Pell grants for prisoners, imposed lifetime bans on welfare for persons convicted of drug offences, and enabled bureaucrats to evict families from public housing if a member had a criminal history, such as an arrest. Consequently, 'by the end of Clinton's presidency,', Alexander writes,

> more than half of working-age African-American men in many large urban areas were saddled with criminal records and subject to legalized discrimination in employment, housing, access to education, and basic

public benefits—relegated to a permanent second-class status eerily reminiscent of Jim Crow.

In the 15 years since these actions, extreme poverty (an income of less than $2 per person per day) doubled to 1.5 million people. Instead of this vast penal system, this money could have been redirected to investments into urban communities to help carry the populations from industrial to service based economies.

In contra-distinction to nonsense theories like the 'culture of poverty' 'color-blindness', or 'post-racism' a forthright historical materialism is a useful approach to adopt when seeking to understand the current outcomes for black people in the US social structure. It is against this backdrop that the militarization of law enforcement should be seen. Police militarization is most acutely felt in what Martin Luther King Jnr. (1967) called the 'other America', where instead of finding the 'experience the opportunity of life, liberty, and the pursuit of happiness in all its dimensions', there is instead a 'daily ugliness'.

Michael Brown's killing is indicative of the intersection of police-citizen encounters that these conditions of daily ugliness produce. It begins with conflicting reports of the events, the fact that the incident was not radioed in for near to an hour, and that the body was left in the road for an excessive amount of time, away from the Brown family. Police deployed SWAT teams who pointed assault rifles at citizens so as to subdue the protesters who had assembled. In the coming days, tear gas, stun grenades, and rubber bullets were deployed against protestors. Journalists were threatened with violence and death (Davidson 2014), and over the next two weeks, over 100 people were arrested, nominally under the pretence of refusing to disperse, but it is unclear whether there was an order and whether it was lawful, and whether this was communicated to protestors (Amnesty International 2014).

These actions were compounded by the Ferguson Police Department's refusal to release Darren Wilson's name, an incomplete incident report, and interference with journalists trying to report on the event. It extends to the Ferguson Police Department where, despite the municipalities population being about two-thirds black, of about 55 officers only three were black. So there was an existing alienated relationship between the police and the community.

This alienation is exacerbated by municipal police forces seeing citizens as a source of revenue. The over-policing of municipalities—like Ferguson—relies on revenue generated by fines and penalties for minor legal infringements such as driving with a broken headlight. The cost of these fines and penalties, and the additional imposition of legal fees, amounts to nothing less than a form of government imposed debt bondage. As blacks are disproportionately poor, and momentarily setting aside whether these practices were motivated by overt racism, they are severely affected by these institutional practices. This is the basis for institutional oppression, the kind that can occurs independent of any overt racist attitudes or actions of the people who enforce these policies.

4.3 The Daily Ugliness of Police Militarization

Sanctioned by the National Defence Authorization Act (1990), the Pentagon has aided the militarization of society through an ongoing transference of $4.3 billion worth of military grade weapons to the police department through the 1033 programme. Since 2006 alone this Act has seen 432 mine-resistant armoured vehicles, 435 other kinds of armoured vehicles, 533 planes and helicopters, and near 94,000 machine guns (see Apuzzo 2014) transferred to municipal police forces. Weapons and hardware, designed for and deployed on battlefields against combatants are now being used in regular policing against US citizens. This program has even reached US campuses where more than 100 campus police forces have received surplus military equipment (Gold 2014). In a notable case, Ohio State received a 19-ton armoured vehicle designed to protect military personal from roadside bombs (Stuart 2013).

As this militarization has become normalized, SWAT units now undertake routine police work like patrols and executing warrants. This indicates a mission creep where these new resources allow the agencies to seek out, envision, and undertake new actionable purposes. Having these weapons on hand introduces a moral cost that is often neglected, in that it elevates possibilities of violent police-citizen incidents into probabilities. Police power is less informed by principles of justice and keeping the peace and rather functions as an instrument of social pacification as it reflects the political goals of the War on Terror and the War on Drugs. In other words, these security agendas have meant that there is a continuous blurring of the distinction between police and military tactics and behaviour, with countless examples of police using excessive, unreasonable, and unnecessary force, acting like a standing occupational army. This erodes the line between the police and the military, making them all state security forces.[27]

As this military equipment belongs to the DoD, police forces cannot sell it. Should police wish to return the items then layers of paperwork, delays in communication, and making police departments carry costs, render the return process burdensome in an effort to stall it. Lastly, the DoD has to approve the return, but they have a vested interest in not carrying the maintenance nor storage costs (Redden 2014).

Advocates for tactical units and military grade equipment suggest these techniques are necessary for modern policing because law enforcement duties place police officers in high-risk environments (cf. Skof 2014). In addition, as SWAT teams impose excessive physical requirements this virtually excludes female officers, subordinating them to support roles. (Dodge, Valcore and Gomez 2011). The combination of an abundance of caution, overwhelming force, and hyper-masculinity is justified as being in the 'public interest', but aside from the nebulous nature of the 'public interest', the approach always presumes a worst-case scenario rather than reasonably judging the likelihood of that kind of outcome. This rationality is how events where 24 police officers with an armoured vehicle were tasked to collect a fine from a 75-year-old man in Stettin, Wisconsin occur, simply because the litter on his property was an apparent eyesore (Chan 2014). This needless aggression is indicative of a social structure where the craft of violence is bifurcated when personal safety is disconnected from the larger social forces that initially produce violence.

Even if one grants that SWAT teams are useful for narrow purposes, the application of extraordinary tactics to ordinary police work creates a climate of fear among citizens and police officers. It is also worth noting that the militarization and the general acquisition of military equipment has occurred without input, consultation, or oversight from the communities that would be policed by this tactic. Indeed, this points to the prime problem; the 1033 programme has been used to deploy military grade weapons to police in case there are radical revolutionary groups, drug dealers, or fundamentalism where extreme force is required. However, not only does this not reflect the situational needs of most police forces, but these purported dangerous groups simply do not have the power that one might presume. This is not the threat is made out to be, so it is but a pretence that reveals the absence of basic democratic governance norms.

As an example of absconding from democratic norms, consider the common enough tactics of forced entry by battering ram to serve warrants. These raids are often predicted upon weak evidence and the fact that a good portion of these people are not charged with a crime mocks the principle of the presumption of innocence. As Tom Nolan explains, 'People who have been charged with no crime aren't only treated like they're guilty; they're made to endure a violent intrusion into their home based on the mere suspicion of low-level crimes' (2014, 1). Furthermore, there are regular reports of bystanders, often African Americans, being hurt in police raids. This is coupled by civil forfeiture and the seizure of assets.

The American Civil Liberties Union (ACLU) (2014) report, *War Comes Home*, is testament to these aforementioned norms. They examined over 800 SWAT incidents between 2011 and 2012, nearly two thirds were for drug searches, while less than one tenth were responses to hostage situations. Part of the reason for this is because of neoliberal public sector resource starvation. To attain funding, police departments have to meet quotas for drug arrests to win federal grants.

When the ACLU requested open records for their report on police militarization, some Massachusetts SWAT teams declined to cooperate, claiming that they operated as law enforcement councils and as such were private entities. Incorporated as 501(c)(3) organizations, they used this legal status to say they are private corporations, not government agencies, and so do not have to comply with open record requests. For example, the North Eastern Massachusetts Law Enforcement Council has about 50 member agencies. They have a wide range of capabilities: As well as a SWAT team METROLEC, has a canine unit, computer crimes unit, motorcycle units, and armoured vehicles. They even applied to the FEA for a drone licence. The ACLU reports that,

> Approximately 240 of the 351 police departments in Massachusetts belong to an LEC. While set up as "corporations," LECs are funded by local and federal taxpayer money, are composed exclusively of public police officers and sheriffs, and carry out traditional law enforcement functions through specialized units such as SWAT teams.

And:

> Police departments and regional SWAT teams are public institutions, working with public money, meant to protect and serve the public's interest. If these institutions do not maintain and make public comprehensive and comprehensible documents pertaining to their operations and tactics, the people cannot judge whether officials are acting appropriately or make needed policy changes when problems arise (2014).

Meanwhile, reminiscent of the Massachusetts Law Enforcement Council hiding behind their incorporation papers, local authorities use corporate non-disclosure clauses as reasons not to respond to judicial requests for information about the various technological devices use in police investigations. For example, between 2008 and May 2015, the NYPD used Stingrays— ISMI catchers— over 1,000 times in local domestic politicking. They did so without a formal policy, nor warrants (New York Civil Liberties Union 2016). The manufacturers, Harris Corporation, sells these products with a non-disclosure clause so it is not known how much they are used. In Baltimore's case, they cited dropped charges rather than disclose their policing techniques and technological capabilities. This is a system where legal and market institutions are used to shield public officials when abusing their power.

Using open source data collection methods, the Justice Policy Institute estimates that police killed 587 people in 2012. In these shootings, young black men were 21 times more likely to be shot than white counterparts. Federal data reports that were collected demonstrated that between 2010 and 2012 there were 1,217 deadly police shootings. Furthermore, of,

> [these] 1,217 deadly police shootings from 2010 to 2012...blacks, age 15 to 19, were killed at a rate of 31.17 per million, while just 1.47 per million white males in that age range died at the hands of police. (Gabrielson, Grochowski Jones, and Sagara 2014)

This data points to the double standard of policing in the US where various agents of the state continue the long chain of suffering that black people have experienced at the hands of the state. Michael Dyson calls this 'America's blue wall of terror' (2017). Still, there is an ideological tendency in parts of the American public imagination wherein taking crime seriously requires unconstitutional policing and inhumane sentences.

Institutional racism sees a willingness of police to use harsh measures to terrorize people of colour. Combined with the widespread criminalization of young black males, the possibility of building trust is squandered when police do kill innocent people. Instead of apologizing and trying to make amends with the families, the police slander their victims, labelling them criminals or thugs. This situation is the antithesis of a civilian police force concerned with safeguarding a democratic polis. Therefore, African Americans' distrust of the police and the criminal justice system as portrayed in Elijah Anderson's *Streetwise* (1990) or Alice Goffman's *On The Run* (2014) is more than reasonable.

When faced with public evidence of wrongdoing, police lie, obfuscate the truth, stonewall investigations, or in the case of New York, the police union threatens labour boycotts, essentially holding cities hostage and applying political pressure to hinder investigations. There are suspicions that prosecutors also collude with police to thwart indictments. Consider that federal indictments by a grand jury are granted in 99.993 per cent of case, but when police are involved it drops to 1.2 per cent. Also consider that about 95 per cent of police shootings are ruled as 'justified', even as body counts rise. Even then, if a case does make it to court, laws forbid prosecutors from informing juries about proper police training and protocols. This means juries do not have resources to judge whether the police action was a deviation from approved behaviour and interaction. This rampant impunity deprives the victims of police homicide the right to a fair public trial.

What these cases show us is that where there is a tendency towards a disproportionate use of force, it is all too often reserved for use against the underclass. There is no due process, and death is deemed acceptable. In the face of such violence, the public use smartphones to record police encounters. However, despite the right to record police action, the police too often confiscate the video footage, or threaten witnesses with arrest. Even when video evidence of unnecessary police brutality against those who do not pose a threat is secured and circulated via social media networks it does not seem to matter. In the case of Eric Garner, whose tragic death was captured on video, the police were seen to choke him into submission—a method prohibited by New York Police departmental policy. Yet even in this case, with video evidence and a coroner report ruling the death a homicide, there was no accountability or punishment for police officer crimes.

There have been suggestions that equipping police with body cameras will limit the abuse of power. Police departments and some reformers are allied on this front. But absent genuine accountability, it is unlikely to have much effect. Consider, for example, the recent history of dashboard cameras: one investigative reporting team examined 1,800 Chicago Police Department maintenance logs (Kongol and Biasco 2015) only to reveal that between September 2014 and

July 2015 there were 90-recorded incidents where there were no functioning microphones in police vehicles. What is particularly troubling about this is that police technicians attribute about 80 per cent of silent audio in dash-cam videos to 'intentional destruction' and that there is a backlog to fix them. There are also records of several vehicles failing to capture video. Even setting aside the lessons from dashboard cameras, where effectiveness depends so much on the police departments' institutional culture and proper archival procedures, this technology has mostly helped police. For example, body cameras have been used to identify and find protestors. With increased computing power and refinements in facial recognition software, this will only become easier. Indeed, it might signal the end of the mob as a historical concept. Reformist aspirations that are devoid of any understanding of power or interest, seemingly unable to recognize that the tools, platforms, and techniques they were celebrating as emancipatory, can be turned against activists, dissidents, or the very causes they are trying to promote.

Nevertheless, given how biases are often encoded into software, given already existing institutional racism, it is likely that software will be used to racial profile populations. Racial profiling is obviously wrong; it presumes a predictive power of race, itself an implicit bias and racially motivated prejudice, and is thus too simplistic for investigative purposes. Not only are these distortions present when arresting, as to are the over-reliance on them, but so are increases in police brutality such as humiliating harassment and verbal abuse. This affects every aspect of a community, especially when the police steal and destroy the property of the people they stop and frisk. The police are rife with misconduct, brutality, and corruption—and they are armed with the tools of war. This simple case demonstrates how technical solutions will not solve social injustice. These developments require us to consider how technological implementations can introduce social problems.

Several of the aforementioned themes can be seen in Chicago's Black Sites. Between 1972 and 1991, more than 100 people were tortured at these sites. This was done with the explicit knowledge of the former Chicago police commander Jon Burge. Mostly African American men were tortured using mock executions, electric shocks, and sleep deprivation. These actions show the institutional willingness to be brutal to the poor and to blacks. In 2003, Governor George Ryan pardoned four of ten death row inmates who say they were subject to torture. Burge was dismissed in 1993 after an internal investigation and convicted in 2010 of perjury during civil proceedings. Involved in those crimes was Chicago detective Richard Zuley. Zuley is notorious for being an interrogator at Guantanamo Bay in 2002. His plan for torturing Mohamedou Ould Slahi was personally signed off by Donald Rumsfeld. Spencer Ackerman's review of court documents filed in Chicago, interviews with Guantanamo Bay prisoners, and Slahi's *Guantanamo Diary* 'suggest a continuum between police abuses in urban America and the wartime detention scandals' (Ackerman 2015a, 1).

Burge and Zuley both began their service with the Chicago Police Department in the 1970s, rising through the ranks. Assigned to different areas—Burge on the south side, Zuley on the north—there is no evidence-showing cooperation between the two. This is perhaps more disconcerting than if they had, for it indicates that impunity is not confined to a select group of officers, but diffused in a system that condones it.

Sadly, Spencer Ackerman's reporting has found that the Chicago Police Department continues to operate an 'off-the-books interrogation compound' at Homan Square on Chicago's west side. Witnesses or suspects, some as young as 15, are detained at the site. As they are not booked at a precinct, there is no public record of these suspects being in custody (Ackerman 2015b). This is akin to the rendition practiced in the early years of the War on Terror. Lawyers and families who have tried to enter Homan Square are turned away, while their clients and relatives are subjected to a routine violation of their rights to legal counsel and coercion into providing statements.

Both are clear violations of the Fifth and Sixth Amendments. Chicago civil rights lawyer Flint Taylor, who has been in practice for 45 years, has said that 'I have reached the conclusion that Chicago police violence is systemic, fundamentally racist, and disproportionally impacts the poor and communities of color' (Taylor in Ackerman 2015c, also see Taylor 2013). This is not an anomaly. It was designed. As Du Bois noted in *Black Reconstruction in America*, 'The whole criminal system came to be used as a method of keeping Negroes at work and intimidating them. Consequently, there began to be a demand for jails and penitentiaries beyond the natural demand due to the rise of crime.' That Du Bois' words still capture many blacks' lived experience is indicative of the salience of this oppression in the development of the American social structure.

This 'daily ugliness' reveals the extent to which the US is a political order structured around violence. Authoritarian and mechanistic in tone, this governance demonstrates how the annihilation of the other is a functional principle of institutional practice that punishes the poor and provides profits for the security-surveillance industry. That these repressive policies are utterly disconnected from human rights shows a militarized police who rarely question the limits of their formal authority because informally they have been tasked with playing a key role in the process of commodifying the bodies of the poor who would otherwise be abandoned due to withdrawn welfare and redistribution services. Left to confront repression by themselves, this one-dimensional understanding of personal safety precludes a social component.

4.4 The Universality of Black Lives Matter

The preceding sections in this chapter addressed how the truly disadvantaged are created by enduring structural injustice. It has also illustrated that co-currently blacks are managed by a method of selectively co-opting a narrow band of blacks into the elite to deflate and diffuse political opposition as well as a kind of rule predicated upon inducing and reproducing weaknesses in poor blacks. The second movement has been aided by off-shoring manufacturing jobs, leaving poor blacks as surplus labourers, partly to undercut any chance of contention, and partly efforts to extract fines and rents by local governments who are themselves operating under neo-liberal resource starvation. Nevertheless, central to these actions is a logic of repression.

The introduction of new modes of repression also opens up new opportunities for a 'double movement' from activists. Whereas, in the late 1970s political scientist Adolf Reed lamented how the US state had adjusted to 1960s black radical protests by incorporating agitators, these new modes of repression bring with them other counter movements. One of these counter movements is Black Lives Matter.

Black Lives Matter, an activist social movement emerged as American citizens saw the death of Trayvon Martin, Michael Brown, Eric Garner, and Tamir Rice as indicative of structural injustice put in place by the racial capitalism discussed in Chapter 1. In combination with the local struggle of Black people in places like Ferguson, where protests lasted more than 100 days, Black Lives Matter sought to blunt racist policing practice across the nation. These needless deaths were emblematic of a nationwide endemic that coalesced into a nationwide demand for justice and the remedy of structural injustice against blacks. An immediate goal of the movement is to stop the criminalization of black life and end the endemic of police harassment, brutality, corruption, and murder.

As Christopher Lebron makes clear, 'the consistent death and abuse at the hands of the police to which blacks have been subject constitutes a form of terrorism under the guise of democratic governance.' Highlighting the 'disturbing parallels between plantation slavery and prisons and correctional facilities convict leasing' Lebron indicates that systematic oppression is in the structure of the US, and that the most recent expressions in stop and frisk, redlining, voter suppression, the War on Drugs is but a continuation of this violence where African American lives are criminalized (2014, 1). African Americans, who as a permanent underclass due to systematic racism, are the main victims of this system. This dehumanizing trauma indicates that blacks' personhood is not recognized nor acknowledged.

Black Lives Matter, and local protestors in Ferguson and elsewhere, are using a 'digital repertoire of contention', to protest and explain American political economy, show the flaws in post-racial theories, and advocate against unlawful extra-judicial police killing and social inequality. These deaths and others reveal that black's everyday life is grounds for suspicion by agents of the state. Granted, the proliferation of cellular devices with internet access, cameras, and broadcast social media platforms add new tactics to the repertoire of contention. These devices can reduce the lag between an incident and public awareness, or undercut fabricated official statements and thus contesting the narrative frame. This is important in Ferguson where cable broadcasters and national newspapers initially ignored the death of Michael Brown. But, while social media is certainly important to the rise of Black Lives Matter, it is neither necessary nor sufficient to explain the politics of this moment and the social dynamics.

Over and above technology, material conditions explain black uprisings. For example, during the Great Recession post-2008, blacks disproportionately suffered versus their white peers, losing an estimated $10 billion. Most of this was due to predatory sub-prime lending practices that targeted aspiring black homeowners who banks suspected would foreclose on mortgages (Henry, Resse and Torres, 2013). Near a quarter of a million blacks did, while others are at risk. As a result, what little blacks had managed to accumulate through intergenerational labour evaporated almost overnight. The ramification is downward social mobility and pauperization. American banks have yet to face indictment for this fraud.

The outcome of the Great Recession was to see even more wealth concentrated in the 1 per cent as the Obama administration did little to redistribute or redress this economic hoarding. As egregious, throughout Obama's presidency, black unemployment was above 10 per cent, while in 2014 black college graduates' unemployment rate was 12 per cent, more than double the white college graduates whose unemployment rate was approximately 5 per cent. Furthermore, since the Recession, median black income fell by near 11 per cent to $33,500, while whites incomes have fallen 3.6 per cent to $58,000, near a third of blacks live in poverty, and over a quarter of blacks are food insecure. Put simply, blacks experience tremendous poverty.[28] Perhaps the biggest indicator of this crushing and systemic poverty is Mariko Chang's shocking and morally indefensible finding that 'While white women in the prime working years of ages 36–49 have a median wealth of $42,600, the median wealth for women of color is only $5' (2010, 3). This is one of the reasons why black women—who carry the consequential burden of the relentless assault on their children, families, and communities—are using coalitional politics guided by labour, feminist and queer theory to undertake the work of liberation.

In *Dissent*, Barbara Ransby (2015) highlights the broad agenda of Black Lives Matter, an umbrella organization seeking a 'bold confrontation with state power', because 'there can be no real economic justice without racial justice.' Adamant that 'the concerns raised by the Black Lives Matter movement reflect the experiences of most black Americans', Ransby says 'they also extend beyond these communities' (2015). The goal of this social movement is less a singular pursuit of representation and diversity in the ruling class, but rather a total revision of the social structure itself to make it more equitable and egalitarian. In other words, this not merely a problem of access to the upper reaches of the social structure, otherwise the Obama administration's legacy would not be so abysmal, rather it is a structural issue that requires structural and material changes. To that effect, the movement is a 'class based struggle' which aims to address salient features of racial capitalism.

The various biographies of leading members demonstrate the extensive, deep, and long-standing commitments to social activism and community organization, much of which is explicitly tied to labour and economic issues. Consider Alicia Garza, Patrisse Cullors, and Opal Tometi, women who, following George Zimmerman's acquittal for Trayvon Martin's death, created and circulated the #BlackLivesMatter hashtag. Ransby portrays them as 'professional organizers working with domestic workers, with immigrants, and against prisons respectively' (2015, 1). Garzam, Cullors, and Tometic are not isolated examples, but show how women are key organizers in the coordination of black resistance and protest. From Marcia Chatelain's vantage, this is an intergenerational participation, and one that includes queer scholars and activists, as they understand how bodies are disciplined. Indeed, as Black Lives Matter promotional material makes clear,

> beyond the narrow nationalism that can be prevalent within Black communities, which merely call on Black people to love Black, live Black and buy Black, keeping straight cis Black men in the front of the movement while our sisters, queer and trans and disabled folk take up roles in the background or not at all.

As Ransby describes the project, 'This is an unapologetic intersectional analysis reflecting the work of black women radicals and feminists such as Sojourner Truth, Angela Davis, Audre Lorde, Barbara Smith, bell hooks, Kimberlé Crenshaw, Beth Richie, Cathy Cohen, and Beverly Guy-Sheftall' (2015, 1). Ransby's listing of this diverse set of scholars and activists is not an imposition to minimize the range and kinds of thoughts amongst those on the list, hide inter-personal rivalries, disagreements, politics or the like. Instead, this kind of grouping is a programmatic spirit orientated towards broad-based emancipation, thereby demonstrating continuity of key elements of late twentieth-century black feminist thought. Angela Davis says as much in her acknowledgements in *Are Prisons Obsolete?* (2003):

> I should not be listed as the sole author of this book, for its ideas reflect various forms of collaboration over the last six years with activists, scholars, prisoners, and cultural workers who have tried to reveal and contest the impact of the prison industrial complex on the lives of people. (2003, 7).

Davis then lists many people and organizations that helped theorize or collect data that informs the project. This wide collaboration with a community of academics and activists is a political and intellectual strength of the prison abolitionist movement, a body of theory that has had profound influence on the shape and concerns of the Black Lives Matter movement. As such, Marcia Chatelain notes that

> Black Lives Matter is feminist in its interrogation of state power and its critique of structural inequality. It is also forcing a conversation about gender and racial politics that we need to have—women at the forefront of this movement are articulating that "black lives" does not only mean men's lives or cisgender lives or respectable lives or the lives that are legitimated by state power or privilege. (Marcia Chatelain and Kaavya Asoka 2015)

On a similar note, consider that in her project to curate black feminist scholarship, Patricia Hill Collins was sensitive to the inclusion of many African American women who's 'multiple voices highlights the diversity, richness, and power of Black women's ideas as part of a long-standing African American women's intellectual community.' The centre of the analysis is thus the division within the black women's experience and is meant to counter 'the tendency of mainstream scholarship to canonize a few Black women as spokespersons for the group and then refuse to listen to any but these select few.'

Much like Reed's analysis of black co-option, selective inclusion is an attempt to curtail access to those scholars seeking redress for social injustices that their work highlights. Indeed, the tokenistic elements are but ways to buy off or stall contention, and so it is but a method to avert greater sharing of resources with subordinate groups in the hope that selective access will stifle and disrupt concerted contention, and possibly invite intra-group scrappy battles around respectability politics and submission by those invited into ruling class or cannon. Moreover, as Collins makes clear, 'assuming that only a few exceptional Black women have been able to do theory homogenizes African-American women and silences the majority.' (2000 viii)

Likewise, Black Lives Matter organizers sit at confluence of the personal and political that seeks to overcome oppressive state apparatus. As Collins explains,

> Like African-American women, many others who occupy societally denigrated categories have been similarly silenced. So the voice that I now seek is both individual and collective, personal and political, one reflecting the intersection of my unique biography with the larger meaning of my historical times. (2000, vi)

In her preface to the second edition of *Black Feminist Thought*, Collins makes clear that 'Black feminist thought's purpose [is], namely, fostering both Black women's empowerment *and* conditions of social justice' (2000 x). The method of social analysis required to achieve this 'place[s] Black women's experiences and ideas at the center of analysis.' Collins readily acknowledges this approach encounters hostility dressed up as epistemological and historical scepticism that attempts to undermine the value of the scholarship: 'For those accustomed to having subordinate groups such as African-American women frame our ideas in ways that are convenient for the more powerful, this centrality can be unsettling' (2000 vii). Even here,

> Oppressed groups are frequently placed in the situation of being listened to only if we frame our ideas in the language that is familiar to and comfortable for a dominant group. This requirement often changes the meaning of our ideas and works to elevate the ideas of dominant groups. (2000 vii)

The last component of Black Lives Matter that we will touch on here is the way the movement employs Collins's adage that 'thought and action can work together in generating theory' as a central political tenet. This social moment takes place with the help of academics, but not for academics. It is scholarly without being beholden to (admittedly withering) disciplinary conventions where self-alienation from subjects is supposedly indicative of good scholarship. In this respect, Black Lives Matter shows that while they will produce good analysis, it is for the broader purpose of the radical overhaul of the social structure. In other words, their analysis is practitioner based and community orientated.

Black women alternate between being an afterthought in public policy, or scapegoated as undeserving of welfare or governmental affirmative action position. Similarly, news media generally is indifferent to the fate of black women. Notwithstanding similar ways and means of activism, the names of Michael Brown, Eric Garner, Freddie Gray received considerable more attention and are better-known than Rekia Boyd, Michelle Cusseaux, Tanisha Anderson, Shelly Frey, Yvette Smith, Eleanor Bumpurs, and others.

The point is not to distract from normalized everyday police brutality, but instead to acknowledge that black women are as susceptible, if not more so, to the everyday violence by state sanctioned agents. They too are victims of shootings, harassments, and racial profiling, while in metropolitan areas, black women are as likely to be evicted as black men are to be imprisoned. As the adage goes, 'black men are locked up, black women are locked out'. These facts tend to inform the prevailing orthodoxy and framing of police violence and its consequences. Nevertheless, black women too, are victims of domestically orientated imperial rule.

Keeanga-Yamahtta Taylor points to the deeper political and social stakes that Black Lives Matter addresses. 'African Americans, of course', she says

> suffer disproportionately from the dismantling of the social welfare state, but in a country with growing economic inequality between the

richest and poorest Americans, austerity budgets and political attacks on social welfare come at the peril of all ordinary people. (2016, 5)

She continues,

It is an example of how, counterintuitively, even ordinary white people have an interest in exposing the racist nature of US society, because doing so legitimizes the demand or an expansive and robust regime of social welfare intended to redistribute wealth and resources from the rich back to the working class. (2016, 5)

For this reason, the ruling class have a stake in perpetuating backlash against this movement.

It is also why police brutality is a good avenue to discuss the oppressive nature of the social structure, something that is at play, but not as evident in voter restriction laws and the efforts to roll back the Voting Rights Act. Acting as the Attorney General within the Obama administration, Holder was proactive in attending to Republican state controlled legislatures efforts to strategically suppress voting rights and discriminatory voting restrictions targeted at poorer and minority voters. He also sought to undertake a broad reform of the criminal justice system seeking to lessen its institutional racism by, for example, supporting the Fair Sentencing Act that eliminated differential sentencing for crimes involving crack and powder cocaine, which themselves skew along racial lines. Another positive development was Holder's role in reduction of mandatory minimum sentences for some crimes, again hoping to ameliorate certain kinds of racial injustice. Nonetheless, these laudable efforts to improve and strengthen regulatory oversight, and anti-discrimination measures sit beside the expansion of the state power detailed above.

What this indicates is that the appropriate target for reform of the social structure requires curtailing then ending capitalism, paired with less imperial aggression abroad. Collins perhaps puts this well when she writes that 'U.S. Black women must continue to struggle for our empowerment, but at the same time, we must recognize that U.S. Black feminism participates in a larger context of struggling for social justice that transcends U.S. borders' (Collins 2000, xi). Yet, ever more as Black Lives Matter addresses the reproduction of capitalism's structures of exploitation and oppression, the movements and its members become a target for capitalism's surrogates, for their contention threatens the established order of things.

While there is still a considerable way to go until liberation, Black Lives Matter has had measurable effects, albeit recognizing, as criminologist David Pyrooz and his colleagues write, 'changes in crime trends are slow and rarely a product of random shocks' (Pyrooz et al. 2016, 1). Some municipalities now require police to wear body cameras, and in other cases officers have been fired.

Additionally, there have been some changes in police practice. Most importantly, the movement has shifted the discourse on crime, police, race ensuring that, for the moment, these topics receive due attention. Likely activists in this movement desire more improvements, but the pressure continues. Even Obama has started to try a reform of the criminal justice system, and to attend to voting rights (he did this at an NAACP national conversion). This is a direct result of Black Lives Matter forcing the federal government to account for the war against black life, to curb its internal state rule practices, and to lessen its militarism.

There are a few key lessons to take away from this discussion. The first is a reminder that surveillance technology disproportionately targets the most vulnerable. The second is that racial subordination is rarely deemed important enough to warrant due attention in mainstream political discourse. For example, to the extent that it is covered in the media, it is often a reaction to protests framed around the legitimacy of protest rather than the structural injustice and the grievances that motivated the protests. This raises a third point. Ever more legitimate civilian political contention is presented as a threat to national security and established order. Fourth, as Wilson's research in the 1980s indicates, black women shoulder the brunt of poverty and discriminatory policies, and even then, their voices and contention are only allowed an audience when they articulate and describe black male suffering. In this respect, it is another point of the dynamic of testimony where women both speak and are silent. These circumstances underscore the importance of a fully-fledged intersectional analysis; meaning that it is not race over class, class over gender, or gender over race—but rather that a proper analysis pay attention to the totality of factors that shape lived experience.

CHAPTER 5

External Rule and 'Free Trade'

From the Revolutionary War to the Second World War, there were over 100 US security force interventions abroad to secure American interests, most of these on behalf of capitalists. Beginning as probes but gradually increasing in intensity and duration, during these interventions the US acquired institutional knowledge about how to use force to establish favourable 'open door' trade policies in Latin America and Japan for example. Actions in these places were ultimately a result of US foreign policy that was Eurocentric, either for commerce or for confinement to limit European influence in the western hemisphere (Stepak and Whitlack 2012). For example, the 1823 Monroe Doctrine proclaiming the entire Americas to be in the US sphere of influence was addressed to a European audience. Thus European stability and economic growth was to be balanced with a degree of military caution as European powers were prime trading partners but also posed the greatest economic and security threats. As interventions elsewhere in the world were attempts to bracket out European influence, the supposition is that imperial actions in a place often have very little intrinsically to do with that particular location; rather they are indicative of politics orientated elsewhere. This is certainly the case of US involvement in the Middle East against the backdrop of the Cold War or Africa in light of the 'global power shift' with China's emerging power.

Whereas the previous chapter emphasized the extent to which the truly disadvantaged bore the brunt of dispossession and subjugation induced by internal US state coercion, in this chapter, I survey the role of military power and the digital components of imperialism that protect resource extraction or the creation of surpluses. The primary concern is with how militarization facilitates the insidious creep of capitalism in international affairs. Here it is important to examine the coercive elements of foreign labour regimes to illustrate that fully functioning capitalism has a tendency to escape the dependence on free labour power.[29]

How to cite this book chapter:
Timcke, S. 2017 *Capital, State, Empire: The New American Way of Digital Warfare.*
    Pp. 99–124. London: University of Westminster Press. DOI: https://doi.org/10.16997/
    book6.f. License: CC-BY-NC-ND 4.0

5.1 Induced Under- and Combined-Development

Following the First World War, wherein oil became a strategic resource, imperial powers jockeyed to control the source via dominating the states that emerged from the collapse of the Ottoman Empire. Initially, Britain had an advantage having occupied Baghdad and Mosul late in the war. Aided by an Arab insurrection and insurgency emanating from a promise of post-war independence, the 1916 Sykes-Picot Agreement between Britain and France outlined the anticipated spoils of the Ottoman Empire, dividing the region primarily between themselves, with a remainder for Russia. Later the League of Nations provided a mandate system redistributing territory held by the defeated Germans and Ottomans. Mandates allowed colonial administration to continue, but without formal annexation. Among other acquisitions around the world, Britain received Palestine and Iraq, and France received Syria and Lebanon.

Blatant imperial action triggered a number of revolts across the Middle East, but these were suppressed and dissenting nationalists exiled. Still, to deflect the appearance of formal colonial incorporation, the British installed Emir Faisal I as King of Iraq through whom the British were able to attain favourable treaties and concessions. After the Second World War, relative hegemonic decline meant Britain had three primary objectives. The first was to extract as much from the empire before these territories acquired independence. The second was to bolster West Germany as it was a buffer to the USSR extending control over Europe. The third was to manage the ascension of the US, particularly as much British capital fled west just prior to and during the First and Second World Wars (see Tooze 2006 and 2014 for details). Domination of the Gulf was one area gradually ceded to US rule.

When nationalist leaders in Middle Eastern states opposed extraction and exploitation, they were overthrown. The quintessential example is Mohammad Mosaddegh in Iran in 1953, two years after he nationalized British Petroleum. The only feasible options for these states were to align with the USSR, another empire, and seek better terms, as did Gamal Abdel Nasser following his 1952 coup in Egypt and nationalization of the Suez Canal thereafter, or to play the empires against one another. In response to this tendency, the US supported the repression of nationalists in their client states, particularly by supplying weapons after worker's strikes in 1953 in Saudi Arabia and Iraq.

In Iraq, the terms of oil extraction concessions heavily favoured Western conglomerations. As these conglomerations also had rights to many oil fields, maximizing long-term profits determined when particular fields were development. With priority placed elsewhere, the conglomerations installations covered 0.5 of the Iraq concession with no foreseeable plans to expand. Out of frustration, between 1958 and 1963, the Iraqi government asserted its political independence. This involved removing the British right to operate the RAF Habbaniya base and withdrawing the undeveloped concessions from Western oil companies. Four days after Prime Minister Qasim announced the formation of a state oil company he was overthrown in a coup.

Meanwhile, the conglomerations' oil production did increase, but not nearly to the extent it did in US client states, Iran, Kuwait, and Saudi Arabia. This meant that Iraq's yield from the concessions was insufficient to undertake developmental projects and the economy stagnated. Having attained power via a coup, the Ba'ath Party nationalized the conglomerations in 1972, and sought technical assistance from the USSR. For the USSR, this was a good regional development, for apart from extending a buffer to the US, Iraq had vast oil reserves, unlike Syria their other regional client.

This nationalism is not without a broader context. Prior to these events, the 1967 Arab-Israeli War severed diplomatic ties between the US and Iraq, and stoked Arab nationalist anti-Western sentiments. With a retreat from Vietnam, President Nixon's decoupling the US dollar from the gold standard, and in 1973 in the wake of the Yom Kippur War, in which OPEC countries asserted their independence by instituting an oil embargo against the West unless higher prices were paid. This resulted in an economic recession in 1974 and 1975. Throughout, sensing weakness, subordinate states—particularly in Latin America and the Caribbean—sought to leave the US sphere of influence. As such, the US caved to OPEC, but as a preventative move, the American ruling class begun to take advantage of cheap labour and move some manufacturing abroad to mitigate future boycotts.

The Gulf States' ruling classes hoarded this new wealth, investing it in Western banks, or purchasing treasury bills. So while the US paid higher prices for oil, most of these funds returned to its financial sector. By contrast, Iraq directed the increased revenue to social spending through infrastructure projects and instituted a domestic industrial policy aimed to lessen imports. It also purchased weapons and undertook a project of military build-up and chemical weapon armament in an attempt to become a regional power. Throughout, the brutal dictatorship repressed dissidents. In 1979, when Saddam became president, military expenditures cost close to 9 per cent of GNP. Meanwhile, in Iran, Mohammad Reza Pahlavi was overthrown in a revolution increasing US concerns about a cascade of similar events throughout the region.

The Iranian Revolution and the oil crisis underscored the rationality for US capital to capture the Persian Gulf. Without such control, US capital accumulation would be vulnerable. In 1980, President Carter issued the Carter Doctrine, which stated, that:

> An attempt by any outside force to gain control of the Persian Gulf region will be regarded as an assault on the vital interests of the United States of America, and such an assault will be repelled by any means necessary, including military force (Carter 1980).

Early in President Reagan's first term, his administration upgraded a Joint Task Force established by Carter to a theater level Command. Central Command has an area of responsibility orientated on the trade flow through the Persian Gulf and is dedicated to analysing and responding to conflicts in the Middle East and East Africa. Initially, one of the Command's primary planning events was to stop the USSR from capturing Iranian oil fields. Since established, the Command has managed major conflicts like the Iran-Iraq War, the Gulf War, the Afghan War, and the Iraq invasion and occupation, as well as several other smaller interventions to limit regional terrorism.

Returning to 1980, when Iraq invaded Iran, many Western companies used it as a proverbial gold rush to sell weapons and military technology to arm Iraq for this brutal conflict (see Timmerman, 1992). The US provided Iraq with information on Iranian troop movements acquired by satellite reconnaissance. Crucially, Iraq used chemical weapons on multiple occasions, although the US voted against UN Security Council statements condemning use thereof. There are also suggestions that the US provided battle plans, such as for the capture of the Fao peninsula in 1988 which brought Iran to negotiation. US security forces were even involved in attacking Iranian ships and oil platforms late in the war.[30] Nevertheless, Iraq accumulated $80 billion in foreign debt to fund the war. This figure gives some indication of the extent to which Iraq and Iran were socially shattered by the war. Iraq especially had neglected social investment and development of the known existing oil fields had stagnated.

There were several reasons for the US supporting Iraq. The first was that Iraq was a strategic retaining wall for Kuwait and Saudi Arabia, both US client states. (The US arranged for these states to loan Iraq funds for war expenditures). Second, by stoking strategic attrition between Iran and Iraq, the US was able to bleed their military capabilities and cripple the countries. Finally, by keeping Iraq weaker than it would have been if it had not engaged in the conflict helped to maintain conditions were it would be easier for the US to install a military base in West Asia to check, if not shrink, the USSR's sphere of influence. With this regional consolidation, the US could advance its interest in dispossessing Iraqi's natural resource endowments.

Given their active role as a buffer for US client states in the region, after hostilities ceased the Iraqi regime presumed there would be debt relief from Gulf States to reconstruct the Iraq economy. But this was not to be as other Arab states increased their production, causing oil prices to dramatically fall, a continuation of a downward trend since 1986. As oil production was half of the Iraqi GDP, this the country's economy contracted. This increase in production functioned to limit Iraq's ability to rearm. Once it emerged the Kuwait was slant drilling into the Rumaila oil field, essentially stealing Iraqi oil, Saddam's regime mobilized to invade Kuwait, using brinkmanship to try bargain debt-forgiveness and curbing other Gulf states' oil production to increase the price of oil and thereby alleviate Iraq's fiscal constraints. Seeing no movement on either of these fronts, Iraq invaded Kuwait to dispossess assets and wealth, but this miscalculation afforded the US the opportunity to create a broad-based coalition, including Arab states, such as Egypt, Syria, and Saudi Arabia, to uphold the principle of sovereignty.

The US-led coalition began bombing Iraq in 1991. Using a broad definition of military infrastructure, over several weeks the scope and scale of the bombing campaign indicated an agenda of systematic destruction. Once a retreat was ordered, many Iraqi troops fled via Highway 80. In accordance with a standing order to destroy all Iraq military equipment, Coalition air forces bombed and strafed a 60-mile stretch of the highway. Once the carnage was broadcast, the event became known as the Highway of Death. After flying over the area to head to post-war negotiations, General H. Norman Schwarzkopf, remarked that 'In every direction we could see the burnt out wrecks of military and civilian vehicles that the Iraqis had used to try flee.' (1992, 482). One reason for the disproportionate brutality of the war to test doctrine and militaries capabilities that they had developed and purchased during the Cold War. How did it work? 'Beyond our wildest expectation' Schwarzkopf wrote (1992, 501).

Meantime, as Jean Baudrillard notes in *The Gulf War Did Not Take Place* (1995), the military press briefings upon which the news media draw from for broadcasting and publication did not correspond with the bigger reality of the conflict, its scale, nor violence. It was a 'dramatic ritual', James Compton writes, framed as 'an emotional confrontation between good and evil, personified in the characters of US President George [H. W] Bush and Iraqi President Saddam Hussein' (2004, 83). In addition, the media emphasis on laser-guided smart bombs—for precise targeting supposedly to limit collateral damage, thus more humanitarian—neglects that about 93 per cent of munitions were unguided, carpet-bombing from B52s. Of the glide bombs, about 70 per cent missed their target causing civilian casualties. Best known is the notorious bombing of the Amiriyah shelter that killed more than 400 civilians in February 1991. (Laser-guided bombs were used). This was but the worst horror of common occurrence (see Human Rights Watch, 1991).

Although there were several reasons for the US not to capture Iraq, chief amongst them was caution at the impending collapse of the USSR. The US had to ensure that there were sufficient troops and resources should they be required for other kinds of missions. Furthermore, Dick Cheney argued, the Coalition did not have enough military resources, nor adequate plans to occupy Iraq, given that an occupation would likely lead to a civil war as the country fragmented: presumably the southern Shiite region would come under the sway of Iran, while Turkey, another US client state, would never permit an independent Kurdist state. Therefore, the US sought options to conclude the war satisfactory.

Throughout the conflict, the US mostly preserved the regime. One possible explanation for this is that the US wanted to create conditions where members of the regime would depose Saddam and a settlement that favoured the

US reached. This would account for the concerted efforts to personify Saddam Hussein as the regime. Be that as it may, Saddam Hussein was not deposed, and so President George H. W. Bush called for an internal Iraq rebellion, hoping to provoke the regime's repression of subjects. It worked. When UNSC 688 (1991) called for Iraq to stop repression, the US and Britain used the resolution as a pretext to implement a no-fly-zone, which nominally limited the Iraq regime from flying north of the 36th parallel or south of the 32nd parallel. The purpose was to use daily bombings to stop Iraq from building air or ground defences in these areas, thus ensuring that if an invasion were to come, it would be easier to execute.

Authorized by UNSC 687, sanctions were to be enforced until Iraq could demonstrate that it had dismantled and decommissioned its 'weapons of mass destruction' and missile programs. These had to verified, thus ensuring a protracted process. Sanctions devastated Iraq: in 1993, the economy was a fifth of that in 1979. This forced the Iraqi state to accept the terms of UNSC 986—the 'oil for food' programme—but this limited the importing of goods to maintain or restore the civilian infrastructure. Unsurprisingly, this had had an awful cascade of consequences in the agricultural sector and rendered the civil services ineffective. Initially, the maximum amount of money paid annually for oil was $170 per Iraqi, of which $51 was set aside for the UN Compensation Commission, a fund created to compensate victims of the Kuwait invasion. Lastly, a disproportionate amount was directed to the Kurds. What little remained was insufficient for effective governance. Later this cap was raised, but sanctions made the full rehabilitation of the Iraqi oil industry near impossible.

Still, the culmination of sanctions had enormous costs, particularly in human life. Inconclusive estimates range from 345,000-530,000 deaths between 1990 and 2002. While there is considerable partisan disagreement on the absolute numbers, methodology, data collection, generalizations, and caveats respectfully, much of this debate seems to miss the point that quibbling for 200,000 fewer deaths do not lessen the severity, redeem the harm, or rebut the function of the sanctions. When asked about the weight of these deaths by Lesley Stahl on *60 Minutes*, US Secretary of State Madeleine Albright replied, 'I think this is a very hard choice, but the price, we think the price is worth it' (see Richman, 2004).

Sanctions presented the US with two binds. First, while they stopped other international investments, they also stopped the exploitation of the existing oil reserves, known to be about 115 billion barrels of oil, and estimated to be twice that. Second, the longer the sanctions were in place, the more deaths accumulated, thus increasing hostility to a US presence when it came. In a Congressional testimony, General Anthony Zinni, then heading Central Command, said that the US 'must have free access to the region's resources' (Testimony to the Senate Armed Services Committee, 13 April 1999). 'Free access' seems to mean direct control of the resources. The 2003 US invasion of Iraq was the geopolitical calculus to ensure an 'open door' to exploit oil but also precluding other states, hopefully at a time when US resentment was manageable by an occupying force.

5.2 Contradictions of Global Rule

Concurrent with these Middle Eastern developments, in the early 1980s the US involved itself in a proxy war in Afghanistan in an effort to undermine the USSR, itself an imperial power. The USSR invaded to support a client regime besieged by Islamic fundamentalists, lest the country end up improving ties with Iran or China, or even give pause to other states in the Soviet sphere to reposition themselves. Implementation of the Carter Doctrine began by the CIA providing material support to Afghan insurgents. For the US, the effort sought to maintain its Middle East footing and thus access to profitable oil reserves. Alongside the Reagan administration's decision to reinvest in US armaments, thereby renewing the Cold War arms race that had been cooled by detente, the insurgency was one of the leading causes for the collapse of the USSR.

Still, during a decade of brutal war the USSR did incredible damage to Afghanistan's infrastructure and government, producing a failed state. Once the Mujahedeen secured power, the country provided a conducive environment for fundamentalist terror networks to grow. One of these networks centered on Osama bin Laden. With the momentum of having defeated the USSR and incensed by the presence of US forces in Saudi Arabia during the Gulf War, plus the ties between the US and Saudi Arabia ruling class, bin Laden funded and recruited fellow Islamic zealots to create al-Qaeda, a terrorist network. During the 1990s, al-Qaeda bombed the World Trade Center, hoping to collapse the North Tower into the South Tower, as well as several terror attacks in Africa including co-ordinated bombings of US embassies in Dar es Salaam and Nairobi. In response, President Clinton authorized cruise missile attacks on targets in Sudan and Afghanistan.[31]

Meanwhile, following the collapse of the USSR, the Bush administration had tasked the DoD to review national security policy. Supervised by Paul Wolfowitz, then undersecretary of policy in the DoD, the final report Defense Planning Guidance (1992) indicated that US strategy 'must refocus on precluding the emergence of any potential future global competitor' (DoD 1992). In the 1990s, the geopolitical policy introspection among the US ruling class and their agents revolved not around whether imperial action was valid, but which approach was best. Multilateralists argued co-ordinated actions helped legitimate imperial rule, and co-opted other countries into this system. Additionally, the emphasis on human rights, promoting procedural democracy, soft power, and ideology could work to sway other states from the inside out. By contrast, unilateralists saw no need for legitimacy, and that indeed multilateral rule and exercise were an unnecessary constraint that hindered flexible and rapid deployment of resources of rule.

In practice, rule was accomplished using both kinds of approaches as the circumstances and conditions dictated. Nonetheless, conspicuous in both approaches was the emphasis on the removal and reduction of barriers to capital. This process involved the creation of the World Trade Organization to complete a regulatory trifecta including the World Bank and International Monetary Fund to cement global capitalism and transfer the costs of economic crisis to the under-developed world. These expansionary dynamics of capital are consistent with long standing trends in the US social structure, like domestic uneven development. In this respect, neoliberalisation, geopolitical foreign policy, and military actions are three different strategic appearances of the same basic impulse catering towards capital accumulation.

While multilateralists and unilateralists debated, the US put economic distance on its rivals throughout the remainder of the twentieth century to reach an unparalleled pre-eminence that allowed near free reign to pursue ambitions. Zbigniew Brzezinski's assessment was that 'geopolitics has moved from the regional to the global dimension, with preponderance over the entire Eurasian continent serving as the central basis for global primacy'. The US, 'with its power directly deployed on three peripheries of the Eurasian continent' was well positioned to establish a 'hegemony of a new type', ascending as the 'the first and only truly global power'. (Brzezinski, 1997, 38, 39). These remarks are indicative of the US ruling class conceiving of its agenda as planetary in scope, and reflecting the accumulative imperative of capital.

The US was perhaps at the pinnacle of its power when bin Laden's al-Qaeda executed a devastating terror attack in New York on 11 September 2001. Trading on the stock market was suspended for four days. When it re-opened, the Dow Jones Industrial Average fell by more than 7 per cent, the worse one day drop up until that point. The US economy contracted by 1.1 per cent in the third quarter of 2011. Still by October 2002, the Dow was down 30 per cent from March 2001. The Institute for the Analysis of Global Security (nd) estimates that the property damage and lost production of goods and services exceeded $100 billion, but factoring in near incalculable stock market losses, the figure approaches $2 trillion.

In retaliation, the US invaded Afghanistan to attempt to kill bin Laden and remove the Taliban government. The US installed Hamid Karzai to head a puppet government. Since 9/11, there has been a noticeable shift in the rhetoric of American statecraft as the libertarian faction of the US ruling class consolidated its ascendance, and used the threat of terror to assert and justify the expansion of overt US imperial power. One area where this is evident is in the National Security Strategy of the United States (2002), which was moulded along the DoD's Defense Planning Guidance (1992) and Project for the New American Century's Rebuilding America's Defenses (2000). In his preamble to the document, President George W. Bush wrote that there was 'a single sustainable model for national success: freedom, democracy and free enterprise' (2002, 1). Invoking the common coded connotations for capitalism, President George W. Bush implied that states that refused to integrate along this model were suspect of being a security threat to the US and thus liable to 'pre-emptive strikes'.

The intellectual background to this unilateral policy comes from many places, but several confluences can be represented by Richard Haass a member of George Bush's National Security Council. In 2000, prior to being appointed Director of Policy Planning in George W. Bush's State Department, he wrote that 'The fundamental question that continues to confront American foreign policy is what to do with a surplus of power and the many and considerable advantages this surplus confers on the United States' (1999). His recommendation was for the US to openly embrace imperial logic, that being the establishment of a global order to accelerate capital accumulation.

Even liberal multilateral scholars like Michael Ignatieff who observe, 'states possess independence in name but not in fact. The reason the Americans are in Afghanistan, or the Balkans, after all, is to maintain imperial order in zones essential to the interest of the United States' (2003a, 61), maintain that 'America's empire is not like empires of times past, built on colonies, conquest and the white man's burden'. On the contrary,

> The 21st century imperium is a new invention in the annals of political science, an empire lite, a global hegemony whose grace notes are free markets, human rights and democracy, enforced by the most awesome military power the world has ever known (Ignatieff, 2003c).[32]

Returning to Haass, he indicated that countries reluctant or refusing to integrate into the US designed world order and allow the exploitation of their resources would be susceptible to 'regime change' and 'nation-building' As far back as 1994, nation building for Haass involved, 'defeating and disarming any local opposition and establishing a political authority that enjoys a monopoly or near-monopoly of control over the legitimate use of force' (Hasss in Foster 2003). As well as creating a market for post-conflict social reconstruction, the bigger prize was opening trade relations and extracting wealth on US terms. Haass writes:

> U.S. efforts to use force to bring about changes in political leadership failed in the cases of Qaddafi in Libya, Saddam in Iraq, and Aideed in Somalia. Force can create a context in which political change is more likely, but without extraordinary intelligence and more than a little

good fortune, force by itself is unlikely to bring about specific political changes. The only way to increase the likelihood of such change is through highly intrusive forms of intervention, such as nation-building, which involves first eliminating all opposition and then engaging in an occupation that allows for substantial engineering of another society. (Hasss in Foster 2003)

The US has attempted to install markets economies in the Balkans, Iraq, and Afghanistan. All three cases have involved 'regime change', to install client governments. In this respect, blatant militarism and state building are a deliberate aggressive attempt to reshape a country to fit the needs of capital accumulation.

Both Haass and Ignatieff allude to the apparently appropriate use to employ military force and hegemonic power to secure conditions for economic dominance and expansion. What difference there is between the two, is where Haass sees no need to morally justify these actions, Ignatieff offers a legitimation exercise for 'empire lite' as 'the lesser evil.' (2003b, 2004) But irrespective of whether there is a lack of pretence for those like Haass, or the easing of conscience for those like Ignatieff, the outcome is the same: greater intervention to shape other states to suit the needs of the US ruling class. In saying as much Haass and Ignatieff recognize that the expansion of commodification is a feature of the American social structure, and of capitalism in general. That these representatives of various wings of the ruling class agree effectively means that changing electoral representatives will not necessarily blunt this drive. It might change its character and appearance, its tone and rhetoric, but not the intention and function. As 2004 Democratic presidential candidate, John Kerry indicated in his particular campaign he would continue to advance the military occupation of Iraq, but seek a multilateral approach, as if a shared security burden is somehow better for the people living under occupation.

As mentioned, the 2003 US invasion of Iraq was a timely resolution to install a base and expand the US sphere of influence and their regime of extraction. The George W. Bush administration used the opportunity afforded by 9/11 to claim that Saddam Hussein's regime had stockpiled weapons of mass destruction. Iraq sought to 'deceive; not to disarm' as Colin Powell said at the United Nations (Powell, 2003). In a retrospective confrontation of his complicity, Powell admitted that prior to the UN presentation, the George W. Bush administration had already committed to using military force (Breslow 2016).

The US invasion was swift, and a new government was installed. It disbanded the army, purged the civil service of Baath party members, and condoned reprisals. Mass unemployment and an eroding civic infrastructure put conditions in place for the emergence of local sectarian self-defence groups, and resulted in cycles of violence of incomprehensible complexity and politics, made more difficult by Iran supporting factions, and an influx of fanatical ideologically motivated combatants seeking to fight the US. This insurgency compounded the developing civil war. Altogether, the invasion produced a failed state, and over thirteen years led to the deaths of approximately 250,000 according to Iraq Body Count. It was a total civic collapse.

To counteract the insurgency, through 2007-8 the US increased troop numbers in a 'surge', but most importantly undertook a program of mass bribery and begun negotiations with Iran. A relative absence of public knowledge about the second and third component has cultivated a myth about the 'surge'. As Daniel Larison points out,

> The mythology is responsible for the hawkish delusion that the Iraq war had been "won" before Obama "lost" it, which gave war supporters an excuse to evade accountability for the catastrophic blunder of the invasion and occupation. (2015)

While somewhat successful in stalling the violence, nevertheless these actions undermined the legitimacy of the new 'democratic' Iraq. Not helping matters was Prime Minster Nouri Al-Maliki excluding and permitting state-based reprisals to sectarians and dissidents. All of this ensured that Iraq was unable to govern its territory.

In neighbouring Syria, the Assad family had reigned as brutal dictatorship since 1970, exploiting sectarian divisions and USSR/Russian support to rule. (Since 1971, the USSR, then Russia operated a naval supply base at Tartus, their only Mediterranean facility). From about mid-2011, mass protests invoking the sentiments of the Arab Spring threatened the Assad government, and cultivated fears of reprisals should it fall. Bashar al-Assad deployed the security forces against demonstrators and executed political enemies. Initially the US sought to arm factions opposed to Assad and exploit the opportunity to pry another country from the Russian sphere of influence. While the factional alliances are impossibly complex to follow, what is important is that the country collapsed into a civil war, causing millions of refugees to flee the region, many heading to Europe producing the longest post-war mass migration.

As the Civil War unfolded, ISIS emerged as a leading faction somewhat able to hold territory in both Syria and Iraq thus drawing support and allegiance from other groups. For a variety of reasons, the Iraqi Army generally retreated rather than engage in combat with ISIS. With minimal resistance, ISIS captured Mosul in 2014 and territory in Northern Iraq, eventually threatening Baghdad. As of writing, alongside the US and North Atlantic Treaty Organization (NATO), the United Arab Emirates and Saudi Arabia are bombing ISIS on a daily basis. Canada and the US have Special Forces operators deployed. So does Russia. Russia's involvement is to maintain their client state lest the area become occupied by US and NATO forces. Still, it is a challenging politics, for both Iraq and Syria are failed states, and some members of the Gulf States ruling class fund ISIS. Currently, the US is in a predicament where it desires the fall of the Assad regime, but is also committed to undermining the very forces that could topple his rule.

The threat of ISIS has also provided a public reason to increase American arms sales to US client states. US Arms sales in 2009 were $31 billion, then $21.4 billion in 2010, tripled to $66.3 billion in 2011, more than 75% of the global arms trade (valued at $85.3 billion in 2011).[33] In a distant second was Russia, with $4.8 billion in sales. This increase is driven by an arms race in the Middle East, as American client states—Saudi Arabia, the United Arab Emirates, and Oman—respond to the Iranian nuclear enrichment program, ISIS, and internal rebellions in the wake of the Arab Spring. Regarding Iran, these sales primarily consist of aircraft—in 2011 Saudi Arabia purchased 84 advanced F-15s adding to 70 F-15s; Oman bought 18 F-16 for $1.4 billion—and missile defence systems, such as the United Arab Emirates' purchase of a Terminal High Altitude Area Defense, a $3.49 billion advanced anti-missile shield that includes radars and is valued at $3.49 billion (Shanker, 2012). The immediate goal is to build, country by country, a regionally integrated missile-shield to protect key sites like oil refineries, pipelines and military bases from missile attacks.

The regional fallout from the Iraq War and Arab Spring, the sectarian proxy wars and the suppression of dissidents in the Middle East has led to more arms sales, the most glamorous being the purchasing of US made aircraft and the missiles to replenish a stockpile depleted from bombings in Yemen, Bahrain, and Syria in 2014. In 2014, Saudi Arabia spent $80 billion on weapons, becoming the fourth largest market for armaments; while the Emirates spent about $23 billion, triple what it spent in 2006. Indeed, American arms manufactures have opened offices in the regions, hoping that sales here will offset shrinkage resulting from a declining US defence budget (Mazzetti and Cooper, 2015). Still, one US policy consideration of Middle East regional arms sales has been to ensure despite sales to Arab states, Israel maintains 'qualitative military edge', a long-standing commitment, but enshrined in law since 2008 (Naval Vessel Transfer Act of 2008).

To conclude this section, in the early twenty-first century the US has sought to consolidate a planetary empire, seeking to dispossess and extract has much surplus value as possible from subordinate states, while cornering out rivals. Still, this process has brought about a number of contradictions. The quintessential one, I believe, is capital having no option but to rule with and through states, either by the use of military forces or regulatory bodies. As Ellen Wood puts it,

> The very detachment of economic domination from political rule that makes it possible for capital to extend its reach beyond the capacity of any other imperial power in history is also the source of a fundamental weakness... National states implement and enforce the global economy, and they remain the most effective means of intervening in it. This

means that the state is also the point at which global capital is most vulnerable, both as a target of opposition in the dominant economies and as a lever of resistance elsewhere. It also means that now more than ever, much depends on the particular class forces embodied in the state, and that now more than ever, there is scope, as well as need, for class struggle (Wood, 2001, 291).

However, the ruling class are seeking to reduce that scope. In reflecting upon 'the indispensability of continued American leadership in service of a just and liberal order', and 'America's bipartisan commitment to protecting and expanding a community of nations devoted to freedom, market economies and cooperation', Hillary Clinton believes there is 'really no viable alternative. No other nation can bring together the necessary coalitions and provide the necessary capabilities to meet today's complex global threats' (2014). Reminiscent of George W. Bush's remarks in the National Security Strategy, what she means is that there is no other social structure suitably amenable for a capitalist ruling class; no other option but uneven development and dispossession will be permitted. Conditional concessions will likely occur, yes, but not at the expense of perpetuating profit.

In pointing out that the US is qualitatively and quantitatively different, Wood's and Clinton's remarks, in different ways and for different purposes, highlight how the US is not only driven by the particular interests of capitalists, but it is burdened with the task of facilitating global capitalism in a world divided into competing nation states. The genuine contradiction is that this expansion appears necessary, but it could be otherwise as there is no natural imperative to accumulate.

5.3 Bases for Commodities and Containment

The US emerged from the Second World War with a nuclear monopoly as well as an extensive system of overseas bases, adding to those acquired during the Spanish American War. As but two examples, Guantanamo Bay and Okinawa have been in operation for near 115 and 70 years respectfully, demonstrating how reluctant the US is to leave a base. It also bears testament to President Truman's stance that in the post-war era, the US was 'going to maintain the military bases necessary for the complete protection of our interests and of world peace' (1945). Indeed, this was more or less the case, particularly during the Cold War when the policy of 'strategic denial', was implemented to limit withdrawal from a base lest they become occupied by the USSR. After the end of the Cold War, President George H. W. Bush reiterated that the 'forward presence' would be maintained, but with a quarter fewer troops while the Clinton administration addressed this problem by using shorter but more frequent deployments.

Bill Clinton's administration oversaw the US establishment of bases in Central Asia, continued bombing Iraq, and intervened in Somalia, the Middle East, the Caribbean, and Eastern Europe. In the last case, the Kosovo bombings were formally to stop genocide; it did facilitate the installation of US troops to secure bases in territory previously in Russia's sphere of influence.

After 9/11 there was a rapid increase in bases, many nominally acquired during occupation of Iraq and Afghanistan, elsewise establishing staging posts in countries like Bulgaria and Uzbekistan for the War on Terror. In their 2009 Base Structure Report, the DoD indicated that they had 716 'sites' in 38 foreign counties (2009, 7). While the majority of these were in Germany (235), Japan (123), and South Korea (87), the locations of the remainder range from the United Kingdom and Italy, to Egypt and Djibouti, Bahrain and Oman and several others (see DoD 2009). These are the declared sites, and do not account for CIA drone bases or Special Forces compounds (See Turse, 2015). Besides expected places like Afghanistan and Pakistan, one can cobble together knowledge of drone bases in Burkina Faso, Chad, Djibouti, Ethiopia, and Niger from press reports (See Whitlock 2011, 2012, 2014, Whitlock and Miller 2013, Londoño 2014).

But as indicated above it is rare that the US willingly initiates a withdrawal, which means that the latent reason for these bases is to expand a geographic sphere of influence to establish favourable conditions for 'free trade'. Much of the base development in the early twenty-first century has been using the War on Terror as an opportunity to consolidate capital accumulation in Eastern Europe, as well as to initiate the same process in Central Asia to check China's westward sphere of influence. For example, bases in Iraq and Bulgaria seek to limit Russian extraction in the Middle East and Eastern Europe respectfully. But Russia and China have sought to counter these efforts. To take a Russian orientated example, in 2014 the Kyrgyzstanian government evicted the US from the airbase in Manas. Rented for $60 million a year, the air base was situated about 400km from the Chinese border and in an area previously part of the USSR. The politics behind this eviction are clear: With the extent to which Kyrgyzstan's economy depends on remittance from and exports to Russia; Russia's backing of Almazbek Atambayev in the 2011 election; as well as their 2012 offer to write off $500 million in debt in return for a base for 15 years, it is clear Russia believed the US was encroaching on its 'territory.'

While the US might have been checked in Kyrgyzstan, it does not mean they have conceded the region. Given relatively more attention in Iraq, the absence of the role of oil and natural gas has been overlooked in the media discussion of the war in Afghanistan. War in this region and regime change has made the construction of the Turkmenistan–Afghanistan–Pakistan–India pipeline politically possible. The deal for the pipeline was signed in 2002, and construction set to begin in 2006, but was delayed due to Taliban control of the development corridor. Following sustained military pressure by the US and NATO forces, it was possible to begin construction in 2015, and set to be completed in 2019. But like Iraq, without a permanent military presence, it would be near impossible to build a pipeline or further capital's extractive ends; the goal is to siphon resources from the Russian sphere of influence.

Following bases closures in Panama in 1999, and aware that domestic politics in Latin America states were not conducive to large military complexes, the US used the War on Drugs as a publically palatable pretext to create many smaller bases in Columbia. Known as 'Plan Columbia', this initiative has created 'cooperative security locations' in Ecuador, Aruba, Curacao, and El Salvador, as well as radar sites in Peru and Colombia. These join bases already in the region in Soto Cano, Honduras, Guantanamo Bay, Cuba, and the Naval station in Vieques, Puerto Pico, which trains Naval Battle Groups before they deploy to the Mediterranean and the Persian Gulf. Elsewhere, the US military uses bases belonging to Latin American security forces, like the Joint Peruvian Riverine Training Center in Iquitos, Peru.

Bases can also be used to exert regime change. For example, and keeping with the Latin America area, the US aided the overthrow of Honduras' democratically elected president Jose Manuel Zelaya in 2009. The State Department, under Hillary Clinton, sought to provide a legal justification for the coup, while President Obama recognized the subsequently installed President Lobo.[34] This destabilization facilitated organized crime as a power vacuum led to violence competition to control drug trafficking. Alongside state sponsored terror and assassinations targeting journalists and human rights activists, the increase in crime has resulted in Honduras having the highest murder rate in the world. In 2012, 87 Representatives from Congress petitioned Hillary Clinton to suspend military and police aid, but she refused (Frank 2012). The reason for all this, according to Dana Frank (2013), is Honduras is intended to be the first domino to push back against the left-wing governments that swept to power in Latin America from around 2005 onwards. Granted, within this wave, some governments, like Venezuela, are authoritarian and display low levels of institutional investment and capacity building, but several, like Brazil, are democratically legitimate.

Aside from security, citadel like bases cement a country's status as a client while from a juridical standpoint sovereignty is preserved. Another benefit of bases is the production of favourable military relationship produced through joint exercises and military assistance programs with the host country's security forces, thus functionally enmeshing them in the US Empire. Bases also allow the US to undertake actions on these bases that is otherwise prohibited in the US. Guantanamo Bay, where prisoners were labelled enemy combatants and so could be held without charge or trial in indefinite detention is the best example. The US can also use these bases to warehouse rapid deployment equipment, for training and the testing of new weapons systems.

There are drawbacks to foreign military bases. The most obvious is 9/11 and the terror directed at the US and its allies. In this instance, the attacks were nominally retaliatory for US bases stationed in Saudi Arabia. The bases are far from populated areas to preserve the appearance of the House of Saud's rule and sovereignty, but Osama Bin Laden created a rhetoric wherein US security forces presence was an occupation of sacred Islamic sites. There are other less extreme examples too. In countries where US troops are allowed off base, like Okinawa, particular merchants benefit from the commerce, but they do so at the expense of other vulnerable members of the community through generating social problems like forced prostitution. There is therefore a tendency for US bases to become an object of domestic politics, co-currently of opportunity and scorn.

For these reasons, and with an eye to costs and returns, many new US bases are rather minimalist outposts that can be built or discarded as required. Even Afghanistan, where the American Army is expected to be deployed until 2024, follows this pattern. As another example, the USS *Ponce*, a former transport ship, has been refitted to become a floating forward operating base. Already deployed to the Persian Gulf, capabilities include helicopter pads and maintenance facilities with the addition of underwater diver support, and barracks to support several hundred Special Forces troops. The advantage of this platform is that it is not dependent on foreign nations to provide land for bases. The Navy is requesting a further $1.2 billion in its budget for two similar but purpose built vessels (Shanker 2012b). This is not to argue for the virtue of American citadels occupying foreign soil, but rather to underscore the shift in military planning where flexible base system and deployment schedule mirrors that of 'flexible accumulation'.

Another blowback results from the culmination of US actions in a particular region. For example, the increased mass migration from Central and South America to the US has much to do with the legacies of US occupation in Nicaragua and the Dominican Republic in the pre-war era, overthrow of governments in Guatemala and Chile in the post-war era, as well as the sponsorship of the Salvadoran and Guatemalan militaries as they committed endless atrocities in the 1980s. Much of this intervention was due to the combination of anti-communism to thwart nationalization of American business interests.

Poverty and crime are endemic by-products as conditions resulting from 'open door' principles for 'free trade' that in turn create uneven-development and pliable client states. Responding to uneven-development and the market for drugs, it was common to see Latin American special forces, many of whom the US trained at the School of the Americas located at Fort Benning, establish drug businesses. Los Zetas are but the most notorious recent incarnation of this process.

While on the topic, in 2014 mass migration from Central America received considerable media coverage due to approximately 70,000 unaccompanied children, and another 70,000 families being smuggled via Mexico to the US border. In 2016, of the unaccompanied children 28 per cent were from El Salvador, 37 per cent from Guatemala, and 15 per cent from Honduras. To stem this, the Obama Administration pressured the Mexican government to increase the capacity of the Southern Border Plan to apprehend migrants before they reached the US border; capturing about 170,000 people in 2015 alone (see Chishti and Hipsman 2016). Internally, the Obama administration was legally limited from undertaking executive action to provide documentation to 5 million migrants who qualified under the Deferred Action for Parents of Americans and Lawful Permanent Residents program (see *US v. Texas*, Liptak and Shear 2016). But while advancing that project is commendable, it is hard to reconcile with that same administration's mobilisation of the security apparatus to intensify mass deportation – about 2.5 million since taking office.

The US international base system is one technique to maintain an economic system predicated upon expanding exploitation and extraction without annexation or colonial settlement, but still exerts political controls over other states. These bases also provide a general condition of coercion that maintain the currents in the existing international system, thus leaving few genuine options for states and regions in the periphery. Overall, bases seek to maintain the political economic hegemony of the US ruling class.

Michael Mann notes how the consequences of climate change will affect food and water supplies, making for climate refugees and amplifying the stakes of existing tensions, conflicts and crises (see Mann and Toles 2016). In the case of crop failure, malnutrition and hunger will be leading drivers of conflicts. Mann and Toles write that 'Climate change will create more competition among a growing global population for less food, less water, and less land—a prescription for a perfect storm of global conflict' (2016).

To be sure, the goals of an integrative political economy and the accompanying blowback brings another contradiction into focus. Asked in 1998 whether he regretted supporting bin Laden's insurgency in Afghanistan given his subsequent turn against the US, Zbigniew Brzezinski, President Carter's National Security Advisor, responded, 'What is most important to the history of the world? The Taliban or the collapse of the Soviet empire?' (Brzezinski quoted in Gibbs, 2000, 241). Events such as 9/11 are by-products, probably inevitable, of this kind of geopolitical exercise of power. Nevertheless, from a cynical geopolitical calculus, perhaps Brzezinski might argue that the prying of Central Europe and Central Asia from the Russian sphere of influence and the creation of US bases in those regions was worth the risk of this blowback. The result of these bases is that Russia is encircled, while China is nearly so. But it comes at the expense of the US homeland being put in direct risk, in effect unleashing a coercive power of the state directed as much internally as externally. As Leo Panitch so eloquently puts it 'the contradictions of ruling the world are great' (2003, 233).

5.4 Securing International Circuits of Production

In the post 9/11 world less than 1 per cent of Americans have served in the military, these troops disproportionately drawn from economically vulnerable and impoverished communities. This '1% army', has been equipped and mobilized to protect and advance the interests of the economic 1 per cent, the power elite who occupy key positions in the security state. But much how the 0.1 per cent, the super-rich, have an outsized role in shaping the economy, so does 0.1 per cent of the military, Special Forces, have an outsized role in shaping military force. In this section I cover how US Special Forces help enforce the prevailing international division of labour. It is this labour regime that organizes 'the production of information and information technology today' (Fuchs, 2016b).

Since the end of the Gulf War, Special Forces have become a key foreign policy instrument, with one analysis calling them the 'most innovative, subtle, and adaptable instruments of national power' (2016, 75). Excluding Iraq and Afghanistan, in 2010 near 4,000 Special Forces troops were stationed in approximately 60 to 75 countries, with efforts to expand both of those numbers. Bearing the hallmarks of a flatter organizational structure and close collaborations with intelligence agencies, these units are designed primarily to respond in unilateral direct covert action. Training and joint operations with security partners, frequently the focus of public attention, are legitimation exercises (Scahill 2010). As these forces are rarely accountable to other branches of government, the effective result is a presidency and the security state are consolidating a private military force, near 66,000 personal and expanding, to complement the CIA (Schmitt, Mazzetti and Shanker 2012). This number has doubled since 2001 and includes military personal and DoD employees, with spending in the same period increasing from $4.2 billion to $10.5 billion. With this funding, 12,000 Special Forces troops have been deployed every day since 2003, with four-fifths located in the Middle East conducting multiple raids each week (Robinson 2012). Therefore, it is an uncontroversial observation that the US state is relying upon Special Forces to an unprecedented degree, and this is particularly fruitful in times of fiscal restraint.

As per Jeremy Scahill's reporting, White House counterterrorism director John O. Brennan has articulated this agenda as the US 'will not merely respond after the fact', but will 'take the fight to al-Qaeda and its extremist affiliates whether they plot and train in Afghanistan, Pakistan, Yemen, Somalia and beyond' (Scahill 2010). Bureaucratically, this traces to George W. Bush's administration order called the Al-Qaeda Network Execute Order that permits Special Forces to deploy beyond the battlefield for lethal and covert operations and sanctions cross-border operations. Reflecting on the pace of deployments, General Tony Thomas, commander of US Special Operations Command describes Special Forces as being, very, very kinetic right now; very direct action because we are trying to rectify five failed states and an extremist phenomenon that's gone rabid. Once we get that back in the box, eventually, I hope, we can have the right sort of access, placement, connective tissue, to retain stability (Thomas as cited by McLeary and Rawnsley 2016).

Similarly, General Donald Bolduc, commander of Special Operations Command Africa is on record as saying that 'terrorists, criminals, and non-state actors aren't bound by arbitrary borders'. Accordingly, he reasons that this requires that Special Forces cannot organize nor recognize traditional borders. 'In fact', he says, 'our whole command philosophy is about enabling cross-border solutions, implementing multinational, collective actions and empowering African partner nations to work across borders to solve problems using a regional approach.' Supporting African states that are waging wars or fighting counter-insurgency, or rebel forces, Bolduc has said that these forces operate in the 'gray zone', which he describes as 'the spectrum of conflict between war and peace' (as cited by Turse, 2016).[35] Due to social media, 'secret wars' are better described as 'low-visibility wars'; conflicts which attract intermittent attention, but which agenda setting minimizes.

Under President Obama, Special Forces have initiated and intensified these 'gray zone' activities. For instance, these forces operate in Somalia, attacking al-Shabaab who have been added to the War on Terror. Around 1,500 disclosed Special Forces operators are deployed in Cameroon, Djibouti, Niger, Egypt, and Libya, many directly in combat roles against African-based terror groups (Obama 2015). But many of these conflicts cannot be 'solved' by military power, and US Generals realise this. For example, when testifying at the Senate Armed Services Committee, the Commander of US Africa Command, General Thomas Waldhauser emphasized how economic scarcity drove insurgencies and rebellions. This is particularly acute among African youth, of whom over 40 per cent of the population is below 15 years of age. 'To protect and promote U.S. national security interests in Africa', Waldhauser testified,

> diplomacy and development are key efforts, and our partnership with the Department of State and the U.S. Agency for International Development (USAID) is key to achieve enduring success. Together, we work to address the root causes of violent extremism, lack of accountable government systems, poor education opportunities, and social and economic deficiencies to achieve long-term, sustainable impact in Africa. (Waldhauser 2017, 2)

Waldhauser is of the opinion that 'soft power', that is economic and cultural hegemony was vital to combat African extremism. It is against that background that Waldhauser illustrates the awareness of a 'global power shift':

> Just as the U.S. pursues strategic interests in Africa, international competitors, including China and Russia, are doing the same. Whether with trade, natural resource exploitation, or weapons sales, we continue to see international competitors engage with African partners in a manner contrary to the international norms of transparency and good governance. These competitors weaken our African partners' ability to govern and will ultimately hinder Africa's long-term stability and economic growth, and they will also undermine and diminish U.S. influence. (Waldhauser 2017, 3)

This was a vital concept to keep in mind as President Trump's budget sought to significantly reduce funding to the State Department's foreign aid and humanitarian budgets.

Military theorists generally presume that industrial democracies are loath to become involved in protracted conflict. This is because citizens carry the costs in the form of taxation or the loss of life as they directly participate in warfare. This sentiment is attributed to General George Marshall that 'a democracy cannot fight a seven-year war'. Therefore, democracies use representative oversight, dissent, and protest to safeguard against needless military efforts. However, should the security state desire protracted conflict; one method to alleviate protest would be to insulate the burden of war from the wider civilian population. Ending conscription does so as a professional military removes the immediate responsibility of war from citizens leaving them relatively untouched by combat. In many respects, a professional military suits the ruling class, military officials, and the public. For the ruling class a professional army eases widespread resentment. For the military, it removes ill discipline and insubordination amongst the troops. And the public, professionals especially, would cease to be unwillingly drafted.

Due to domestic politics, in August 2011, the Obama administration began defence spending cuts totalling nearly half a trillion dollars over 10 years.[36] In part, the latent rationale is to produce a military that is more efficient by, for instance, eliminating obsolete procurement, closing unnecessary bases, and streamlining commands. Included in this plan is a reduction of military personnel by almost 100,000 by 2017, four fifths of which would be Army personnel.

This budgetary squeeze coincides with the US's reorientation from the Middle East to the Asia-Pacific region. While I will detail this development below, put simply, it means that the US state will try to move beyond both counterinsurgency and counterterrorism operations and towards more strategic concerns. The ramification for the Army is its attempt to remain central to this new strategic re-orientation while active involvement in major combat operations is curtailed. But given the strategic reorientation, the former Army Chief of Staff General Odierno conceded that the army will be side-lined and relegated to conducting strategically secondary missions such as peacekeeping, regime stabilization, and counterinsurgency (Odierno 2012). Odierno predicts that these operating environments will feature 'regular military and irregular paramilitary or civilian adversaries, with the potential for terrorism, criminality, and other complications' (2012, 1).

To meet this diverse mission mandate, the Army is seeking to put logistic hubs in key locations, while units seeking regional alignment will have specialist equipment, and be provided with linguistic and cultural training to attend to different missions and different physical, political, and cultural environments. The goal is to have an army that is used as a deterrent as part of a broader security plan. Odierno says 'This means maintaining a force of sufficient size and capacity so that potential adversaries understand clearly our ability to compel capitulation if necessary.' He continues, 'we will increasingly emphasize activities aimed at deepening our relationships with partners and demonstrating our country's commitment to global security. Ideally, a focus on prevention and shaping will keep future conflicts at bay' (2012).

To supplement this regional realignment, the United States has used private military contractors (PMCs)—mercenaries—as auxiliaries to publically claim that they have fewer troops committed to an area of operations. In August 2011, for example, there were more than a quarter of a million mercenaries in Iraq and Afghanistan (Commission on Wartime Contracting, 2011).

By using volunteers and contractors to undertake military labour, the conditions exist to go to war for extended periods without genuine accountability to the public. Indeed, the security state can bypass attempts to garner public legitimacy for conflicts and military interventions. In other words, citizens' views are not central to ascertaining the costs of military adventurism and occupation. Moreover, a volunteer military tends to encourage the ideologically predisposed to sign up. This further distances the military from the values within American society.

An additional feature of the Army recalibration of military planning and operations are efforts to fully integrate technological capabilities into frontline units, thereby extending advanced technology and the information revolution to the individual solider. Although Odierno admits that goal is still years away from operational deployment, certainly a research agenda involves the construction of an 'operator suit' to serve as an infantry force multiplier. Initial specifications for this computerized suit include night vision and other tools to enhance situational awareness, enhanced strength, ballistic protection, and a life support infrastructure. This means that the state requires fewer soldiers to deploy similar levels of force, effectively concentrating the skills and capability of warfare with a selected and narrow warrior elite.

Internally, the state seeks to lionize the military in an attempt to forestall critical appraisals of its activities. This is evident in the rhetorical pairing and purposeful conflation of unreserved support of troops with unreserved support for the operations in which they are involved. These moves seek to quash criticism while ordinary people unreservedly repeat war apologetics, thereby capitulating to ideological dogma. Indeed, the military and its personnel are publically positioned as beyond reproach. The military being a prime delivery instrument of humanitarian aid and the subject of gaming and cinematic narratives assist in internal public relations exercises. This has been so successful that even allegations of atrocities are met with undue suspicion and an unqualified blanket defence before an investigations take place. Overall, this culture of solider worship blinds the public to the realities of war and occupation, obscuring rather than addressing the issue of imperial conflict.

These forces have more presidential access under President Obama than previous administrations, as he is allowing these forces to act in an aggressive, secretive, and pre-emptive manner. Emblematic of this mode of operation is the group formally known as Task Force 714, a 'direct-action' unit conducting 'high-intensity hits' (Ackerman in Horton, 2010). One should not discount the policy sway of Special Forces in advocating a move away from large missions to more flexible operations (see Ackerman 2009). Special Forces Command has been advocating for more autonomy to position troops and equipment as per their judgement about global affairs (Schmitt, Mazzetti and Shanker 2012), ostensibly to be able to respond rapidly to broad and emerging threats, while avoiding large-scale foreign interventions and occupations. Accordingly, Special Forces are seeking new kinds of missions. However, there is dissent in some areas of the Pentagon—particularly area commanders and the State Department—that believe the request for more autonomy would bypass the Joint Chiefs of Staff and the Defence Secretary, thus missing democratic oversight (Schmitt, Mazzetti and Shanker 2012). This issue here is not legitimacy of using covert forces, but who maintains authority.

The political turf wars seem to be regularly won by Special Forces. For example, then Defence Secretary Leon Panetta, upon the request of Special Forces, broadened their operational purview by granting it a global combatant command. In addition to global responsibility, this command status effectively gave Special Forces the ability to reallocate troops to regional commanders, bypassing Pentagon oversight.[37] This modification grants Special Forces a greater degree of autonomy to determine threats as per their intelligence operations, although operations would still be directed by the president. This allows Special Forces to conduct missions that could otherwise be stalled by the Pentagon, effectively making them akin to the Praetorian Guard.

The dominant place and influence of Special Forces is so entrenched that the US Army, in an effort to remain relevant, is seeking to train its general-purpose units to provide logistical support, menial labour, and regional specialization to Special Forces units (see Odierno 2012). Cheerleading this development Linda Robinson (2012) remarks,

> These changes will allow special operators to deploy in an integrated fashion with other elements of the U.S. government, including conventional military forces, in well-thought-out campaigns that will last not days but years and achieve durable positive effects.

Even as the military downsizes and refocuses on the Asia-Pacific region there is no indication that the Special Forces budget will be reduced, or that unit deployments will be curtailed. Rather it appears that their troop levels will stay consistent, just reallocated to other regions (see Schmitt, Mazzetti, and Shanker 2012). It is envisioned that their missions will be to stay on call for direct action against terrorist targets and hostage rescue operations. Further, using the pretence of training and liaison missions, they will be used to collect information in unorthodox ways. In short, the Obama administration has made Special Forces a central tool in enforcing global rule.

As mentioned, Special Forces operate on the African continent where one of their main tasks is to protect international circuits of production. The conflicts in the Great Lakes region and the Iraq War are associated—even driven to a certain extent—in an international circuit of production that use conflict minerals to create networked and handheld computing (see Fuchs, 2014). These devices are assembled in China using energy secured by the US in Iraq. Furthermore, the Great Lakes War is aided and abetted by arms manufacturers that sell small arms to African countries as a business venture to keep states fragile, and thus make it relatively easier to extract resources and wealth; deliberately destabilized just enough to make resource extraction efficient. Lastly, these international circuits of production have obvious racial significance.

5.5 The Military Response to a 'Global Power Shift'

Given a 'global power shift', (Hoge 2004) US Foreign Policy is becoming Sinocentric. Arguably, the Nixon administration's opening of relations with China to exploit a Sino-Soviet split was the first step in the direction, but with the collapse of the USSR, Clinton's administration deemphasized a Eurocentric posture, and undertook military planning with a rising China in mind (Stepak and Whitlack 2012). This was a defence priority in the George W. Bush administration until 9/11 provided an opportunity to advance interests in the Middle East. However, the Obama administration reinitiated a 'pivot to Asia'.

This reorientation is present in the various Presidential and Pentagon Strategic documents (see Department of Defense 2012a, 2012b, Daggett 2010, Obama 2007). In much the same way that the US viewed European economic growth and trade as beneficial while being circumspect about security concerns, the US has adopted the same stance to China in an attempt to cater simultaneously towards strategic balancing and economic development. To accomplish this goal, the US will continue trading with China while establishing and maintaining military superiority (see Department of Defense 2012a, 2012b, Daggett 2010). This military presence takes the form of large naval exercises with allies, redistributing troops from Japan and South Korea to the Philippines, and Australia, and other parts of the region, and donating equipment (Burke 2013, Gonzanga 2013). Other actions include deploying littoral combat ships in Singapore. This is because the Malacca Strait is an energy chokepoint for China: as the majority of the country's energy flows through this region, it is ripe for blockade. These developments are acute additions to an existing infrastructure of bases in Japan and South Korea, and aside to ongoing military support for Taiwan.

Given that much trade travels via sea, the orthodox understanding of global trade is that it is underwritten by naval power. States that have the ability and power to enforce the movement of goods in such a way that they are insulated from regional violence are the economic hegemons. In line with orthodoxy, the US deploys its Navy to enforce trade on its terms. This power is backed by the ability to direct sustained combat operations on, over, under, and adjacent to the sea using naval aircraft, marines, or missiles. China, while not yet possessing the naval presence or the force for direct confrontation nevertheless has, the US believes, sufficient force to disrupt US hegemony in the Western Pacific. This force is characterized by the deployment of the *Liaoning*, China's first aircraft carrier, which reports indicate became combat ready in November 2016. A second carrier is being built (CSIS 2016a). Although the *Liaoning* is not as capable as US aircraft carriers, it can be supported by land-based aircraft. Finally, China's military spending went from about 25 billion US dollars in 1990 to over 200 billion by 2015 (SIPRI 2016).

In the 21st century the US stance towards China involves a combination of engagement, interdependence and competition, with the US aware of Chinese intentions to become the regional hegemonic power and so diminishing US influence in the Western Pacific. Much of this comes to a head in the South China Sea as China seeks to use the Spratly Islands to assert its claims within the nine-dash line. Multiple states—like Philippines, Vietnam, and Malaysia—have claims in the region, and these interests play off one another, increasing tensions. As of late 2016 'China appears to have built significant point-defense capabilities, in the form of large anti-aircraft guns and probable close-in weapons systems (CIWS), at each of its outposts in the Spratly Islands' (CSIS 2016b). The public analysis by the Centre for Strategic and International Studies indicates that,

> China has nearly completed structures intended to house surface-to-air missile (SAM) systems on its three largest outposts in the Spratly Islands. The deployment of SAM batteries to Fiery Cross, Mischief, and Subi Reefs would be in keeping with China's efforts to extend its defense capabilities throughout the nine-dash line. (CSIS 2017)

Periodically the US conducts freedom of navigation exercises with destroyers in the South China Sea or training exercises with carrier battle groups in the Western Pacific (Perlez 2016). Some of these exercises pass well within what would be considered Chinese territory if the US legitimated the claims. The stakes are significant: $5 trillion of trade passes through the South China Sea each year. And so little surprise that the Chinese state spends $10 billion per year on international public relations, some of this is used to recruit client states to support China's regional interest.

It is with strategic caution over economy hegemony that despite military spending cuts, the Navy will not reduce any of its 11 aircraft carrier task forces (*New York Times* Editorial 2012), while 34 of the 57 US nuclear submarines are based in the Pacific (Heginbotham and Samuels 2016). Rather, there is renewed investment into these kinds of military resources. Take for instance the new Ford class carrier. This is the first new aircraft carrier class since the USS *Nimitz* in 1968, and America's first new carrier of any kind since the USS *George H.W. Bush* was completed in 2003. At 47,000 tons this carrier class features a redesigned flight deck to launch and recover aircraft far more efficiently than the currently operating *Nimitz* generation. Additional improvements include new designed propulsion systems, reactors, and radar (Terdiman 2013). Carrier groups are re-locatable airports, bases, and factories and are used to coordinate force projection; a form of twenty-first-century gunboat diplomacy. At the same time, the development of three Zumwalt stealth destroyers will cost approximately $22 billion, and the first is expected to be combat ready in December 2019. Reportedly, these ships can fire precision projectiles 70 miles.

The aforementioned orthodoxy holds that military pre-eminence yields significant economic benefits through reducing security tensions thereby assuring safety to investors. That said, Dan Drezner (2013) is sceptical about the extent to which this naval orthodoxy fulfils the promise of structured economic benefit. Roughly, his reasoning is that international security threats are less likely for stable states, but rather more likely for failing states and those resisting global integration, so there is no need for a sizable naval presence. Here US military bases in the Middle East are intended to safeguard against energy insecurity by countering the hegemony while concurrently deterring Russian or China from entrenching their presence in the region. However, year by year the US becomes less reliant on foreign oil supplies, in part through domestic fracking shale reserves. Presently, less than a quarter of gas consumed in the US is imported, and of that figure less than a fifth comes from the Middle East. So there may be some reconsideration about the degree to which the US needs to secure this region. At the same time, both Russia and China will for the foreseeable future lack the capability to project more than token military power into the Gulf. In Russia's case this is because of domestic economic weaknesses, and in China's case, their present priority is the South China Sea. But even then, the resources in this region are consumed more by China and India and decreasingly by the US—so there should be burden sharing.

Nevertheless, Drezner's argument is one of degree, not one of kind. What I mean is that he does acknowledge how the US Navy allows the US to dictate the terms of global economic and political integration. The purpose of the US Navy is not to expunge rivals, but to use the prospect of force to consolidate control over economic activity, and the standards and norms that govern that activity. David Graeber's observations about military force and contemporary international political economy complement this view. He argues that a state can use their military power to control financial liquidity.

> The essence of U.S. military predominance in the world is, ultimately, the fact that it can, at will, drop bombs, with only a few hours' notice, at absolutely any point on the surface of the planet. No other government has ever had anything remotely like this sort of capability. In fact, a case could well be made that it is this very power that holds the entire world military system, organized around the dollar, together. (Graeber 2011, 365)

To elaborate, the US uses their money supply to act as an international reserve currency. Much like how once Britain established the gold standard, the network externalities and path dependency of British imperial rule meant that other states had to consider the benefits of monetary convergence, so too do states have to weigh the incentives of monetary convergence on the US dollar. This technique is particularly effective when there is 'gunboat' issuing of US treasury bonds as a form of tribute together with the aggressive deployment of financial instruments and institutions in rolling out and maintaining US hegemony.

Considered from this vantage, what appears as the loss of centralized US control of capital is rather a strategy of indirect extraction that involves demanding that other states pay tribute to the US. Within this order, transnational enterprises are enabled by US policy to further entrench indirect rule. In return, the US, through the Navy and other agencies, provides security to corporationsto do business. This is accomplished through either rigging international treaties, capturing international organizations, or lobbying and bullying for favourable business relations in host countries. In short, the US security state seeks to create global governing structures to maintain a rule in which other countries must abide, and in which labour is suppressed, and surpluses are channelled to the US.

CHAPTER 6

Minds, Brains, and Disciplinary Programs

In this last chapter I discussed the general turn to quantified cognitive-behaviourism, particularly its combination of abstracted empiricism and psychologism, as it seeks to forge a 'Grand Theory' of the social sciences from the mind and its genetic basis and then apply this model in matters of governance. Accordingly, I want to consider the ideological assumptions that underwrite a series of turns occurring in a broad range of fields, including behavioural economics, cognitive science, evolutionary psychology and information systems as well as elements within artificial intelligence research as they seek to examine how the universally shared features of human cognition code and recode historically specific forms of cultural practice. To their credit, proponents and practitioners in these disciplines rightly do think that cognitive findings—when put in their social, historical, and comparative context—are truly illuminating.[38] Nonetheless, I argue that they fall foul of cognitive behaviourism because they have a weak and unsustainable theory of the mind. My inquiry considers the ramifications of these paradigms as they have sought to integrate with one another based upon several common commitments to a kind of computational economy in the brain, and that once understood, can be replicated in information systems, but can also explain historical and social development by referring to the brain. Indeed, despite these diverse elements, I argue that they are manifestations of a definable core insofar that these disciplines share strong claims are over-interpretations of small evidence and reflect more the prevailing ideological conditions than genuine insight. In the course of this chapter, I explain why this intellectual artifice is not only an alienated understanding of human beings, but one that when backed by institutional sanction via 'nudge' like programs, will create new techniques of oppression, ensure social stratification, and further legitimate exploitation.

Altogether, the goal in this chapter is to address several interrelated kinds of questions, which include the evolution and social nature of the human

---

How to cite this book chapter:
Timcke, S. 2017 *Capital, State, Empire: The New American Way of Digital Warfare.*
    Pp. 125–143. London: University of Westminster Press. DOI: https://doi.org/10.16997/
    book6.g. License: CC-BY-NC-ND 4.0

brain, the possibility of embodied intersubjectivety through mirror neurons and the extent to which social life has neuro supports, the neurosociology of emotion and its relation to cognition and decision making, and the degree to which consciousness is computational. What is more, this development trades on the promise that it can reveal the cognitive continuities that underlie particular collective responses to cultural forms. In doing so, the project seeks to explain how particular mental rules cross boundaries of time and place and underlie perceptual and cognitive abilities. This implies that groups of persons are not only historically socially situated, but historically cognitively situated. Underwriting all of this is the presumption of the convergent combination of the cognitive-computational revolution that will be the most far-reaching intellectual development of the early twenty-first century. Still, I think there are several conceptual errors that require attention before one wholeheartedly boards this train.

Animating my critique is a principled rather than practical end. To elaborate, what I mean is that my critique does not aim at a premature project that has not yet been able to deliver on its promises. Rather, this project is built upon several suppressed contradictions that beget errors in axiomatic reasoning that then accumulate. This is not a pedantic exercise: what is at stake is the interlinking nature of knowledge, cognition, and reality as they inform prospects for human flourishing. By this, I mean how events are described and explained, how factual reports are constructed and how cognitive states are attributed. Too often mental states are said to orientate themselves to discursive constructions, themselves predicated upon an interplay between a person's situated cognition and material context; thus these are expressions of the context of their occurrences. Therefore, to a speaker their own mind is unknown; but it is available to the expert whose hermeneutic hammer beats down on a person's lived experience and intentions. This makes the analyst have final say over the descriptions and meanings of social actions. To me, too much sway is given to the discursive power of cognitive behaviourism. This dominant stage presence in current intellectual inquiry is a peculiar naturalization that sidelines more plausible explanations.

I begin by tracing some key developments in the attempts to date, on the part of researchers and theorists, to constitute an interdisciplinary venture on cognitive behaviourism axioms, and to develop links between different projects. I address both pioneering and transitional attempts to describe cognition in terms of the computational process of coded symbols and the relation to embodied experience. Thereafter I show how the accumulation of errors in axiomatic reasoning combined with unwarranted enthusiasm for cognitive behaviourism and cherry-picking evidence harms social science. These emblematic cases seem to me to go most directly to the heart of what is at stake in the general turn to cognitive behaviourism. In this respect, I am interested in the social production of the substantive claims.

Much of this debate would be conceptual, except that cognitive behaviourism is already being used to guide policy makers. Although carried out in technical terms, and so rendered neutral and natural, the implementation of cognitive behaviourism functions to limit political struggle and judgements about politics. As such, there is much at stake, particularly when one recalls how many fashionable twentieth-century social policies appealing to rationality qua neutrality were extremely harmful. Similarly, this practice of presuming that persons can be better understood and governed by social policy informed by cognitive behaviourism is the application of misguided assumptions, which once coded in bureaucratic decision systems would then condition much of our life and leave little room to contend. To better understand this development, one needs some familiarity with post-war twentieth-century American social thought.

6.1 The First AI Revolution and the Legacies of Political Behaviourism

During the Second World War, political science in the United States came into its own as the study of order. This meant that the study of politics was less textual and canonical, leaving behind its philosophical and legal-historical orientation, and instead was put in service of the state to understand political behaviour and social cohesion (Skocpol 1985, 4). This project even drew in many of the European émigrés such as Theodor Adorno, Max Horkheimer, Herbert Marcuse and other political refugees who proverbially 'had to pay the rent' and spent their wartime activities modelling personality, propaganda, and the influence of information exchange (Wilson, 2004, Chapter 2). This project borrowed significantly from psychology and organizational economics, but it was also influenced by nascent behaviourism.

Behaviourism, as practiced by B. F. Skinner, reduced behaviour to the simple set of associations between an action and its subsequent reward or punishment. This approach applied an empirical statistical analysis to predict the future as a function of the past. Here 'a vague sense of order emerges from any sustained observation of human behaviour'. Furthermore, 'direct observation of the mind comparable with the observation of the nervous system has not proved feasible'. This brackets aside intentions, along with other 'conceptual inner causes' a valid science of behaviour (Skinner, 1953, 16, 29, 31). With its success, there were spill over effects for other disciplines, and became the foundation of what Robert Dahl (1961) called the 'behavioural revolution' in the social sciences.

This approach was meant to reconcile the differences between expectations and practice with persons in organizational settings, and the extent to which people did not follow rules and procedures, and how did they become influenced to do what actions as well as their attitudes to events. Part of this research agenda was enabled by the technologies of mass public opinion surveying that informed researchers of discrepancy between normative and institutional rationality and people's everyday decision-making practices.

The critical error that behaviourists of all kinds made was ruling out the importance of subjective, mental phenomena simply because it was difficult to observe or measure. Deficiency of method is insufficient grounds for a conceptual grounding; this points to the social setting of this idea. Accordingly, Noam Chomsky's 1967 critical review of Skinners' *Verbal Behaviour* torpedoed Skinner's attempt to explain linguistic ability by behavourial principles. Instead, Chomsky (1959) argued that the human mind had a linguistic capacity founded on a universal grammar which itself was innate. Languages could only be developed if they conformed to the deep structure of the brain.

Along with advances in computer science, the computational turn reduced behaviourism's stranding in American social sciences. Following the Second World War, computer scientists actively sought to build machines that could compute rationally to mimic human cognitive processes. The computational turn pulled from Alan Turing (1950) and the Claude Shannon's (1948) information science—which itself relied upon formal mathematical logic developed by Gottlob Frege and Bertrand Russell—whose work argued that computers resembled the human brain, and that these machines would eventually manifest an artificial intelligence indistinguishable from human intelligence. In the 1950s, computer scientist John McCarty (1979) called the study of intelligence and its replication of essential features on a computational system artificial intelligence. The goal of this project was to create intelligent devices and robots that could undertake labour while also demonstrating how biological intelligence functioned. Herein computation is understood as anything that can be represented as information can be computed.

This project intersected with Chomsky insofar that his work uses natural attributes to explain ordinary language practice and linguistic ability. In making the deep structure of the brain responsible for syntax, effectively giving it priority over semantics, Chomsky's critics argued that he could not account for meaning (cf. Searle 1972). This focus on the biological rather than the social pushed both social sciences and cognitive scientists to shift attention to trace the distinct patterns produced by the brain so that computers could replicate these patterns, hoping that this would replicate the form of consciousness.

These successes, however, were arguably limited. This was because there were severe errors with the foundational assumption about rationality. While computer programs could be written to manipulate symbols within logical finite systems this was not successful outside those systems. The scope of comprehension for a computer using natural language was limited, and computer scientists encountered the same barriers as philosophers of language in the ideal and ordinary language debates (see Rorty 1967).[39]

A good demonstration of these conceptual inadequacies can be represented by John Searle's (1980) famous 'Chinese Room' argument wherein he presents a strong case for the distinction between meaning making and information processing. Herein symbol manipulation via a set of predetermined logical rules cannot match how humans relate symbols to meaningful events. This fits with Chomsky's conception of language wherein the complexity of internal representations is a result of a genetic endowment maturing in an environment. This opens up the possibility of rich, creative, meaningful activity. This simply cannot be reduced to computational associations as practiced by behaviourists. Chomsky's approaches to the understanding of the mind are anathema to behaviourism. Their emphasis on the internal structure and characteristics enable it to perform a task is different from the external associations formed by relying on patterns of past behaviour and the environment.

As meaning making is still out of reach of computation, Hubert Dreyfus has good grounds to state that, 'the research program based on the assumption that human beings produce intelligence using facts and rules has reached a dead end, and there is no reason to think it could ever succeed' (1992 ix). In short, the first artificial intelligence (AI) revolution was limited by an overly rational model of mind wherein consciousness was understood as the computation of information processing as opposed to making meaningful interactive relationships and associations with the world.

6.2 The Second AI Revolution and Embodied Computation

Following Chomsky's critique of artificial intelligence and the jettisoning of positivist logic methodology, there was an emergence of technological power in the computation area. The aforementioned critiques of 'good old fashioned AI' heralded a turn to probabilistic and statistical models and analysis. This was in part attributed because advancements in engineering and robotics, achieving goals, being successful, was more professionally rewarding than addressing fundamental scientific questions. This led AI researchers to use computers to model the architecture of the brain. The advanced computing power allowed models of networks rather than logical serial processing.

There was also an additional development where there was some limited modification to the presumptions to the mind. Cognitive scientists tended to understand a mind that is biological, embodied, and affective, that is linked to thought processes that are apparently 'illogical' relative to previous models of the mind that stressed the separation of emotions from cognition that was endemic to early cognitive theory. However, the empirical methodological re-orientation of the second AI revolution saw mental processes classified as information processing, and moreover, the best model for a cognitively active human being is a computer running a program. This change is a selective inversion of the where the mind does not pre-exist discourse or culture, but rather is continually accomplished in and through its production and interpretation. This newer approach sought out alternatives to a strictly logical view of cognition and incorporated findings and axioms from psychology, anthropology, and linguistics, in short stressing the network nature of cognition as a computational problem.

These intellectual sentiments, supported by cognitive linguistics, demonstrate the complex and reciprocal relationship between culture and the embodied mind in forming the human subject; here the brain is the material site where language, culture, and the body meet and form each other. These sentiments are present in Foucauldian philosophical anthropology regarding the contextual shaping of cultural artefacts that then redirects questions about the author's cognitive process to questions of authorship in material culture more broadly. An axiom in this analysis is that there needs to be a thorough understanding of the existence, circulation, and disciplining of a discourse within the author's material body. By inference, reading texts can reveal ideological formations, but also cognitive processes. There seems to be a contradiction between the role given to the shaping power of culture on the brain, while seeking to preserve and stress universal innate constrained cognitive actions that hold across cultural and historical eras. A similar impulse is present in the Derridean critique of rationalism, wherein rational thought is not a reflection of natural functioning of human cognition. As Jacques Derrida argues, 'there is nothing outside the text.' The key difference between post-structuralism deconstruction and Chomskian cognitive science is where Derrida kept good portions of Saussurean arbitrariness, although making it less phonocentic, Chomsky argued that meaning was not arbitrary, but rather motivated by innate characteristics bounded by physical attributes that were refined by environmental factors.

From the Chomskian vantage, cognitive science embraces a framework wherein culture intersects with human cognition and material forces as they influence and shape each other. There is an emphasis on how human cognition is deeply tied to materiality and embodiment, even to the extent that persons are themselves unaware of the process by which the brain is the site where culture and biology meet and shape each other.

Nonetheless, current renditions of AI are little more than behavioural principles cloaked by sophisticated computational techniques. This can be seen in the reliance on statistical learning techniques to better mine massive datasets. Implicit in this endeavour is the assumption that with sufficient statistical tools and enough data, interesting signals can be isolated from the noise of hereunto poorly understood systems. While the urge to gather more data is strong, it is not always clear whether this is a path to meaningful explication. What I mean relates to the conception of the purpose of scientific practice and emblematic of the struggle between the efficiency of using computing power to distinguish between signal and noise, or whether it is more meaningful to find the essential basic principles that underlie and provide explanatory insights of the system. This is reminiscent of Sydney Brenner's dismissal of the sequencing revolution in the biological sciences as 'low input, high throughput, no output science' (Friedberg, 2008). What the second AI revolution is attempting is to reverse engineer systems and networks whose nature is a mystery, although it is not always clear what theoretical framework this data fits. To paraphrase David Berry, 'the destabilizing amount of knowledge' produced by this computational turn 'lack the regulating force of philosophy' (Berry, 2011). Appreciating physical differences can help limit claims of the comparative similarity between brains and computers.

Aside from the major difference that brains have bodies, while computers are digital, brains are analogue. Neurons can fire in relative synchrony or relative disarray and fluctuating membrane potentials are a factor. Additionally, computers use byte-addressable memory, but memory in the brain is associational. Another appreciable difference is that computers are modular and serial whereas the brain has distributed and domain-general neural circuits. For example, the hippocampus is important for memory, but also imagination, navigation, and other functions. This means that unlike computers, processing and memory are performed by the same components in the brain. Moreover, the brain has no system clock akin to the speed of a microprocessor. Together these differences show that synapses are far more complex than electrical logic gates. Lastly, the brain can repair itself after injury. In this respect, the brain is a self-organizing system and adapts to experience in ways that simply do not happen with microprocessors.

In short, attempts to develop artificial neural networks to replicate the brain are nowhere near like the actual intricate and massive connection of neurons. This means that they are limited in how useful they are in testing theories about basic cognitive functions. Moreover, there is a kind of paradox: the attempt to prove that the mind is logically computational, and thus digitally replicable, trades upon associational strategies, biases, and biological things.

6.3 The Role of Economics and Psychology

Reminiscent of ethnology, evolutionary psychology roughly states that the mind is the way that it is because of adaptions to the environment, and that insights of evolutionary biology can be used to bring new light onto the human brain, and human behaviour more generally. These neo-Darwinists have sought to apply natural selection to social organization much like Herbert Spencer's meek justification that the social stratification and colonial domination of expansionist industrial capitalism reflected natural selection. Evolutionary psychology takes mundane observations—such as cells being spherical—to claim that physical principles provide channels of development that extend up to individual action and social organization. It does so by explaining human behaviour by referencing a competitive environment as understood by cost and benefits anchoring in economic modelling. Here the presumption is that everyday human behaviour can be well explained by this framework, where replication of genetics is the purpose of human beings, and that this action is guided by calculations undertaken by the brain directly and indirectly largely at the unconscious level regarding an economy of energy consumption and expenditure.

This has the hallmarks of Gary Becker's project, which he described as 'the economic approach to analyse social issues that range beyond those usually considered by economists', (Becker, 1992) or as he said elsewhere, an 'approach to human behavior' (Becker, 1976). However, the crucial oversight of this project is that market rationality is substituted for pure rationality, meaning that social interactions are assessed in relation to the market. This treats all social interactions as transactions. Having set all relations to the market metronome, the market is presented as an omnipresent system of distributing goods, rewards, and privileges. However, this presumption is unwarranted; rather a case must be made for relating things to the market, not the other way round. So the mistake is presuming what ought to be proven.

Construing ecology as economy does not explain much because there are always retrospective appeals to the two principles of mutation and selection to explain humanity's remarkable attributes. The paradigm is so flexible that it is immune to experimental and observational tests. Therefore, when evolutionary psychologists are found wanting they can simply weasel out by saying that they now have more information at their disposal. In doing so they seek to escape assessing, whether in principle their research agenda is theoretically well grounded. This does not explain much and so is not satisfactory. Like Spencer, it is philosophically convenient for social Darwinism to skip over the political installation of institutions such as the market. Instead, social adaption has less to do with natural and biological processes than political and social processes.

To the extent that one can see the economic principles of Gary Becker's project in evolutionary psychology, similarly one can see the economics of Daniel Kahneman who sought to model the 'intuitive mode in which judgments and decisions are made automatically' in affect theory (Kahneman 2002, 470). In Kahneman's theory, 'an automatic affective valuation – the emotional core of an attitude – is the main determinant of many judgments and behaviors.' (Kahneman 2002, 470). As this applies to the affective turn, there is the latent promise that it can account in some cases for how the material environment triggers specific kinds of intensities of awareness which elude description, representation, or intentional formation, but which Kahneman speculates, developed in 'evolutionary history' (Kahneman 2002, 470).

Kahneman's research demonstrated that persons are susceptible to anchoring, availability, and representativeness biases. When combined with a lack of knowledge in strategic settings, inertia, and sunk costs, the general claim is people are fallible and do not act in accordance with strict rationality. Further to that, one tenet of affective evolutionary psychology is that brains evolve to develop and function in social networks and have an appreciation of the costs of reproduction, and that these are impulses that shape our actions, oftentimes which are not well understood by persons themselves, that there are pre-conscious motives that drive action.

This is hardly controversial—indeed, it can be understood as necessary humanization of economic research to acknowledge that preferences are not consistent. However, a quick follow up proposition is that persons are 'predictably irrational' to use Dan Ariely's (2009) turn of phrase, and so they can be systematically and strategically manipulated by savvy architects of choice. These architects are often employers and governments—those with power—and depending on their intentions, the architecture can be for social amelioration or exploitation.

The depoliticized language of 'nudges' cloaks this manipulation as if to connote mild direction rather than paternalistic intervention by the ruling class. Proponents of nudges like Richard Thaler and Cass Sunstein point out that as policy is the architecture of choice and so can be used to correct for a person's predictably irrational preferences (Thaler & Sunstein 2008). But people have contradictory and inconsistent views and practices, so it falls to the nudges and their preferences as to how they will design the architecture that informs the setting of other's choices: for if consistent preferences do not exist then there is no way to nudge people to what they want or need; it can only be what paternalists think they want, which is but what paternalists want. In this respect, nudging is more than creating incentives that a person can then exercise options over, but rather an intervention to try rig the system that triggers an affect in a person so they then undertake the ruling class's subjectively preferred behaviour. Additionally, as nudging is built into a social system it is a cost effective means to shape subjects (See McMahon, 2015, Cromby & Willis Martin, 2014, Leggett, 2014).

The ethics of this kind of governance warrant scrutiny. While Thaler (2015) claims that there is little chance of manipulative nudges causing harm because most nudges are visible, even if one suspends disbelief simply on his say so, his defence neglects to incorporate the need for the transparency over, and indeed justification for, active intervention to shape subjects. In doing so Thaler overlooks that the political purpose of nudging is to for policy to make itself inconspicuous and so circumvent a public gaze.

There are other problems here too. While certain decisions which were once thought to be self-consciously produced are automatic, this does not mean that all or most of our actions are automatically pre-conscious or without intent. So when affective evolutionary psychologists use neuroscience to underwrite behavioural economics they have little to say about the individual person or even consciousness. Accordingly, when using the same axiomatic paradigm it is unlikely to have anything valid to say about social organization and politics.

6.4 Computing Means and Social Ends

The social and political consequences of the computational turn have a near unprecedented impact on governmental practice. Setting aside for present purposes the role of government in collecting information and creating profiles of people—itself extremely problematic in nature—there are other kinds of insidious epistemic problems that skew the conception of persons and their actions. In this section, I use the example of algorithmic regulation to demonstrate that there are principled arguments for keeping neuroscience out of social policy.

Algorithmic regulation is an approach to governance that seeks to apply AI learning principles to process the data produced by sensors to adapt to changing circumstances, induce stability, and shape social actions. The main promise of algorithmic regulation is that it makes governance more effective, and thus harnesses the state for democratic purposes by improving service delivery. This is justified by harnessing 'a deep understanding of the desired outcome', as one proponent calls it (O'Reilly 2013, 289). But make no mistake, algorithmic regulation is a political programme that seeks to quell politics.

Algorithmic regulation marries anticipatory adaption of the environment with the various kinds of technologies of surveillance such as dynamic biometrics and smart environments of those same environments to guide public interventions according to what particular people are susceptible to do. It does so to 'nudge' or influence a person's decisions to adopt preferred social actions. In doing so, it seeks to minimize the contingency of human actions for governors to better stabilize their regimes. In other words, its target is to delimit what a person could do and prevent those actions from being actualized.

It has a pre-emptive character that seeks to create affects or nudge persons based upon an anticipatory evaluation of what a person could do and what the political regime wants them to do. It then masks this gentle pressure as a person's agency to decide to act. This means that algorithmic regulation undermines the person as a moral agent because it seeks to even slightly displace their preferences and intentions for the regime's own.

The error here is disconnecting the means of doing politics from its ends, and so reveals the several simplistic and naïve assumptions about politics and power. The fault is presuming that behaviours discovered via data mining are independent of power, and overlooks how the process of politics shapes the contents of politics. This political agnosticism can be seen in cases where the imperative to evaluate and demonstrate efficiency, results, and the like presupposes that the goal of policy is optimising the already agreed upon, or already instituted. So positioned, algorithmic regulation is posed as politically neutral and thus able to generate objective and inoffensive universal remedies to social ills.

It neglects that most political discussions and struggles are about beliefs, and so are not amenable to quantifiable. So the appeals to efficiency and rationality in the form of 'crunching numbers' does not improve on weaknesses of human judgement, rather the profiling and digital transcription enabled by predictive data mining bypasses human interpretation altogether. This in turn changes a person's relationship to knowledge as it is applied in a social setting.

To be clear, the issue is not quantification, or statistics. Quantification requires epistemic communities that evaluate interpretations, uses, and findings. By contrast, automated algorithmic regulation is not accountable to an epistemic community at large. Rather it is privy to proprietary bureaucracies whose programmers and administrators are not directly accountable to the people they seek to nudge. The lack of transparency emerges again when dealing with methodological concerns. The absence of a broader epistemic community that is not employed by these bureaucracies means that there is no independent process of testing and evaluating the code.

The computational turn has a pretence to an analysis anchored in empirical experiment and deductive–causal—logic. Rather it interpolates people through induction as shadows of themselves. This indifference to causes in heterogeneous contexts has a direct impact on the presumed existence of causal interactions particularly with how to understand a person's actions and intentions. Algorithmic systems are appealing because it relieves governors from the burden of being accountable and transparent in their assessments of people. This phenomenon deflects attention away from causality and intentional agency or individual and collective ability to give account of their actions and related encumbered meanings thereof.

In doing so, it is seen as the ability to disrupt existing deliberate governance, and instead 'hack' people. Here, getting people to adopt a welfare program, or forestall civil disobedience. The commonality between these two kinds of actions is that they are treated as an equation that needs a solution suitable to an epistemic government problem, the problem being inducing people to be lessen radical indeterminacy and the incommensurability of contexts and behaviours. In doing so, this upends existing conventions regarding the production and enforcement of norms.

One can contrast this to circumstances where persons encounter institutional due processes. This particular kind of interaction requires persons to use intentional language to provide explanations and motivations for their actions. In this respect, it is a moment for people to give account of themselves and in so doing, the institution provides a moment for a person to challenge the norms that organize that very process as the norms are relatively more visible, intelligible, and contestable. It is not automated and scripted by code.

As the purpose of algorithmic regulation is to assist bureaucracies anticipate what bodies could do, and then nudge these bodies to undertake subjectively desirable actions, this undermines the agency that is foundational to the person-as-citizen. Rather people are objectified, while the process itself is concurrently mystified and reified such that accounts for and about the data and its uses are unexamined. This kind of regulation limits a person's capacity to develop as an autonomous agent who engages in collective action.

This has the hallmarks of Marcuse's one-dimensional society. Recall that he argued that the process of near total social integration due to consumer and administrative driven logics flattens the scope for discourse, imagination, and understanding. Instead what is substituted is the perspective of the dominant order which uses various mechanisms to create social closure. While the mechanical forms he identified—punditry and media systems—are different, the mechanical functional remains the same: the appearance of contentment in service of capital, but not essential contentment independent thereof.

Rendering politics devoid of class concerns, the struggle for power to distribute goods, or disagreements about belief, relegates contention and confrontation to but accepting different unintentional driven tastes and preferences. I cannot see how this could be considered emancipatory, for it renders democratic governance as aesthetic rather than normative.

6.5 Lazy Definitions and Weak Epistemology

In at least one strand of contemporary philosophy of mind, talk of perception has fallen out of favour. Indeed, most writers deny perception altogether, or claim it does not matter. Instead, they reduce perception to reality, or speak of the 'really real'. Perceptions are said to be 'nothing but' particles or waves or structured brain events. Paul Churchland (1996) replaces the perceiver with functioning biological bodies. The perceiver is reduced to an organized body, mind becomes the brain, body motions become actions, man becomes the person. Churchland redefines phenomenal qualities as being nothing but properties of the brain. Cognitive events such as understanding, recognising, feeling, and perceiving are replaced with neural analogues. Here psychological events are treated solely as neural events. Here this is always already nothing but the really real of matter and motion. And this is the prevailing view in cognitive science.

These contemporary materialists have two claims. This first claim is that all perceptions can be explained in terms of or by reference to neural events and the like. The second claim is that there are only neural events (and other physical events in the environment). At the heart of the dismissal of perception is the combination of two beliefs. The first is that science, especially neurological science, has access to reality; and second, the distrust of perceiver-dependent events.

The critique is that neuroscience practices an epistemology that seeks to associate properties. Take connectomics for example. Here the goal is to map the neurons in the human cerebral cortex as a preliminary step to digitally reproducing that circuitry (see Alivisatos et al. 2012). Google Brain is a very good example of this kind of project. Then again, this approach is an error: it merely seeks the surface manifestation rather than the logic and operations that performs the task, what is the brain actually doing. Therefore, it is difficult to discover this by seeing where synaptic connections are being strengthened or where there is neural activity. Information of this sort may well be useful, but it does not address the fundamental question about mechanisms.

In part, this is because there are real problems with the working definition. Describing consciousness as 'the feeling of processing information' cannot be correct because it implies consciousness is perceived by something else. This is a problem when trying to construct computationally based artificial intelligence: For unless a mathematical pattern can perceive its own existence, then consciousness is but well described by that mathematical pattern.

Besides, considering humans' have approximately 100 trillion possible arrangements of synapses, even if were possible to map out the exact pattern of brain waves that gives rises to a person's momentary complex of awareness, that mapping would only explain the physical correlate of these experiences, but it would not be them. Experiences are irreducibly real, but different from brain waves. Still, it is an error to mistake consciousness as being well described by mathematics or computation for being mathematical or computational. Presuming otherwise is to reify a description. Overall, these are incomplete representations and partial understandings of physical, biological, psychological, and social reality.

There are other methodological errors. Researchers rely upon fMRIs to compare brain activity with visual stimuli by examining increases in blood flow in order to infer associations. But this neuroimaging is little more than neo-phrenology and misleading. Four points are relevant here. First, as Lilienfied et al. (2015) point out, 'the bright red and orange colors seen on functional brain imaging scans are superimposed by researchers to reflect regions of higher brain activation.' Moreover, this increased illumination is not a direct measure of neural activity; rather 'they reflect oxygen uptake by neurons and are at best indirect proxies of brain activity.' So changes in blood flow are not a clear indicator of what the precise relationship between cerebral blood flow and neural activity happens to be (Sirotin & Aniruddha, 2009). Besides, it is not as if other parts of the brain are dimmed when there is a stimulus. As Lilienfied et al. write, 'the activations observed on brain scans are the products of subtraction of one experimental condition from another. Hence, they typically do not reflect the raw levels of neural activation in response to an experimental manipulation.' So increased blood flow indicates little about what is occurring in other parts of the brain that are active. So controversies regarding the assumptions read 'into' and 'out of' brain scans are left unattended (see Dumit 2004), or dealt this at the level of technical improvements of data capturing technology at the larger expense of what is trying to be captured, in others words, a poor understanding of the problem, hoping that the technical refinements will provide insights. However, this largely leaves the question of how thoughts and consciousness relate to each other under-attended.

One final point Lilienfied et al. raise is that 'depending on the neurotransmitters released and the brain areas in which they are released, the regions that are "activated" in a brain scan may actually be being inhibited rather than excited.' So functionally, it could be that these areas are be being 'lit down' rather than 'lit up'. In other words, it is premature to try to isolate individual components from a working whole. Even the most basic tasks require the integrated unit.

Granted, researchers tend to study what they know how to study, but this points to the deficiency of the developing experimental techniques or methods that seek to find the right target. While more data and better statistical analysis can provide a better approximation to mapping mechanical relations, it reveals little about the principles behind those mechanical relations. Statistical analysis is all well and fine, but one should not confuse understanding what is happening for why it is happening. Moreover, one can be easily mislead by data mining that seems to work because one does not know enough about what to look for.

A more appropriate approach is to understand the fundamental principles. Take the example of medical practice. Without a strong grounding in biological principles a doctor will not be able to examine and explain variations to bodies, all they will have is knowledge of techniques that come in and out of fashion, and while these techniques may be successfully applied, their use does not demonstrate fundamental knowledge of a human body's biological processes. So their medical knowledge is predicated upon techniques rather than principles, which is a problem, should techniques change or a new kind of variation is uncovered. Without fundamental knowledge of the causal processes, one is only in the catalogue business, and this does not tell us about how structures were acquired or developed. In short, one is dealing with a different conceptual problem.

Probability theory and statistics are misapplied to biology and cognitive science because they seek to find correlations within noisy data rather than examining how biological and cognitive systems select and filter out the noise; these systems are not trying to duplicate the noise, but rather to filter it out. Using the example of human infants, although initially confronted by noise, they reflexively acquire language because they have the genetic endowment to do so.

In addition to theoretical problems inherent in using statistical induction, practical problems emerge when researchers use or amalgamate large data sets.

This is because of unknowns in the selection criteria and quality of data. These limitations produce errors that compound upon each other and are rarely acknowledged. So there are intrinsic limitations to data as well as interpretive elements involved so it would be an egregious mistake to believe that quantification necessarily brings social science closer to objective truths.

A popular stance is the definition that assumes that all mental representations derive from brain activity, and so every mental state has an associated neural state. The difficulty with this definitional understanding of consciousness is that it does little to aid and address the more relevant question, at least for the present discussion, about how it arises. In avoiding the metaphysical grounding of consciousness it becomes trapped in a circle where the contents of consciousness consist of whatever we happened to be aware of. In this respect, the present generation of AI researchers are describing perception, not consciousness.

Cognitive functionalists posit that 'the mind is what the brain does', as two commentators put it (Kosslyn and Koenig 1992, 4), while Paul Churchland explains this, 'whether or not mental states turn out to be physical states of the brain is a matter of whether or not cognitive neuroscience eventually succeeds in discovering systematic neural analogs for all the intrinsic properties of mental states' (1996, 206). But this way of understanding the mind is premature, for the model—the computational theory of mind—is hardly a settled question in the philosophy of mind. It is rather, as Thomas Nagel has written a kind of 'physical-chemical reductionism' (Nagel 2012, 5). To give some background, John Searle regards the mind body problem as resting upon the faulty presumption that these terms reflect 'mutually exclusive categories of reality.' It exists because there is a reluctance to see that 'our conscious states qua subjective, private, qualitative etc. cannot be ordinary physical, biological features of our brain.' (Searle 2007, 39). Searle writes that if we drop the mutually exclusive criteria then a solution is possible. To his mind,

> All of our mental states are caused by neurobiological processes in the brain, and they are themselves realized in the brain as its higher level or system features. So, for example, if you have a pain, your pain is caused by sequences of neuron firings, and the actual realization of the pain experience is in the brain. (Searle, 2007, 39–40).

But, this introduces a problem insofar that it requires one to specify how conscious states come into being. This attends to not only questions of making sense of perceptions and experience, but also the extent to which a person's consciousness is evoked by material circumstances independent to the body. This defence requires us to defend the person as a perceiving agent; the nature of the object of perception; the role of mental contents; and the causal and significatory relation between perceptions and objects.

Keeping these points in mind, it is worth returning to the AI research. These efforts, as notable as they have been in their disciplines, are mimicking intelligence. In addition, AI is deterministic: if presented with the same inputs, it will produce the same outputs if the program were run again.[40] Beyond practical problems, in principle there remains little understanding of the brain. Presently, cognitive behaviourists describe intelligence in a way that boils down to 'being able to do everything person can do'. This circular reasoning demonstrates that scientists do not know what these computations are trying to mimic. So even once we set aside the hubris from executives who seek to sell software systems, there is considerable distance between producing things that even remotely resemble the breadth of actual human intelligence, let along consciousness. To reiterate the points made above, without a principle-based understanding of consciousness there is little way to know what you have designed to act in a particular way is actually successful in being sentient. The working definitions of intelligence in artificial intelligence are descriptive low bars and are nowhere near self-awareness or consciousness.

In the attempt to remedy the faulty theory of mind, social scientists would do well to reassess their relationship with metaphysics, and discard the coextensive hyper-materialism that characterizes the AI researcher paradigm. Treating perceptions, ideas and emotions as little more than electrical impulses misses the emergent properties where the whole is greater than the sum of its parts. This perspective, it seems to me, stems from a cramped, hyper-reductive view of causality: one that is materialist, but not historical, instead of viewing the mind and its mental activity as distinct from mere and reductive material impulses. So one needs to take seriously that minds are a distinct realm of existence that cannot be fully explained by physicalists. In other words, there is a remainder after taking account of cognitive evolution, computational models, or the economy of mind. Neither chemical reactions predicated upon a base economy of natural selection can account for the creation of the mind. While physical evolution is causally necessary, by itself it is an insufficient condition for consciousness. These bold claims about neurological support are but an epistemology of excessive reductionism.

There is one last bit of hubris where researchers believe that mathematically based speculations resolve or dissolve long standing political conundrums, but do so without seriously engaging with those philosophical debates. It is related to the belief that all reality can be fully comprehended in terms of physics. But this is a fantasy. While it is easy to understand, for instance, the interaction of light and nerve impulses, this cannot account for the gaze outwards. Cognitive behaviourism falls at this first hurdle while still being far away from being able to account for other aspects of human consciousness like the formation of intentions and undertaking voluntary action. So if cognitive functionalism has little to say about the person and consciousness, it is certainly not well positioned to claim relevant meaningful contributions to social policy.

6.6 The Psychologism of Abstracted Empiricism

Having discussed potions of the intellectual inheritance of cognitive behaviourism from twentieth-century social thought, I now want to turn my attention to a critical branch of sociological thought from the same period to assist in analysing this set of ideas. C. Wright Mills worked in the immediate post-war period as a research assistant to Elihu Katz and Paul Lazarsfeld's research on the media effects of mass communication. The majority of their work sought to understand the persuasive influence of mediated messages in print and broadcast communication technologies to shape and control the ideas, attitudes, and behaviours of members of a society. Mills thought that most of the findings suggested that the media effects of mass communication sat in concert, if not over-determined, by other factors like differentiated cultural practice of composite audiences and their agency. And for this reason, he never shook his distaste for behaviourism and its presuppositions.

Shaped by this post-war infatuation with coding mass behaviour and his critique thereof, in *The Sociological Imagination*, Mills identified the emergence of Grand Theory (the term Mills used to mock Talcott Parsons's work) and Abstracted Empiricism (a comment on Daniel Bell's work). Stemming from his close experience with large public opinion survey research and alongside questions about the legitimacy of power, epistemologically, Mills was dissatisfied with the attempt to induce correlative relations but at the expense of understanding social forces. With an excessive focus on individuals, these aforementioned studies did not consider social relations, real world politics, nor were they well grounded in the sociological theoretical tradition. Altogether, this reflected what Mills described as a pervasive 'psychologism.' What he meant by this was 'the attempt to explain social phenomena in terms of facts and theories about the make-up of individuals' (Mills 2000, 67 fn 12). He writes,

> Historically, as a doctrine, it rests upon an explicit metaphysical denial of the reality of social structure. At other times, its adherents may set forth a conception of structure which reduces it, so far as explanations are concerned, to a set of milieux. In a still more general way…pyschologism rests upon the idea that if we study a series of individuals and their milieux, the results of our studies in some way can be added up to knowledge of social structure. (Mills 2000, 67 fn 12)

Abstracted empiricists, had according to Mills, adopted a research approach that sought to replicate the demonstrated success of the physical sciences, but in doing so had prioritized method over substance. In this respect, it was 'systematically a-historical and non-comparative' (Mills 2000, 68). Quantitative survey methods were presumed to be more rigorous than other kinds of social inquiry. But this kind of research was costly, required significant staff to distribute, collect, and tally the findings in preparation for basic computational analysis. These actions required large budgets and resources, and so led to the bureaucratization of social research that resembled industrial scale production. In this industrial scale, research the sunk costs of the scale of investment trumps self-critique and modification. This mind-set makes it difficult to understand change and contradiction in social, economic, and political institutions let alone wider social and political development. As Mills observed:

> one reason for the thin formality or even emptiness of these fact-cluttered studies is that they contain very little or no direct observation by those who are in charge of them. The 'empirical facts' are facts collected by a bureaucratically guided set of usually semi-skilled individuals. It has been forgotten that social observation requires high skill and acute sensibility; that discovery often occurs precisely when an imaginative mind sets itself down in the middle of social realities. (Mills 2000 70 fn 13)

Together, these enable the pre-conditions for the domestication of critique. So being enamoured with cognitive behaviourism often leads to but one kind of approach to the study of human action. But this has direct and distinct disadvantages because the information produced tends to be a-historical and decontextualized. This kind of theoretical mindset makes it difficult to deal with change in social, economic, and political institutions.

Abstraction, without context, Mills believed, led to disengaged scholarship, alienated from the true dimensions of the problems under investigation. Excessively functional, behavioural, and naïve empirical approaches fail to perceive the wider social and political settings that organize those particular arrangements. These approaches count the countable because they are easily countable. This is not to elevate context above all else, but to suggest that historical circumstance, contingency if one will, cannot be discounted in any analysis. So, the spirit of Mills' critique is perhaps as important now, given that there is a prevailing belief that technological management is necessarily required given the rise of ever more complex societies and the discussions over the selection of basic values is closed.

As I have demonstrated throughout this chapter, the psychologism produced by Grand Theory and Abstracted Empiricism has come about through the dismissal of reasoning and intention. This is the product of two beliefs: the first is that science, especially neurological science, has access to reality; and second, the distrust of perceiver-dependent events. But this is little more than bringing the hermeneutic hammer down on lived experience, holding that people are not best positioned to relate to an observer their reasons for actions. Instead, one has the judgement of the theorist or unaccountable bureaucratic code. Moreover, it concedes that the investigation of social problems can be best approached via methodologies defined by computation not humanism; this is disciplinary supplication, not supplementation.

All of this is to say that there is a tremendous intellectual stake in cognitive behaviourism being correct. So much so that criticisms are brushed away and considered professional contrarians rabble rousing for their attention. This neglects though that in the attempt to impose a synthesis on approximately 25 years of research, the hubris and generalisations that have emerged therefrom there has been a significant intellectual citadel build upon a shaky foundation of over generalized eclecticism. It has created a messy soup in which the 'cognitive' elements are insufficiently grasped by the technicians, and the technical elements are insufficiently grasped by the social sciences, all of which creates a few leads and insights but much commotion and confusion. While this piecemeal approach presumes as-yet-unconnected little particulars to be the whole, it is rather nothing but a kind of naïve empiricism.

To conclude, capitalism's rule requires more than military force, more that favourable laws, more than coercion and legitimation. A dangerous, impoverished, exploited and oppressed, urban class requires the development of a system of beliefs with several mechanisms to get the subjects themselves to justify the prevailing social inequality and social order. Calculated nudges are helpful in that regard. So, notwithstanding C. Wright Mills 'well known critique of methodological, conceptual, and organizational flaws American social science research has continued to accommodate the wishes of the US ruling class, and has heeded calls to serve the state. Ultimately, and this is what is at stake with this epistemology, is that the anticipatory uses of big data will destroy the concept and practice of habeas corpus.

CONCLUSION

Digital Coercion and the Tendency Towards Unfree Labour

Triumphant in the Cold War, wary of decline, and compelled by capitalism to expand, the US' imperialist inclination has expressed itself on continental, hemispheric, and global scales. Still, the goal has not been to control but one part, several parts, or even large parts of the globe. Rather is it the attempt to control the planet itself. In this sense, US imperialism is a manifestation of the desire to create space and mechanisms for the accumulation of value, a more basic component of capitalism than profit. It concerns forming a world dedicated to capital accumulation primarily benefiting the US ruling class, and, as a secondary consideration, the ruling classes of tribunes and client states such that they continue to support US rule. However, it is social structure that also produces increasing inequality and authoritarianism almost everywhere, whether that be in the America itself or other places in the international system. Thomas Jefferson called this the 'empire of liberty'. But the rhetoric clouds the extent to which dispossession, exploitation, and oppression are the mechanisms of this expansion.

Capitalism is a globally expansive system, one hierarchically structured between metropole and hinterland, core and periphery; which seeks to open up the later with its supply of cheap raw materials and labour for investment, extraction of surplus value, and a site for exporting surplus goods. Since the emergence of capitalism in Europe, economies in the periphery have been restructured to meet the needs of the core, rather than their own needs, and as but one example, this has resulted in debt bondage for poor states. Indeed, capitalism requires an expansionary dynamic to postpone economic crises. This postponement can be achieved by using indirect or direct coercion from security forces, or the establishment of domestic and international institutions to structurally adjust places to serve the interests of the US ruling class.

How to cite this book chapter:
Timcke, S. 2017 *Capital, State, Empire: The New American Way of Digital Warfare.* Pp. 145–148. London: University of Westminster Press. DOI: https://doi.org/10.16997/book6.h. License: CC-BY-NC-ND 4.0

Put in different terms, the US security state is the outcome of a capitalist state, using its security forces to 'accumulate by dispossession', oversee the extraction of commodities, and to enforce a global labour regime that to one degree or another has an elective affinity with unfree labour practices. These are features present in both internal and external components of the New American Way of War. The harnessing of this labour power is used to extract surplus value that in turn is converted into a 'security surplus' that is spent to enforce a global imperial order that in service of the aforementioned regime of accumulation. Politically, it is a system that no longer seeks the basic pretence of governing with public accountability in mind. Militarily, it is a system with the capacity to deploy force against internal dissidents and rivals at will. Internationally, it is a system of indirect rule on a global scale.

So the more violence seems unavoidable and incomprehensible, the more it is an expression of an underlying social structure, and irrespective of whether it is carried out by security forces, or patterns of investment, the outcome is to strengthen the position of the ruling class. When and where rulers have a monopoly of force and can acquire their resources without necessarily bargaining with producers that rulers can extract at a rate of their discretion. This combination creates an unstable social system prone to inequalities. Domestically, the struggle between subjects and rulers that led to democratization will likely be eroded as increasingly portions of the subject-population cannot offer items rulers require for their strategic pursuits. Therefore, these persons are deemed politically dispensable and basic services and welfare provisions are curtailed or withdrawn because this mode of accumulation has no functional need to be accountable to those who provide the necessary labour power required to produce the state. Instead, the state will make strategic selections catering to those it deems valuable or whose support it requires to continue ruling. This has domestic as well as global ramifications for governance. If this social structure continues, it is likely that arbitrary rule, militarization, and wide inequality will be the order of the day. How this politics is meant to promote the well-being and human flourishing of ordinary Americans and persons living elsewhere, is unclear.

This is a good place to revisit the main topic of this book: the relationship of capital to constraint. I have illustrated contemporary constraint as being organized by a security state managing a particular labour regime (Chapter 1) which itself has long institutional antecedents (Chapter 2), but which now works through various mechanisms like calculated conflict (Chapter 3). One can see the securitization dynamics internally, for instance in policing the most vulnerable (Chapter 4), and externally, for instance in international uneven-development (Chapter 5). New techniques of ideological manipulation are being developed to mystify this process (Chapter 6).

Common to all of these processes is the role of unfree labour. Indeed, given the intensity and scope of exploitation in capitalism, the need for a reserve army of labour, debt bondage, market dependency for social and personal reproduction, and induced underdevelopment, without a doubt unfree labour is a labour model in fully-functioning capitalism. One might say that there is a tendency to replace free labour with unfree equivalents. This is telling about the prospects for mass prosperity.

Amongst apologetic analysts, unfree labour is normally attributed to momentary instances of dispossession as previously unconnected parts of the globe are being integrated into the global economy. In this kind of explanation, it is temporary measure that will apparently subside, leading to free wage labour as fully functioning capitalism takes hold. Setting aside the questionable assumption that dispossession and fully functioning capitalism are incompatible, the main deficiency of this interpretation is that it neglects the extent to which labour power is unfree precisely because of the capital accrued by the ruling class, which itself is because of an extended period of accumulation by dispossession through extraction, expropriation and exploitation. Related, apologists proclaim that the need for labour-power to be a freely traded commodity in a capitalist economy. But nothing prohibits unfree labour from being bought and sold. If anything, it is the preservation of this hard distinction that obscures one from witnessing the mechanics of capital in places with unfree labour while furthering dividing workers to ensure that they cannot form and then act upon a proletariat class-consciousness. The exploitation of unfree labour then is a sign of mature capitalism and is the imposition of class struggle 'from above' to ensure than labour-power is entirely directed by their discretion and intentions, and ultimately to keep value of commodities higher than the value of labour.

The rise of unfree labour is related to two economic considerations. The first is that unfree labour is easier to control than free labour, thus making it cheaper to employ and reproduce. With global markets, ruthless competition, and demands for maximum profit, unfree labour becomes an option to reduce labour costs, perhaps even a preferred form of labour regime in the twenty-first century in the absence of economic growth and with the rate of profit falling. To be clear: this does not mean that all labour will become unfree, rather that first there are degrees of freedom, and second that the tendency to adopt this practice when competition is most acute where class struggle 'from below' could jeopardize profit making.

Returning to the apologists for unfree labour, they claim that the remuneration in this set of production relations is beneficial to the worker, for at least it provides some subsistence, thereby providing opportunities that those persons might not otherwise had have, and indeed the possibility of increased status. However, such positive appraisals wilfully dismiss the many reports about working conditions in the garment industry in South East Asia, construction in the Emirates, or assembly plants in China. Here, workers are worked to death, in unsafe environments, and face sexual harassment with limited recourse to report abusers. Still, it is telling about the apologists' moral character to suggest that even an oppressive subsistence job is sufficient for a person. However, aside from this, the existence of unfree labour is a functional by-product of class struggle 'from above' where capitalists seek to lower pay to increase profits.

Attention to the spectrum of free and unfree labour is vital for two reasons. The first is the extent of coercion that hinders class struggle 'from below', thus limiting prospects for the development of not only class-consciousness, but also the necessary organizing required to make this consciousness a prominent political force able to contest for racial structural transcendence. Further to this point, a labour regime that seeks to convert a workforce from free to unfree needs to understand the conditions under which this is likely, and so informs class struggle.

There are two problems here. The first is that the imposition of unfree labour means that it is difficult for workers to form a proletariat class-consciousness; instead their subjugation means that they defer to social pre-political identities that ensure their particularity and otherness. Here class identity is replaced by an identity based in race, gender, sexuality, vocation, leisure, or nationalism. In this respect, one of the benefits of unfree labour is that capitalists can stall, retard, or diminish the production or reproduction of class-consciousness. There other identities are reifications that displace a politics of society for one of particularity. This is a form by which capitalists are successfully able to restructure and thwart opposition; it is successful class struggle 'from above.'

In the end, American imperialism is the net result of politics, policies, corporation actions, and trade relations, the nurturing of local collaborators in dependent societies, and fiscal instruments to compliment security forces seeking to ensure that there are no insurmountable barriers to capital accumulation. Demilitarisation is a necessary step to reduce the power of fully functioning capitalism. Granted the orderly conversion and redirection of human and material resources employed in military activities to human and environmental development can do much to help the truly disadvantaged. While this process will have short-term costs, such as assisting industries in transition, the 'peace dividend' will be considerable. Ending unchecked US imperialism will not issue in an era of global lawlessness and war. If anything, the opposite is more likely because great wars are the result of uneven development. While this will do much to limit the coercive constraints of capitalism, the elimination of security forces is necessary but insufficient. Accordingly, it is vital to move beyond a narrow understanding of demilitarisation and end the accumulation drive itself. Doing so requires taking away the capitalist ruling class source of power, the private ownership of property.

Notes

[1] Data collected by the Centre for Responsible Politics, https://docs.google.com/spreadsheets/d/1-7PdCI2NawSgP1QE-cGYVYedetYqepR-4jBweaJyqFo/edit#gid=1782600961. Since 9/11, less than 150 Americans have been killed by terrorist attacks, while 450,000 have been killed in domestic gun violence. In 2015, there were about 165,000 separate gunshots recorded in 62 different urban municipalities (Frankel, 2016).

[2] Uber, Airbnb, YouTube, Snapchat, Instagram, Twitter, Fitbit, Spotify, Dropbox, WhatsApp, Tumblr, Pinterest are examples of billion dollar companies created after 2005.

[3] In March 2016, Google had 32 billion visitors, while Facebook had 30 billion (See Eavis 2016).

[4] See http://www.bostondynamics.com/robot_Atlas.html.

[5] By no means are these contradictions universal. Nor are they 'necessary inconvenient truths' or general empirical facts about the unfortunate by-product of economic development, but rather specific features of rule by capital.

[6] The DoD also manages 826,000 in the National Guard and a benefits program that serves over 2 million persons.

[7] It is worth remembering that 'Capital is dead labour that, vampire-like, only lives by sucking living labour, and lives the more, the more labour it sucks. The time during which the labourer works, is the time during which the capitalist consumes the labour-power he has purchased of him.' (Marx 1977, 342).

150 Capital, State, Empire

8   The mechanisms for producing this wealth, accumulation and inequality involve a diverse number of causes. An abbreviated list includes how the fall of the Soviet Union allowed capitalism to unilaterally dictate global trade conditions, the deindustrialization of North America paired with outsourcing to the Global South, the displacement of labour by automation, intensifying work concurrent with a general suppression of wages, the developmental state capitalism of China with its vast cheap and unorganized labour pool lowering production costs, the induction of demand for products through consumerism, re-regulation to create corporate financial rentierism, and the creation of new markets in information and communicative technologies as the rate of profits fell in established sectors. Common to all of these mechanisms is widespread domination and exploitation, oppression and coercion which comes at the expense of a more stable and equitable economy. This points towards how production is controlled.

9   Although as Supreme Command of the Allied Powers, General Douglas MacArthur, during the Occupation of Japan, can be considered as a Viceroy – as can Paul Bremer in his role as Presidential Envoy to Iraq at the Coalition Provisional Authority.

10 Genuine free labour implies: first, that workers chose their jobs voluntarily; second, that the terms are specified and well understood by each party; third, that workers have unrestrained exit rights; and fourth, incentives are financial rather than coercive. This is a standard that most jobs in capitalism fail to meet, because as Marx notes, almost all work in this social structure is really exploitation or subordination. What appears to be 'freedom' is essentially coercion. But this coercion is mystified by the rise of a bourgeois ideology.

11 Historically, dispossession was a feature of colonized territories were destroyed by the forced labour or indigenous people, or importing slaves; in Europe, industrialism required the destruction of traditional ways of life to force a migration from rural areas to cities to create a new factory labour force. Overall, colonialism and commodification were intertwined with the continued strengthening in European societies creating new means for subjugating and governing populations all in the pursuit of profit.

12 The moral sanction and badness of theft hinges on depriving a person of the means to reproduce their life, and this is particularly acute in circumstances where a person's labour was vital in producing the item. But the moral harm is reduced with digital items because as they can be easily reproduced, no thus one is deprived. Digital ownerships rights then are more a matter of law, and less a moral bad.

13 Much of this theory develops out of the study of European polities. While Tilly cautions against universalizing the European state-formation modal for other spaces and times 'our ability to infer the probable events and sequences in contemporary states from an informed reading of European history is

close to nil' (1975, 82)—he nevertheless thinks it is useful for regional and historical comparative and contrastive work. He writes that 'the European historical experience, for all its special features, is long enough, well-enough documented, and a large enough influence on the rest of the world that any systematic conclusions which did hold up well in light of that experience would almost automatically become plausible working hypotheses to be tried out elsewhere.' (Tilly, 1975, 13–14).

[14] Notwithstanding the value that Polanyi offers by correctly rendering reciprocity and redistribution as social, he incorrectly fails to label the market economy as stemming from the same social system. Instead he views it is as disembedded and distinct and so able to devour the social.

[15] The 'end of monetary policy history' was a commitment was to price stability above all else using inflation targeting at around 2 per cent to lower market volatility. This was accomplished using an operationally politically insulated central bank using one instrument (the short-term interest rate,) for one objective (controlling inflation via a consumer price index,) over a medium term (six to eight quarters,) using assert prices to detect emerging financial imbalances thereby minimising excessive fluctuations. Transparent communications was deemed importance around the uses and rationale of that instrument as a way to smooth out micro-fluctuations.

[16] Abstractly, the Great Recession was just another partial capitalist economic crisis that comes from the contradiction between the individual desire for profit and the necessity of a social division of labour. Specifically, it was caused by Wall Street using digital technical to implement 24-hour trading, improve records management, and invest into emerging markets due to better oversight. Aside from the rapid inflows and outflows of capital causing economic and social instability, the speculative investment into new online businesses and enterprises eventually led to the 2000 dot.com crash that in turn heralded a new regime of low interest rates. Bankers took advantage of these conditions and invested into property speculation and debt, deliberately using sub-prime mortgages to financed people unlikely to pay them. Returns on investments were good because of a high interest rate on the debt. When defaults occurred, assets could be seized or refinanced, thus yielding better returns. These financial instruments were bundled with other loans and packaged as investment funds. While selling these products to clients, banks themselves insured against these debts. Being so exposed to these risks, when one financial house fell it had a cascading effect across the financial sector leading to a good portion of the economy falling into recession.

[17] This is why from about 1915 onwards solders were equipped with metal helmets to protect them from head injuries. This was one of many military changes that states made to adapt to the circumstances and conditions of modern industrial warfare. A modern solder's personal equipment still more or less reflects this concern.

18 Comparatively, in the Second Boer War, 1899–1902, it is estimated that the British Army fired 273,000 rounds. One outcome of the war was a rapid modernization program to design and equip artillery as a good portion of the guns fielded in the conflict had been in service in the Crimean War. The new specifications were for a gun that could fire a 12.5lb shell 6,000 yards (Norris, 2000, 164-165).

19 Petraeus was then appointed to command in Iraq, where he had some success. He was later appointed to command in Afghanistan to replace General Stanley McChrystal, before making his way to the CIA.

20 Roberto Gonzalez (2015) argues that the program had an internal ideological function in that it sought to do public relations work with American citizens to convince then that there were humanitarian motivations attached to the occupation, and that social science was being enrolled to limit the use of force and limit cultural conflicts that might lead to unnecessary casualties. It sought to counter the narrative and images of the US occupation as brutal that emerged after Abu Ghraib.

21 See http://minerva.dtic.mil/funded.html, http://semantics.ling.utexas.edu/, http://vivo.cornell.edu/display/grant72804.

22 See http://www.apa.org/news/press/statements/interrogations.aspx – also see Senate Select Committee on Intelligence published a voluminous account of the CIA's program.

23 See http://chronicle.com/blogs/conversation/2013/03/22/tom-coburn-doesnt-like-political-science/ http://crookedtimber.org/wp-content/uploads/2009/10/Coburn_NSF.pdf, http://www.nature.com/news/nsf-cancels-political-science-grant-cycle-1.13501.

24 When Risen initially drafted the article in 2003 for the *New York Times*, he asked the CIA for comment. In April 2003, George Tenet and Condoleezza Rice, the director of the CIA and the National Security Advisor respectfully, met with Risen and Jill Abramson, the *Times* Washington bureau chief. Appealing to national security and the possible endangering of a CIA agent's life Tenet and Rice requested that the *Times* hold the article. The *Times* complied.

25 The Senate Judiciary Committee passed, by a bipartisan margin of 13–5, such a proposed law, but it did not receive a Senate vote.

26 There is also something to be said about the latent presumption that Black intergrate and adapt the behavioural norms associated with 'whiteness.'

27 Granted, the 1033 program does also include the distribution of items like blankets, office furniture, computers and so on. See http://www.dla.mil/dispositionservices.

28 Relatively smaller compared to the great Recession, but still nevertheless still worth noting, due to justifiable affirmative action the 2013 US government shutdown disproportionately affected Blacks. The shutdown was due to a showdown over funding the Affordable Care Act (2010), legislation

which would have dramatically improved the conditions for at least 16 million people, most of whom are persons of color (U.S. Department of Health & Human Services 2015).

29 One result of an unfree labour regime is that it generates a crisis of underconsumption, usually because it drives down wages or leads to job losses in other contexts; thus the consumption practices of workers are affected by this capitalist restructuring of the labour regime. In this respect, unfree labour is a contributing factor in a capitalist economic crisis.

30 The US redacted 8,000 pages prior to non-permanent Security Council member states viewing the report on Iraq's weapon's program.

31 A Hollywood film, *The Siege*, (1998) starring Denzel Washington and Bruce Willis, revolved about a hypothetical situation where a terrorist leader Ahmed bin Talal—a facsimile for bin Laden—was captured, kickstarting terror attacks in New York.

32 Normatively, a coercive imposition of democracy is an intellectual contradiction in orthodox democracy theory.

33 With a combined profit of $16.2 billion, in 2014, the combined sales of Lockheed Martin, Boeing, Raytheon, Northrop Grumman and General Dynamics, five of the world's largest arms manufacturers defence companies, amount to $125 billion out of global combined arms sales of $401 billion, account for about 0.001 per cent of the US $16.77 trillion Gross Domestic Product (2013). Together they employ 450,000 people in the US and abroad. While each company has multiple business lines ranging from electronic systems, to aeronautics, and naval systems, all aside from Boeing, receive the majority of their business from arms sales, both domestic and foreign.

34 Few other heads of state did.

35 Special Forces have also supported the Drug Enforcement Agency in Latin America (Scahill 2010) as well as conducting independent operations. For example, in Honduras Special Forces use Forward Operating Base Mocoron to train counter-narcotics Honduran troops in counter-insurgency tactics (Turse 2012). Even more worrying in some respects is that using military forces in an international policing capacity, involves the militarization of police forces and other government agencies. For instance, there is little to differentiate a DEA Foreign deployed Assistance & Support Team agent from a Special Forces operator. The same has held for tactical units in domestic policing for some time (Kraska and Kappeler 1997, Shank and Beavers 2013).

36 Although discretionary spending is set to increase by approximately $109 billion, see http://www.whitehouse.gov/sites/default/files/omb/budget/fy2013/assets/defense.pdf.

37 Regional commands could appeal to the Pentagon for adjudication, but given that Special Forces are shielded by Presidential authority, the Pentagon's scope for discretion is it is not yet clear.

38 While there are few critical, sociological engagements with the social shaping of neuroscience (cf. Pickersgill 2013), this is not to downplay or diminish the achievements of neuroscience research and its medical treatments. It is the opposite. Efforts to treat neuroscience seriously involve ensuring it does not become a discursive pawn to supplement ideological claims that techno-shaman sell as they misinterpret medical research in an effort to peddle their intellectually unsatisfying speculative philosophy.

39 The similarity I want to stress is disagreement as to whether the cognitive can be understood either through reforming models of cognition to become more computational, or rather to pursue a better understanding of the mind's abilities.

40 One could quibble here and point to random numbers included in calculations and so on. However, this pseudo-randomness must be written into code. If pseudo-random numbers were the same, the output would be the same.

References

Acemoglu, Daron, and Robinson, James. 2012. *Why Nations Fail: The Origins of Power, Prosperity and Poverty*. London: Profile Books.

Ackerman, Spencer. 2009. 'Special Operations Chiefs Quietly Sway Afghanistan Policy'. *The Washington Independent*. 9 November.

Ackerman, Spencer. 2015a. 'Bad Lieutenant: American Police Brutality, Exported from Chicago to Guantánamo'. *The Guardian*. 18 February 2015. Retrieved from http://www.theguardian.com/us-news/2015/feb/18/american-police-brutality-chicago-guantanamo.

Ackerman, Spencer. 2015b. 'Homan Square Revealed: How Chicago Police "Disappeared" 7,000 People'. *The Guardian*. 19 October 2015. Retrieved from http://www.theguardian.com/us-news/2015/oct/19/homan-square-chicago-police-disappeared-thousands.

Ackerman, Spencer. 2015c. 'How Chicago Police Condemned the Innocent: A Trail of Coerced Confessions'. *The Guardian*. 19 February 2015. Retrieved from https://www.theguardian.com/us-news/2015/feb/19/chicago-police-richard-zuley-abuse-innocent-man.

American Civil Liberties Union (Massachussetts) 2014. 'Our Homes are Not Battlefields: Reversing the Militarization and Federalization of Local Police in Massachusetts'. Privacy SOS. Retrieved from https://privacysos.org/swat/#secrecy.

Adams, Ralph James Q. 1978. *Arms and the Wizard: Lloyd George and the Ministry of Munitions 1915–1916*. London: Texas A&M University Press.

Ahmed, Akbar. 2012. 'Deadly Drone Strike on Muslims in the Southern Philippines'. *Brookings*. 5 March 2012. Retrieved from http://www.brookings.edu/research/opinions/2012/03/05-drones-philippines-ahmed.

Alcoff, Linda. 1991. 'The Problem of Speaking for Others'. *Cultural Critique* 20: 5–32.

Alexander, Michelle. 2016 'Why Hillary Clinton Doesn't Deserve the Black Vote'. In *The Nation*, 29 February. Available at https://www.thenation.com/article/hillary-clinton-does-not-deserve-black-peoples-votes/

Alivisatos, Paul, A. et al. 2012. 'The Brain Activity Map Project and the Challenge of Functional Connectomics'. *Neuron* 74(6) pp. 970–4.

American Civil Liberties Union. 2014. *War Comes Home: The Excessive Militarization of American Policing*. New York: American Civil Liberties Union. Retrieved from https://www.aclu.org/sites/default/files/assets/jus14-warcomeshome-report-web-rel1.pdf.

Amnesty International. 2014. 'On the Street of America: Human Rights Abuses in Ferguson'. New York: Amnesty International.

Anderson, Elijah. *Streetwise: Race, Class, And Change In An Urban Community*. Chicago, IL: University of Chicago Press.

Apuzzo, Matt. 2014. War Gear Flows to Police Departments. *New York Times*, 8 June 2014. Retrieved from http://www.nytimes.com/2014/06/09/us/war-gear-flows-to-police-departments.html?_r=3.

Ariely, Dan. 2009. *Predictably Irrational: The Hidden Forces That Shape Our Decisions*. New York, NY: HarperCollins.

Bahre. Erik. 2014. No time, no money: Why do people work for free? *Transformations*, 15 September 2014. http://transformations-blog.com/no-time-no-money-why-do-people-work-for-free

Barker, Dean. 2011. *The End of Loser Liberalism*. Washington DC: Center for Economic and Policy Research.

Baudrillard, Jean. 1995. *The Gulf War Did Not Take Place*. Bloomington, IN: Indiana University Press.

Baum, Dan. 2016. 'Legalize it All'. *Harpers*, 25 March 2016. Retrieved from https://harpers.org/archive/2016/04/legalize-it-all.

Beaumont, Peter. 2012. 'Are Drones Any More Immoral Than Other Weapons of War?' *The Observer*. 19 August 2012. Retrieved from http://www.guardian.co.uk/commentisfree/2012/aug/19/peter-beaumont-drone-warfare-debate.

Becker, Gary. 1976. *The Economic Approach to Human Behaviour*. Chicago, IL: University of Chicago Press.

Becker, Gary. 1992. 'The Economic Way of Looking at Life'. Nobel Lecture. 9 December 1992. Retrieved from http://www.nobelprize.org/nobel_prizes/economic-sciences/laureates/1992/becker-lecture.pdf.

Beckert, Sven. 2014. *Empire of Cotton*. New York: Alfred A. Knopf.

Belcher, Oliver. 2013. The Afterlives of Counterinsurgency: Postcolonialism, Military Social Science, and Afghanistan, 2006-2012. Unpublished PhD dissertation, University of British Columbia.

Bell, Derrick A. 1995. Who's Afraid of Critical Race Theory? *University of Illinois Law Review* (4).

Bernanke, Ben. S. 2013. 'Monitoring the Financial System, Speech at the 49th Annual Conference on Bank Structure and Competition sponsored by the Federal Reserve Bank of Chicago'. Chicago, IL. 10 May 2013.

Berry, David M. 2011. 'The Computational Turn: Thinking About the Digital Humanities'. *Culture Machine (12)*. Retrieved from http://www.culturemachine.net/index.php/cm/article/view/440/470

Boghosian, Heidi. 2013. *Spying on Democracy*. San Francisco, CA: City Light Books.

Boot, Max. 2003. 'The New American Way of War'. *Foreign Affairs*, July/August 2003. Retrieved from http://www.cfr.org/iraq/new-american-way-war/p6160.

Booth, Robert and Ian Black. 2010. 'Wikileaks Cables: Yemen Offered US "Open Door" to Attack al-Qaida on its Soil'. *The Guardian*, 3 December 2010. Retrieved from http://www.theguardian.com/world/2010/dec/03/wikileaks-yemen-us-attack-al-qaida.

Booz Allen Hamilton. 2014. 'Booz Allen Hamilton Sponsoring Legislation: Digital Accountability and Transparency Act (DATA)'. Retrieved from http://www.boozallen.com/media-center/calendar-of-events/2014/09/digital-accountability-and-transparency-data-act-data.

Bouir, Jamelle. 2015. 'Where Black Lives Matter Began'. *Slate*. 23 August 2015. Retrieved from http://www.slate.com/articles/news_and_politics/politics/2015/08/hurricane_katrina_10th_anniversary_how_the_black_lives_matter_movement_was.html.

boyd, danah and Crawford, Kate 2012. 'Critical Questions for Big Data: Provocations for a Cultural, Technological, and Scholarly Phenomenon', *Information, Communication and Society*, 15(5) 662-679. DOI http://dx.doi.org/10.1080/1369118X.2012.678878

Brass, Tom. 2011. *Labour Regime Change in the Twenty-First Century: Unfreedom, Capitalism and Primitive Accumulation*. Leiden, NL: Brill.

Breslow, Jason, M. 2016. 'Colin Powell: U.N. Speech "Was a Great Intelligence Failure"'. *PBS*. 17 May 2016. Retrieved from http://www.pbs.org/wgbh/frontline/article/colin-powell-u-n-speech-was-a-great-intelligence-failure.

Brock, Thomas. 2010. 'Young Adults and Higher Education: Barriers and Breakthroughs to Success'. *Transition to Adulthood* 20(1).

Bronner, Etham, Savage, Charlie, and Shane, Scott. 2013. 'Leak Inquiries Show How Wide a Net U.S. Cast'. *New York Times*. 25 May 2013. Retrieved from http://www.nytimes.com/2013/05/26/us/leaks-inquiries-show-how-wide-a-net-is-cast.html.

Brophy. Enda. 2011. Language put to Work: Cognitive Capitalism, Call Center Labor, and Worker Inquiry. *Journal of Communication Inquiry* 35(4) 410-416. DOI: 10.1177/0196859911417437

Brophy. Enda 2015. Revisiting the Digital Assembly Line: New Perspectives on Call Centre Work. *Labour / Le Travail* 75, 211-230.

Brzezinski, Zbigniew. 1997. *The Grand Chessboard: American Primacy and its Geostrategic Imperatives*. New York: Basic Books.

Bureau of Justice Statistics. 'Justice Expenditure And Employment Extracts, 2012 – Preliminary'. Retrieved from http://www.bjs.gov/index.cfm?ty=pbdetail&iid=5239 (accessed March 2016).

Burke, Matthew. 2013. '20,000 US Troops Descend on Australia for Training'. *Stars and Stripes*. 17 July 2013. Retrieved from https://www.stripes.com/news/pacific/20-000-us-troops-descend-on-australia-for-training-1.230775#.WPYVyVPyvtc.

Carney, Mark. 2013. Monetary Policy After the Fall, Eric J. Hanson Memorial Lecture University of Alberta Edmonton, Alberta, 1 May 2013. Retrieved from http://www.bankofcanada.ca/wp-content/uploads/2013/05/remarks-010513.pdf.

Carr, David. 2012. 'Blurred Line Between Espionage and Truth'. *New York Times*. 26 February 2012. Retrieved from http://www.nytimes.com/2012/02/27/business/media/white-house-uses-espionage-act-to-pursue-leak-cases-media-equation.html.

Carrigan. Mark. 2017. 'Digital Labour and the Epistemic Fallacy'. 4 February 2017. Retrieved from https://markcarrigan.net/category/an-inquiry-into-digital-capitalism/the-intensification-of-work.

Carter, Jimmy. 1980. State of the Union Address 1980. 23 January 1980. Retrieved from http://www.jimmycarterlibrary.gov/documents/speeches/su80jec.phtml

Center for Strategic and International Studies. (CSIS) 2016a. 'How Does China's First Aircraft Carrier Stack Up?' *China Power*, http://chinapower.csis.org/aircraft-carrier.

Centre for Strategic and International Studies. (CSIS) 2016b. 'China's New Spratly Island Defenses'. *Asia Maritime Transparency Initiative*. 13 December 2016.

Centre for Strategic and International Studies. (CSIS) 2017. A Look at China's Sam Shelters in the Spratlys. 23 February 2017. Retrieved from https://amti.csis.org/chinas-new-spratly-island-defenses.

Chan, Aleksander. 2014. 'Wisconsin Police Take Armored Tank to Collect Fine From 75-Year-Old Man'. *Gawker*. 29 October 2014. Retrieved from http://gawker.com/wisconsin-police-takearmored-tank-to-collect-fine-from-1652293887.

Chang, Mariko. 2010. 'Lifting as We Climb: Women of Color, Wealth, and America's Future'. Insight Center for Community Economic Development. Retrieved from http://www.mariko-chang.com/LiftingAsWeClimb.pdf.

Chatelain, Marcia and Asoka, Kaavya. 2015. 'Women and Black Lives Matter: An Interview with Marcia Chatelain'. *Dissent*. Summer 2015. Retrieved from https://www.dissentmagazine.org/article/women-black-lives-matter-interview-marcia-chatelain.

Chin, Warren. 2007. Examining the Application of British Counterinsurgency by the American Army in Iraq. *Small Wars & Insurgencies* 18(1): 1–26.

Chishti, Muzaffar, and Hipsman, Faye. 2016. 'Increased Central American Migration to the United States May Prove an Enduring Phenomenon'. Migration Policy Institute. 18 February 2016. Retrieved http://www.migrationpolicy.org/article/increased-central-american-migration-united-states-may-prove-enduring-phenomenon.

Chomsky, Noam. 1959. 'Review of *Verbal Behavior*, by B.F. Skinner'. *Language* 35: 26–57.

Churchland, Paul. 1996. *The Engine of Reason, The Seat of the Soul: A Philosophical Journey into the Brain.* Cambridge, MA: MIT Press.

Clinton, Hillary Rodham. 2014. 'Hillary Clinton reviews Henry Kissinger's "World Order"'. *The Washington Post.* 4 September 2014. Retrieved from https://www.washingtonpost.com/opinions/hillary-clinton-reviews-henry-kissingers-world-order/2014/09/04/b280c654-31ea-11e4-8f02-03c644b2d7d0_story.html?utm_term=.fe498022154e.

Clinton, Yvette et al. 2010. 'Congressionally Directed Assessment of the Human Terrain System'. *CNA Strategic Studies.* November 2010.

Coates, Ta-Nehisi. 2013. 'How the Obama Administration Talks to Black America'. *The Atlantic.* 20 May 2013. Retrieved from http://www.theatlantic.com/politics/archive/2013/05/how-the-obama-administration-talks-to-black-america/276015.

Cohen, Nicole, 2011. 'The Valorization of Surveillance'. *Democratic Communiqué.* 22(1): 5.

Cole, David. 2014. 'We Kill People Based on Metadata'. *The New York Review of Books.* 10 May 2014.

Collins, Patricia Hill. 2000. *Black Feminist Thought.* New York, NY: Routledge.

Collins, Randall. 2004. 'Gorski and the Military-Fiscal Theory of State Penetration'. *Comparative & Historical Sociology* 15(4): 5-6.

Comaroff, Jean and Comaroff, John. 2012. 'Theory from the South: A Rejoinder. Theorizing the Contemporary'. *Cultural Anthropology.* 25 February 2012. Retrieved from https://culanth.org/fieldsights/273-theory-from-the-south-a-rejoinder.

Commission on Wartime Contracting. 2011. 'Transforming Wartime Contracting, Final Report to Congress'. August 2011. Retrieved from https://cybercemetery.unt.edu/archive/cwc/20110929213820/ http://www.wartimecontracting.gov/docs/CWC_FinalReport-lowres.pdf.

Compton, James. 2004. *The Integrated News Spectacle: A Political Economy of Cultural Performance.* New York: Peter Lang.

Connell, Raewyn. 2007. *Southern Theory: The Global Dynamics of Knowledge in Social Science.* Malden, MA: Polity Press.

Cook, J. et al. 2013. Quantifying the Consensus on Anthropogenic Global Warming in the Scientific Literature. *Environmental Research Letter* 8(2).

Correct the Record. 2016. 'Barrier Breakers 2016: A Project Of Correct The Record, Correct the Record Press Release'. Retrieved from http://www.politico.com/f/?id=00000154-3082-d20b-a1fc-b3e3368b0000.

Crawford, Neta. 2016. 'US Budgetary Costs of Wars through 2016: $4.79 Trillion and Counting'. Watson Institute, Brown University. Retrieved from http://watson.brown.edu/costsofwar/files/cow/imce/papers/2016/Costs%20of%20War%20through%202016%20FINAL%20final%20v2.pdf.

Crilly, Rob. 2011. 'Protest Against American Drone Attacks in Northern Pakistan'. *The Telegraph*. 20 June.

Cromby. John and Willis Martin, E. H. 2014. 'Nudging into Subjectification: Governmentality and Psychometrics'. *Critical Social Policy* 34(2): 241–59.

Daggett, Stephan. 2010. 'Quadrennial Defence Review 2010: Overview and Implications for National Security Planning'. Congressional Research Service. Retrieved from https://fas.org/sgp/crs/natsec/R41250.pdf.

Dahl. Robert A. 1961. The Behavioral Approach in Political Science: Epitaph for a Monument to a Successful Protest. *The American Political Science Review* 55(4): 763–72.

Davis, Angela 2003. *Are Prisons Obsolete?* New York, NY: Seven Stories Press.

Davidson, Amy. 2014. 'Drawing a Gun in Ferguson'. *The New Yorker*. 20 August 2014. Retrieved from http://www.newyorker.com/news/amy-davidson/drawing-gun-ferguson.

de Peuter, Greig, Cohen, Nicole S., and Brophy, Enda. 2015. 'Interrogating Internships: Unpaid Work, Creative Industries, and Higher Education'. *tripleC* 13(2): 329–35.

Department of Defense. 1992. FY 94-99 Defence Planning Guidance (Draft) 18 February 1992, partially un-redacted. The National Security Archive, George Washington University. Retrieved from http://nsarchive.gwu.edu/nukevault/ebb245/doc03_full.pdf.

Department of Defense. 2009. 'Base Structure Report'. Office of the Deputy Under Secretary of Defense, Installations and Environment. Retrieved from https://www.defense.gov/Portals/1/Documents/pubs/BSR2009Baseline.pdf.

Department of Defense. 2012a. Sustaining US Leadership: Priorities for 21st Century Defense. January 2012. Retrieved from http://archive.defense.gov/news/Defense_Strategic_Guidance.pdf.

Department of Defense. 2012b. 'Joint Operational Access Concept'. January 2012. Retrieved from https://www.defense.gov/Portals/1/Documents/pubs/JOAC_Jan%202012_Signed.pdf.

Department of Defense. 2017. About the Department of Defense (DOD). Retrieved from https://www.defense.gov/About.

Diamond, Larry. 2015. Facing Up to the Democratic Recession. *Journal of Democracy* 26(1): 141–55.

Dodge, Mary, Valcore, Laure, and Gomez, Frances. 2011. 'Women on SWAT Teams: Separate but Equal'. *Policing* 34(4): 699–712.

Draper. Nicholas. 2010. *The Price of Emancipation: Slave-Ownership, Compensation and British Society at the End of Slavery,*. Cambridge: Cambridge University Press

Dreyfus, Hubert. 1992. *What Computers Still Can't Do*. Cambridge, MA: MIT Press.

Drezner, Dan. 2013. Military Primacy Doesn't Pay (Nearly As Much As You Think). *International Security* 38(1): 52–79.

Drucker, Jesse. 2012. 'Google Avoided about US$2B in Taxes Last Year by Stashing US$10B in Bermuda Haven', *Financial Post*, 10 December 2012, http://business.financialpost.com/technology/google-dodged-about-us2b-in-taxes-last-year-by-stashing-us10b-in-bermuda-haven

Du Bois, W.E.B. 2013. *Black Reconstruction in America*. New Brunswick: Transaction Publishers.

Dumit, Joseph. 2004. *Picturing Personhood: Brain Scans and Biomedical identity*. Princeton, NJ: Princeton University Press

Dyer-Witheford, Nick and de Peuter, Greig. 2009. *Games of Empire: Global Capitalism and Video Games*. Minneapolis, MN: University of Minnesota Press.

Dyson, Michael Eric. 2017. America's Blue Wall of Terror. *New Republic*. 19 January 2017. Retrieved from https://newrepublic.com/article/139940/americas-blue-wall-terror.

Eavis, Peter. 2016. How You're Making Facebook a Money Machine. *The New York Times*. 29 April 2016. Retrieved from https://www.nytimes.com/2016/04/30/upshot/how-youre-making-facebook-a-money-machine.html.

Echevarria, Antulio. 2004. 'Towards an American Way of War'. Strategic Studies Institute. Retrieved from http://www.dtic.mil/futurejointwarfare/ideas_concepts/echeverria_american_way_of_war.pdf.

The Economist. 2016. 'Tinker, Tailor, Hacker, Spy'. *The Economist*. 10 November 2016. Retrieved from http://www.economist.com/news/special-report/21709773-who-benefiting-more-cyberisation-intelligence-spooks-or-their?fsrc=scn/tw/te/pe/ed/technologytinkertailorhackerspy.

Entous, Adam, Gorman, Siobhan and Rosenberg, Matthew. 2011. 'Drone Attacks Split US Officials'. *The Wall Street Journal*. 10 June.

Ertman, Thomas. 1997. *Birth of the Leviathan: Building States and Regimes in Medieval and Early Modern Europe*. Cambridge: Cambridge University Press.

Feenberg, Andrew. 2009. 'Critical Theory of Communication Technology'. *The Information Society* 25(2): 77–83.

Ferguson, Niall. 2004. *Colossus: The Price of America's Empire*. New York: Penguin Press.

Finer, Samuel. 1997. *The History of Government From the Earliest Times*. New York: Oxford University Press.

Finn, Peter. 2011. 'A Future for Drones: Automated Killing'. *The Washington Post*. 19 September.

Foster, John Bellamy. 2003. 'Imperial America and War'. *Monthly Review* 55(1).
Frank Dana. 2013. 'Hopeless in Honduras? The Election and the Future of Tegucigalpa'. *Foreign Affairs*. 22 November 2013.
Frank, Dana. 2012. 'In Honduras, a Mess Made in the U.S.'. *New York Times*. 26 January 2012. Retrieved from http://www.nytimes.com/2012/01/27/opinion/in-honduras-a-mess-helped-by-the-us.html.
Frankel, Todd. 2016. 'This May be the Best Way to Measure Gun Violence in America'. *The Washington Post*. 23 April 2016. Retrieved from https://www.washingtonpost.com/news/the-switch/wp/2016/04/23/this-may-be-the-best-way-to-measure-gun-violence-in-america/?utm_term=.f8781ffc71f3&wpisrc=nl_tech&wpmm=1.
Friedberg, Errol. C. 2008. 'An Interview with Sydney Brenner'. *Nature Reviews Molecular Cell Biology* 9: 8-9. January 2008.
Fuchs, Christian. 2016a. *Critical Theory of Communication: New Readings of Lukács, Adorno, Marcuse, Honneth and Habermas in the Age of the Internet*. London: University of Westminster Press. DOI: https://doi.org/10.16997/book1
Fuchs, Christian. 2016b. Digital Labor and Imperialism. *Monthly Review* 67(8), https://monthlyreview.org/2016/01/01/digital-labor-and-imperialism
Fuchs, Christian. 2014. *Digital Labour and Karl Marx*. New York: Routledge.
Fuchs, Christian, and Dyer-Witheford, Nick. 2012. 'Karl Marx @ Internet Studies'. *New Media & Society* 15(5): 782–96.
Fuchs, Christian and Winseck, Dwayne. 2011. 'Critical Media and Communication Studies Today. A Conversation'. *tripleC*, 9(2).
Fukuyama, F. 2012. *The Origins of Political Order: From Prehuman Times to the French Revolution*. New York: Farrar Straus & Giroux.
'FY 94-99 Defence Planning Guidance (Draft)'. 18 February 1992. Partially unredacted. The National Security Archive, George Washington University. Retrieved from http://nsarchive.gwu.edu/nukevault/ebb245/doc03_full.pdf.
Gabrielson, Ryan, Grochowski Jones, Ryan and Sagara, Eric. 2014. 'Deadly Force, in Black and White'. *ProPublica*. 10 October 2014. Retrieved from https://www.propublica.org/article/deadly-force-in-black-and-white.
Gandy, Oscar 2009. *Coming to Terms with Chance: Engaging Rational Discrimination and Cumulative Disadvantage*. Farnham: Ashgate Publishing
Gartzke, Erik. 2013. 'The Myth of Cyberwar: Bring War in Cyberspace Back Down to Earth'. *International Security* 38(2): 41-73
Gibbs, David, N, 2000. 'Afghanistan: The Soviet Invasion in Retrospect'. *International Politics* 37: 233–46.
Giddens, Anthony. 1985. *The Nation-State and Violence*. Berkeley, CA: University of California Press
Gilbert Burnham et al. 2006. 'Mortality After the 2003 Invasion of Iraq: A Cross-sectional Cluster sample Survey'. *The Lancet*. Vol. 368. No. 9545, pp. 1421–8
Goffman, Alice. 2014. *On the Run: Fugitive Life in an American City*. Chicago, IL: University of Chicago Press.

Gold, Hannah. 2014. 'The Pentagon Is Giving Grenade Launchers to Campus Police'. *VICE*. 5 September 2014. Retrieved from http://www.vice.com/read/the-pentagon-is-giving-grenade-launchers-to-campus-police-904 1/5.

Gomes, Peter. 2000. Introduction to Tillich, Paul. *The Courage to Be*. New Haven, CT: Yale University Press.

Gonzaga, Robert. 2013. 'Philippine War Games Tied to US Pivot Strategy in Asia'. *Stars and Stripes*. 28 June 2013.

Gonzalez, Roberto. 2015. 'The Rise and Fall of the Human Terrain System'. *Counter Punch*. 29 June 2015. Retrieved from http://www.counterpunch.org/2015/06/29/the-rise-and-fall-of-the-human-terrain-system.

Gosztola, Kevin. 2013. 'NSA Sent Home Talking Points for Employees'. *The Dissenter*. 2 December 2013. Retrieved from http://dissenter.firedoglake.com/2013/12/02/nsa-sent-home-talking-points-for-employees-to-use-in-conversations-with-family-friends-during-holidays.

Gourley, Jim. 2014. 'Welcome to Spartanburg!: The Dangers of this Growing American Military Obsession'. Retrieved from http://ricks.foreignpolicy.com/posts/2014/08/27/welcome_to_spartanburg_the_dangers_of_this_growing_american_military_obsession.

Graeber, David. 2011. *Debt: The First 5000 Years*. New York, NY: Melville House.

Grandin, Greg. 2016. 'Henry Kissinger, Hillary Clinton's Tutor in War and Peace'. *The Nation*. 5 February 2016. Retrieved from https://www.thenation.com/article/henry-kissinger-hillary-clintons-tutor-in-war-and-peace.

Greaves, Matthew. 2015. 'The Rethinking of Technology in Class Struggle: Communicative Affirmation and Foreclosure Politics'. *Rethinking Marxism* 27(2).

Greenwald, Glenn. 2014. *No Place to Hide*. New York: McClelland and Stewart.

Gregory, Derek. 2011. 'From a View to a Kill: Drones and Late Modern War'. *Theory, Culture, Society* 28(7-8): 188–215.

Grotelueschen, Mark. 2001. *Doctrine Under Trial: American Artillery Employment in World War I*. Westport, CT: Greenwood Press.

Gruneau, Rick. 1996. 'Introduction: Why TVTV?'. *Canadian Journal of Communication* 21(1).

Haass, Richard. 1999. What to do with American Primacy. Brookings Institute. 1 September 1999. Retrieved from https://www.brookings.edu/articles/what-to-do-with-american-primacy.

Harvey, David. 2007. *A Brief History of Neoliberalism*. Oxford: Oxford University Press.

Hay, Colin. 1999. 'Marxism and the State'. In *Marxism and Social Science*, Andrew Gamble, David Marsh, and Tony Tant (Eds). MacMillan: London.

Hedges, C. 2013. 'The Shame of America's Gulag'. *Truthdig*. 17 March 2013. Retrieved from http://www.truthdig.com/report/item/the_shame_of_americas_gulag_20130317.

Heginbotham, Eric and Samuels, Richard, J. 2016. 'Poor Substitute'. *Foreign Affairs*. 5 March 2016. Retrieved from https://www.foreignaffairs.com/articles/australia/2016-05-03/poor-substitute.

Henry, Ben, Reese, Jill and Torres, Angel. 2013. 'Wasted Wealth, Alliance for a Just Society'. May 2013 http://allianceforajustsociety.org/wp-content/uploads/2013/05/Wasted.Wealth_NATIONAL.pdf.

Herman, E. S. and Chomsky, N. 2002. *Manufacturing Consent: The Political Economy of the Mass Media*. New York, NY: Pantheon.

Hines, James and Rice, Eric M. (1994) 'Fiscal Paradise: Foreign Tax Havens and American Business'. *The Quarterly Journal of Economics*, Vol. 109:1, 149-182

Hobson, John. 1965. *Imperialism: A Study*. Ann Arbor, MI: University of Michigan Press.

Hodges, Jim. 2012. 'US Army's Human Terrain Experts May Help Defuse Future Conflicts'. *Defense News*, 22 March.

Hoge, James F. Jnr. 2004. 'A Global Power Shift in the Making'. *Foreign Affairs*. July/August 2004.

Hope, Wayne. 2016. *Time, Communication and Global Capitalism*. Houndmills: Palgrave Macmillan.

Horton, Scott. 2010. 'DIA and the Black Jail at Bagram'. *Harpers*. 17 May 2010. Retrieved from http://harpers.org/blog/2010/05/dia-and-the-black-jail-at-bagram.

Hudson, Linda, Owens, Colin, and Flannes, Matt. 2011. 'Drone Warfare: Blowback from the New American Way of War'. *Middle East Policy* 18(3): 122–32.

Human Rights Watch. 1991. *Needless Deaths In The Gulf War: Civilian Casualties During the Air Campaign and Violations of the Laws of War*. New York: Human Rights Watch.

Human Terrain System. 2008. *Human Terrain Team Handbook 2008*. Fort Leavenworth, KS. Retrieved from http://www.vho.org/aaargh/fran/livres9/humterrainhandbo.pdf.

Huntington, Samuel 1975 The United States, in Crozier, M, Huntington, S. P., Wataniki, J., (eds) *The Crisis of Democracy: Report on the Governability of Democracies to the Trilateral Commission*, New York: New York University Press

Huws, Ursula. 2014. *Labor in The Global Digital Economy: The Cybertariat Comes of Age*. New York: Monthly Review Press.

Ignatieff, Michael. 2003a. 'The Challenges of American Imperial Power'. *Naval War College Review*. Vol. LVI, No. 2.

Ignatieff, Michael. 2003b. *Empire Lite: Nation-building in Bosnia, Kosovo and Afghanistan*. Toronto: Penguin Canada.

Ignatieff, Michael. 2003c. 'The Burden'. *The New York Times Magazine*. 5 January 2003. Retrieved from http://www.nytimes.com/2003/01/05/magazine/05EMPIRE.html?pagewanted=all.

Ignatieff, Michael. 2004. *The Lesser Evil: Political Ethics in an Age of Terror*. Edinburgh: Edinburgh University Press.

Ignatieff, Michael. 2012. 'Drones Give Democracies No Cause for War'. *Financial Times*. 12 June, Retrieved from http://www.ft.com/cms/s/0/10a03278-b3b3-11e1-a3db-00144feabdc0.html.
James, Cyril L. R. 1938. *A History of Negro Revolt*. New York: Haskell House Publishers.
James, Cyril L. R. 1989. *The Black Jacobins*. New York: Vintage Books.
Jessop, Bob. 1990. *State Theory: Putting the Capitalist State in Its Place*. Cambridge: Polity.
Jin, Dal Yong. 2013. 'The Construction of Platform Imperialism in the Globalization Era'. *tripleC* 11(1): 145–72. Retrieved from http://www.triple-c.at/index.php/tripleC/article/viewFile/458/446.
Johnson, Walter. 2013. 'King Cotton's Long Shadow', *The New York Times*, 30 March 2013. Retrieved from http://opinionator.blogs.nytimes.com/2013/03/30/king-cottons-long-shadow.
Justice Policy Institute. 2012. 'Rethinking the Blues: How We Police in the U.S. And at What Cost?'. Retrieved from http://www.justicepolicy.org/uploads/justicepolicy/documents/rethinkingtheblues_final.pdf.
Kahneman, D. 2002. 'Maps of Bounded Rationality: A Perspective on Intuitive Judgement and Choice'. Nobel Prize Lecture. 8 December 2002. Retrieved from http://www.nobelprize.org/nobel_prizes/economic-sciences/laureates/2002/kahnemann-lecture.pdf.
Karp. Matthew. 2016. *This Vast Southern Empire Slaveholders at the Helm of American Foreign Policy*. Cambridge, MA: Harvard University Press
Keeanga-Yamahtta, Taylor. 2014. *From #BlackLivesMatter to Black Liberation*. Chicago, IL: Haymarket Books.
Kello, Lucas. 2013. 'The Meaning of the Cyber Revolution: Perils to Theory and Statecraft'. *International Security* 38(2): 7–40.
Kendzior, Sarah. 2013. Meritocracy for Sale. *AlJazeera* 4 May 2013. http://www.aljazeera.com/indepth/opinion/2013/05/20135371732699158.html
King Jnr, Martin Luther. 1967. 'The Other America', Speech at Stanford University. 10 March 1967. Retrieved from http://www.thekingcenter.org/archive/document/other-america#.
Klaidman, Daneil. 2012. 'Drones: How Obama Learned to Kill'. *Newsweek*. 28 May. Retrieved from http://mag.newsweek.com/2012/05/27/drones-the-silent-killers.html.
Konkol, Mark and Biasco, Paul. 2016. 'Chicago Police Hid Mics, Destroyed Dashcams to Block Audio, Records Show'. *DNAinfo*. 27 January 2016. Retrieved from https://www.dnainfo.com/chicago/20160127/archer-heights/whats-behind-no-sound-syndrome-on-chicago-police-dashcams.
Kosslyn, Stephen, and Koenig, Olivier. 1992. *Wet Mind: The New Cognitive Neuroscience*. New York: Free Press. p. 4.
Kramera, Adam, D. I., Guilloryb, J. E. and Hancock, Jeffrey T. 2014. 'Experimental Evidence of Massive-scale Emotional Contagion Through Social

Networks'. *Proceedings of the National Academy of Sciences* 111(24): 8788–90.

Kraska, Peter and Kappeler, Victor. 1997. 'Militarizing American Police'. *Social Problems* 44(1): 1-18.

Krippner, Greta. 2011. *Capitalizing on Crisis: The Political Origins of the Rise of Finance.* Cambridge, MA: Harvard University Press.

Krugman, Paul. 2007. *The Conscience of a Liberal.* New York, NY: W.W. Norton & Company.

Kulikoff, Allan. 1986. *Tobacco and Slaves, The Development of Southern Cultures in the Chesapeake, 1680–1800.* Chapel Hill, NC: University of North Caroline Press.

Kulikoff, Allan. 1992. *The Agrarian Origins of American Capitalism.* Charlottsville, VA: University Press of Virginia.

Lanier, Jaron. (2013) W*ho Owns the Future?* New York, NY: Simon and Schuster.

Langer, Ralph. 2013. 'Stuxnet's Secret Twin'. *Foreign Policy.* 19 November. Retrieved from www.foreignpolicy.com/articles/2013/11/19/stuxnets_secret_twin_iran_nukes_cyber_attack.

Lapidos, Juliet. 2013. Banks Above the Law. *New York Times.* 7 March. Retrieved from http://takingnote.blogs.nytimes.com/2013/03/07/banks-above-the-law

Larison, Daniel. 2015. 'The Iraq War and the Mythology of the "Surge"'. *The American Conservative.* 10 August. Retrieved from http://www.theamericanconservative.com/larison/the-iraq-war-and-the-mythology-of-the-surge.

Lebron, Christopher. 2014. 'Hypocrisy Democracy'. *The Critique.* 5 November. Retrieved from http://www.thecritique.com/articles/hypocrisy-democracy.

Leggett, Will. 2014. 'The Politics of Behaviour Change: Nudge, Neoliberalism and the State'. *Policy & Politics* 42(1): 3–19.

Lerner, Daniel. 1958. *The Passing of Traditional Society: Modernizing the Middle East* Glencoe, IL: Free Press.

Levi, Margaret. 1997. *Consent, Dissent, and Patriotism.* Cambridge: Cambridge University Press.

Levy, Josh. 2013. 'NSA's Surveillance Programs are the "Most Serious Attacks on Free Speech We've Ever Seen"'. *Boing Boing.* 22 August, Retrieved from http://www.boingboing.net/2013/08/22/opinion-nsas-surveillance-p.html.

Lilienfeld, Scott O. et al. 2015. 'Fifty Psychological and Psychiatric Terms to Avoid: A List of Inaccurate, Misleading, Misused, Ambiguous, and Logically Confused Words and Phrases'. *Frontiers in Psychology*, 3 August. Retrieved from http://journal.frontiersin.org/article/10.3389/fpsyg.2015.01100/full.

Liptak, Adam and Shear, Michael D. 2016. 'Supreme Court Tie Blocks Obama Immigration Plan'. *New York Times*, 23 June. Retrieved from http://www.nytimes.com/2016/06/24/us/supreme-court-immigration-obama-dapa.html?_r=0.

Lipton, Eric, and Savage, Charlie. 2011. 'Hackers Reveal Offers to Spy on Corporate Rivals'. *New York Times*. 11 February. Retrieved from http://www.nytimes.com/2011/02/12/us/politics/12hackers.html.

Lohaus, Phillip. 2016. 'Special Operations Forces in the Gray Zone: An Operational Framework for Using Special Operations Forces in the Space Between War and Peace'. *Special Operations Journal* 2(2): 75–91.

Londoño, Ernesto. 2014. 'U.S. Deploys 80 Troops to Chad to Help Find Kidnapped Nigerian Schoolgirls'. *The Washington Post*. 21 May.

Mcafee, Andrew and Brynjolfsson, Erik 2012. 'Big Data: The Management Revolution'. *Harvard Business Review*, October 2012, Vol.90(10) https://hbr.org/2012/10/big-data-the-management-revolution

Maier, Charles. 2006. *Among Empires: American Ascendency and its Predecessors*. Cambridge, MA: Harvard University Press.

Manjoo, Farhad. 2017. 'Tech's Next Battle: The Frightful Five vs. Lawmakers'. *The New York Times*. 4 January. Retrieved from https://www.nytimes.com/2017/01/04/technology/techs-next-battle-the-frightful-five-vs-lawmakers.html.

Mann, Michael and Toles, Tom. 2016. *The Madhouse Effect*. New York: Columbia University Press.

Markoff, John. 2016. 'Pentagon Turns to Silicon Valley for Edge in Artificial Intelligence'. *The New York Times*. 11 May. Retrieved from https://www.nytimes.com/2016/05/12/technology/artificial-intelligence-as-the-pentagons-latest-weapon.html.

Marx, Karl. 1977. *Capital, Volume I*. New York: Vintage.

Marwick, A. (2013). 'Big Data, Data-Mining, and the Social Web. Governments, Corporations and Hackers: The Internet and Threats to the Privacy and Dignity of the Citizen'. Privacy, Power and the Internet: *New York Review of Books* conference, Scandinavia House, New York, NY, 30-31 2013. http://www.tiara.org/blog/wp-content/uploads/2013/10/marwick_2013_datamining_talk.pdf

Massey, Douglas, and Denton, Nancy A. 1993. *American Apartheid: Segregation and the Making of the Underclass*. Cambridge, MA: Harvard University Press.

Maxwell, Richard. 2003. *Herbert Schiller*. Lanham: Rowman & Littlefield

Mayer, Jane. 2016. *Dark Money: The Hidden History of the Billionaires Behind the Rise of the Radical Right*. New York: Doubleday.

Mayer-Schönberger, Viktor and Cukier, Kenneth. 2013. *Big Data : A Revolution That Will Transform How We Live, Work and Think*. London: John Murray.

Mazzetti, Mark. 2011. 'US Is Intensifying a Secret Campaign of Yemen Airstrikes'. *The New York Times*. June 8.

Mazzetti, Mark and Cooper, Helene. 2015. 'Sale Of U.S. Arms Fuels The Wars Of Arab States'. *The New York Times*. 18 April.

McCarty, John. 1979. 'Ascribing Mental Qualities to Machines'. In Ringle, Martin (Ed.) *Philosophical Perspectives in Artificial Intelligence*. Brighton: Harvester Press.

McDuffee, Allen. 2013. 'Army Scores a Super-Stealthy Drone That Looks Like a Bird'. *Wired*. 27 November. Retrieved from http://www.wired.com/dangerroom/2013/11/army-maveric-microdrone.

McLeary, Paul and Rawnsley, Adam. 2016. 'SitRep: Long War Gets Longer, Special Ops Leaders Brace For It.' *Foreign Policy*. 26 May. Retrieved from http://foreignpolicy.com/2016/05/26/situation-report-long-war-gets-longer-special-ops-leaders-braced-for-continued-conflict-raqqa-not-yet-in-crosshairs-vietnam-being-careful-about-the-way-ahead-and-lots-more.

McMahon John. 2015. 'Behavioral Economics as Neoliberalism: Producing and Governing "Homo Economicus"'. *Contemporary Political Theory* 14: 137–58.

Meiners, Roger (1995) 'In Service to the State' in Sommer, John W. (ed.) *The Academy in Crisis: The Political Economy of Higher Education*. New Brunswick, NJ: Transaction Publishers.

Menn, Joseph. 2013. 'Secret U.S. court approved wider NSA'. *Reuters*. 19 November. Retrieved from http://www.reuters.com/article/2013/11/19/us-usa-nsa-spying-idUSBRE9AI11Y20131119.

Middlebrook, Martin. 1971. *The First Day on the Somme*. London: Allen Lane.

Miliband, Ralph. 1969. *The State in Capitalist Society*. New York, NY: Basic Books.

Miller, Greg. 2012. 'U.S. Drone Targets in Yemen Raise Questions'. *The Washington Post*. 2 June.

Mills, C.W. 1948. *New Men of Power: America's Labor Leaders*. Oxford: Oxford University Press.

Mills, C.W. 1951. *White Collar: The American Middle Classes*. New York, NY: Oxford University Press.

Mills, C.W. 1956. *The Power Elite*. New York: Oxford University Press.

Mills, C.W. [1959] 2000. *The Sociological Imagination*. Oxford: Oxford University Press.

Mindell, David. 2002. *Between Human and Machine: Feedback, Control, and Computing before Cybernetics*. Baltimore, MD: The John Hopkins University Press.

Morgan, Edmund S. 1978. *The Challenge of the American Revolution*. New York, NY: W.W. Norton.

Mosco, Vincent. 1986. 'New Technology and Space Warfare'. In Becker, J., Heldebro, G., and Paldan, L. (Eds). *Communication and Domination: Essays to Honor Herbert Schiller*. Norwood, MI: Ablex Pub Corp., pp. 76—83.

Mosco. Vincent. 2014. *To the Cloud: Big Data in a Turbulent World*. Boulder, CO: Paradigm Publishers.

Mosco. Vincent. 2016. 'Marx in the Cloud'. in Fuchs. Christian and Mosco. Vincent. (eds) 2016. *Marx in the Age of Digital Capitalism*. Leiden: Brill

Mosco, Vincent. 2017. 'Weaponized Drones in Military Information System'. *Science as Culture*. Vol. 26 2: 276–81.

Mosco, Vincent and Schiller, Dan (Eds.). 2001. *Continental Order? Integrating North America for Cybercapitalism*. Lanham, MD: Rowman & Littlefield Publishers.

Mossman, Matt. 2016. 'Paying Their Dues'. *Foreign Affairs*. 25 February. Retrieved from https://www.foreignaffairs.com/articles/2016-02-25/paying-their-dues.

Nagel, T. 2012. *Mind and Cosmos*. New York, NY: Oxford University Press.

National Oceanic and Atmosphere Administration. 2013. 'CO_2 at NOAA's Mauna Loa Observatory Reaches New Milestone: Tops 400 ppm'. Press Release. 10 May. Retrieved from http://www.esrl.noaa.gov/gmd/news/pdfs/7074.pdf.

National Security Agency. 2007. *SIGINT Mission Strategic Plan, FY2008-2013*. Retrieved from https://www.eff.org/files/2013/11/15/20131104-nyt-sigint_strategic_plan.pdf.

National Security Agency. 2013. *SIGINT Strategy 2012-2016*. 23 February.

The National Security Strategy of the United States of America. 2002. September. Retrieved from http://www.state.gov/documents/organization/63562.pdf.

Neff, Gina. 2012. *Venture Labor: Work and the Burden of Risk in Innovative Industries*. Cambridge, MA: MIT Press.

Neff. Gina. and Nafus, Dawn. 2016. *Self-Tracking*, Cambridge, MA: MIT Press

New York Civil Liberties Association. 2016. 'NYPD Has Used Stingrays More Than 1,000 Times Since 2008'. Retrieved from http://www.nyclu.org/news/nypd-has-used-stingrays-more-1000-times-2008.

New York Times Editorial. 2012. 'New Strategy Old Pentagon Budget'. *New York Times*. 29 January .

Nigh, Norman. 2012. 'An Operator's Guide to Human Terrain Teams'. *CIWAG Case Study Series 2011-2012*. Andrea Dew and Marc Genest (Eds). Newport, RI: US Naval War College, Center on Irregular Warfare and Armed Groups.

Nolan, Tom. 2014. 'Stop Arming the Police Like a Military'. *Defense One*. 24 June. Retrieved from http://www.defenseone.com/ideas/2014/06/stop-arming-police-military/87163/ 1/7.

Norris, John. 2000. *Artillery: A History*. Stroud: Sutton Publishing.

Obama, Barack. 2007. 'Renewing American Leadership', *Foreign Affairs* 86(4).

Obama, Barack. 2008. Ebenezer Baptist Church Address, Delivered 20 January 2008, Ebenezer Baptist Church, Atlanta, GA. Retrieved from http://www.americanrhetoric.com/speeches/barackobama/barackobamaebenezerbaptist.htm.

Obama, Barack. 2015. 'Letter From The President – War Powers Resolution'. The White House. 11 December. Retrieved from https://www.whitehouse.gov/the-press-office/2015/12/11/letter-president-war-powers-resolution.

Odierno, Raymond. 2012. 'The U.S. Army in a Time of Transition'. *Foreign Affairs* 91(3).

Olson, Keith W. 1973. 'The G. I. Bill and Higher Education: Success and Surprise'. *American Quarterly* 25(5).

O'Reilly, Tim. 2013. 'Open Data and Algorithmic Regulation'. In Goldstein, B. and Dyson, L. (Eds). *Beyond Transparency*. San Francisco, CA: Code for America Press. p. 289.

Oumar, Jemal. 2012. 'Mystery Airstrike kills Azawad Terrorists'. *Magharebia* 22 June. Retrieved from http://magharebia.com/en_GB/articles/awi/features/2012/06/22/feature-01.

Palmer, Bryan D. 1990. *Descent into Discourse: The Reification of Language and the Writing of Social History*. Philadelphia, PA: Temple University Press.

Panitch, Leo. 2003. 'September 11 and the American Empire'. *Intervention* 5(2).

Peck, Jamie. 2010. *Constructions of Neoliberal Reason*. Oxford: Oxford University Press.

Perlez, Jane. 2016. 'U.S. Carriers Sail in Western Pacific, Hoping China Takes Notice'. *New York Times*, 18 June. Retrieved from https://www.nytimes.com/2016/06/19/world/asia/us-carriers-sail-in-western-pacific-hoping-china-takes-notice.html?smid=tw-nytimesworld&smtyp=cur&_r=0.

Peters, Charles. 1982. 'A Neo-Liberal's Manifesto'. *The Washington Post*. 5 September. Retrieved from https://www.washingtonpost.com/archive/opinions/1982/09/05/a-neo-liberals-manifesto/21cf41ca-e60e-404e-9a66-124592c9f70d/?utm_term=.c1b49bca3c62.

Pew Research Center. 2013. 'Keystone XL Pipeline Draws Broad Support: Continuing Partisan Divide in View of Global Warming'. 2 April. Retrieved from http://www.people-press.org/2013/04/02/keystone-xl-pipeline-draws-broad-support.

Pickersgill, Martyn. 2013. 'The Social Life of the Brain: Neuroscience in Society'. *Current Sociology* 61(3).

Polanyi, Karl. 1957. *The Great Transformation*. Boston, MA: Beacon Press

Pooley, Jefferson. 2008. 'The New History of Mass Communication Research'. In Park, David W. and Pooley, Jefferson. *The History of Media and Communication Research*. New York, NY: Peter Lang.

Posen, Barry. 2003. 'Command of the Commons: The Military Foundation of U.S. Hegemony'. *International Security* 28(1).

Powell, Colin, L. 2003. 'Remarks to the United Nations Security Council. 5 February. Retrieved from http://2001-2009.state.gov/secretary/former/powell/remarks/2003/17300.htm.

Price, David. 2008. *Anthropological Intelligence: The Use and Neglect of American Anthropology in the Second World War*. Durham, NC: Duke University Press.

Price, David. 2016. *Cold War Anthropology: The CIA, the Pentagon, and the Growth of Dual Use Anthropology*. Durham, NC: Duke University Press.

Pyrooz, David et al., 2016. 'Was There a Ferguson Effect on Crime Rates in Large U.S. Cities?' *Journal of Criminal Justice* 46. September.

Ransby, Barbara. 2015. 'The Class Politics of Black Lives Matter'. *Dissent*. Fall 2015. Retrieved from https://www.dissentmagazine.org/article/class-politics-black-lives-matter.

Rappeport, Alan. 2016. 'Gloria Steinem and Madeleine Albright Rebuke Young Women Backing Bernie Sanders'. *New York Times*. 7 February. Retrieved from http://www.nytimes.com/2016/02/08/us/politics/gloria-steinem-madeleine-albright-hillary-clinton-bernie-sanders.html.

Rashid, Ahmed. 2000. *Taliban: Militant Islam, Oil and Fundamentalism in Central Asia*. New Haven, CT: Yale University Press.

Rawls, John 1971. *A Theory of Justice*. Harvard, MA: Harvard University Press.

Redden, Molly. 2014. 'Police Want to Get Rid of Their Pentagon-Issued Combat Gear. Here's Why They Can't'. 30 September. Retrieved from http://www.motherjones.com/politics/2014/09/police-departments-struggle-return-pentagon-military--surplus-gear.

Reed, Adolph and Zamora, Daniel. 2016. 'Bernie Sanders and the New Class Politics'. *Jacobin*. 8 August. Retrieved from https://www.jacobinmag.com/2016/08/bernie-sanders-black-voters-adolph-reed-trump-hillary.

Richman, Sheldon. 2004. 'Iraqi Sanctions: Were They Worth It? Global Policy Forum'. January 2004. Retrieved from https://www.globalpolicy.org/component/content/article/170-sanctions/41952.html.

Risen, James 2006. *The State of War: The Secret History of the CIA and the Bush Administration*. New York, NY: Free Press.

Risen, James and Poitras, Laura. 2013a. 'NSA Gathers Data on Social Connections of US Citizens'. *New York Times*. 28 September.

Risen, James and Laura Poitras. 2013b. 'NSA Report Outlined Goals for More Power'. *New York Times*, 22 November

Robinson, Cedric J. 1997. 'In the Year 1915: D. W. Griffith and the Rewhitening of America'. *Social Identities: Journal for the Study of Race, Nation and Culture* 3(2).

Robinson, Cedric J. 2016. *The Terms of Order: Political Science and the Myth of Leadership*. Chapel Hill, NC: University of North Carolina Press.

Robinson, Linda. 2012. 'The Future of Special Operations'. *Foreign Affairs* 91(6).

Rorty, Richard (Ed.). 1967. *The Linguistic Turn: Recent Essays in Philosophical Method*. Chicago, IL: University of Chicago Press.

Rushton, Katherine. 2013. 'Amazon Received More Money from UK Grants Than it Paid in Corporation Tax', *The Telegraph*, 15 May 2013, http://www.telegraph.co.uk/finance/personalfinance/tax/10060229/Amazon-received-more-money-from-UK-grants-than-it-paid-in-corporation-tax.html

Sandoval, Marisol. 2013. 'Foxconned Labour as the Dark Side of the Information Age: Working Conditions at Apple's Contract Manufacturers in China'. *tripleC* 11(2).

Savage, Charlie. 2013. 'C.I.A. Is Said to Pay AT&T for Call Data'. *New York Times*. 7 November. Retrieved from http://www.nytimes.com/2013/11/07/us/cia-is-said-to-pay-att-for-call-data.html?_r=0.

Savage, Charlie, and Weisman, Jonathan. 2015. 'N.S.A. Collection of Bulk Call Data Is Ruled Illegal'. *New York Times*. 7 May. Retrieved from http://www.nytimes.com/2015/05/08/us/nsa-phone-records-collection-ruled-illegal-by-appeals-court.html.

Scahill, Jeremy. 2010. 'Obama's Expanding Covert War'. *The Nation*. 4 June.

Scheve, Ken and David Stasavage (2010) 'Democracy, War and Wealth: Evidence of Two Centuries of Inheritance Taxation'. *American Political Science Review* 106: 81-102.

Schiller, Dan. 2000. *Digital Capitalism: Networking the Global Market System*. Cambridge, MA: MIT Press.

Schiller, Dan. 2011. 'The Militarization of US Communications'. In Wasko, Janet, Murdock, Graham and Sousa, Helena (Eds). 2011. *The Handbook of Political Economy of Communication*. Chichester: Wiley Blackwell.

Schiller, Herbert. 1969. *Mass Communication and American Empire*. New York: Augustus M. Kelly.

Schmitt, Eric and Thom Shanker. 2013. A Commander Seeks to Chart a New Path for Special Operations. *The New York Times*, 1 May

Schmitt, Eric, Mark Mazzetti, and Thom Shanker. 2012. 'Admiral Seeks Freer Hand in Deployment of Elite Forces'. *New York Times*. 12 February.

Schwarzkopf, H. Norman. 1992. *It Doesn't Take a Hero*. New York, Bantam Books.

Sealey, Roger. 2010. 'Logistics Workers and Global Logistics: The Heavy Lifters of Globalization, Work Organisation'. *Labour & Globalisation* 4(3).

Searle, J. 1972. 'Chomsky's Revolution in Linguistics'. *New York Review of Books*. 29 June. Retrieved from http://www.nybooks.com/articles/archives/1972/jun/29/a-special-supplement-chomskys-revolution-in-lingui.

Searle, John. 1980. 'Minds, Brains, and Programs'. *Behavioral and Brain Sciences* 3 (3).

Searle, John. 2007. *Freedom and Neurobiology*. New York, NY: Columbia University Press.

Seib, Gerald. 2017. 'Ash Carter Says Putin Is Making It Harder for U.S. to Work With Russia'. *The Wall Street Journal*. 6 January. Retrieved from https://www.wsj.com/articles/ash-carter-says-putin-is-making-it-harder-for-u-s-to-work-with-russia-1483698600.

Shah, Hemant. 2011. *The Production of Modernization*. Philadelphia, PA: Temple University Press.

Shane, Scott. 2012. 'No Charges Filed on Harsh Tactics Used by the C.I.A.' *New York Times*. 30 August. Retrieved from http://www.nytimes.com/2012/08/31/us/holder-rules-out-prosecutions-in-cia-interrogations.html?pagewanted=all&_r=0.

Shank, Michael, and Elizabeth Beavers. 2013. 'America's Police are Looking More and More Like the Military'. *The Guardian*, 7 October.

Shanker, Thom. 2012a. 'U.S. Arms Sales Make Up Most Of Global Market'. *New York Times*, 26 August.

Shanker, Thom. 2012b. 'Floating Base Gives U.S. New Footing in the Persian Gulf'. *New York Times*, 11 July.

Shannon, Claude E. 1948. 'A Mathematical Theory of Communication'. *Bell System Technical Journal*. Vol. 27.

Singh, Joseph. 2012. 'Betting Against a Drone Arms Race'. *Time*. 13 August. Retrieved from http://nation.time.com/2012/08/13/betting-against-a-drone-arms-race/#ixzz2h54oZUZx.

Sirotin, Yevgeniy, B. and Das, Aniruddha. 2009. 'Anticipatory Haemodynamic Signals in Sensory Cortex not Predicted by Local Neuronal Activity'. *Nature* 457. Retrieved from http://www.nature.com/nature/journal/v457/n7228/abs/nature07664.html.

Skinner, B. F. 1953. *Science and Human Behavior*. New York, NY: Macmillan.

Skocpol, Theda. 1979. *States and Social Revolutions: A Comparative Analysis of France, Russia, and China*. Cambridge: Cambridge University Press.

Skocpol, Theda. 1985. 'Bringing the State Back In: Strategies of Analysis in Current Research'. In Evans, P. Rueschemeyer, D. and Skocpol, T. (Eds.). *Bringing the State Back In*. Cambridge: Cambridge University Press.

Skof, Matt. 2014. 'Police "Militarization: Angle is Overblown'. *Ottawa Citizen*. 20 August. Retrieved from http://ottawacitizen.com/news/world/skof-police-militarization-angle-is-overblown.

Slahi, Mohamedou Ould. (ed. Siems, Larry) 2015. *Guantánamo Diary*. New York, NY: Little, Brown.

Smith, Neil. 2006. 'There's No Such Thing as a Natural Disaster'. *SSRC*. 11 June. Retrieved from http://understandingkatrina.ssrc.org/Smith.

Smythe, Dallas W. 1981. *Dependency Road: Communications, Capitalism, Consciousness, and Canada*. Norwood, NJ: Ablex Publishing Corp.

Sokol, Ronald. 2010. 'Can the US Assassinate an American Citizen Living in Yemen?' *The Christian Science Monitor*. 29 September.

Spiegel Staff. 2013. 'How the NSA and GCHQ Spied on OPEC'. *Spiegel Online*. 11 November. Retrieved from www.spiegel.de/international/world/how-the-nsa-and-gchq-spied-on-opec-a-932777.html.

Stepak, Amir and Whitlack, Rachel. 2012. 'The Battle over America's Foreign Policy Doctrine'. *Survival: Global Politics and Strategy* 54(5).

Stockholm International Peace Research Institute (SIPRI) 2016. SIPRI Military Expenditure Database, https://www.sipri.org/databases/milex [downloadable spreadsheet]

Stockman, Farah. 2016. 'On Crime Bill and the Clintons, Young Blacks Clash With Parents'. *New York Times*, 18 April. Retrieved from http://www.nytimes.com/2016/04/18/us/politics/hillary-bill-clinton-crime-bill.html.

Strawer, Bradley. 2012. 'The Morality of Drone Warfare Revisited'. *The Guardian*. 6 August. Retrieved from http://www.theguardian.com/commentisfree/2012/aug/06/morality-drone-warfare-revisited.

Stuart, Heather. 2013. 'Ohio State University Acquires Military-Style Armored Truck'. *The Huffington Post*. 18 September. Retrieved from http://

www.huffingtonpost.com/2013/09/18/ohio-state-university-armored-truck_n_3949750.html.

Taylor, Alan M. and Williamson, Jeffrey G. 1994. 'Capital Flows to the New World as an Intergenerational Transfer'. *Journal of Political Economy* 102(2).

Taylor, Flint. 2013. 'Police Torture and the Death Penalty in Illinois: Ten Years Later'. *The Nation*. 11 January. Retrieved from https://www.thenation.com/article/police-torture-and-death-penalty-illinois-ten-years-later.

Taylor, Keeanga-Yamahatta. 2016. *From #BlackLivesMatter to Black Liberation*. Chicago, IL: Haymarket Books

Terdiman, Daniel. 2013. 'America's first next-gen aircraft carrier takes high tech to sea'. *CNET News*. 10 November. Retrieved from news.cnet.com/8301-11386_3-57611603-76/americas-first-next-gen-aircraft-carrier-takes-high-tech-to-sea.

Thaler, Richard. 2015. *Misbehaving: The Making of Behavioural Economics*. Allen Lane: London.

Thaler, Richard and Sunstein, Cass. 2008. *Nudge: Improving Decisions About Health, Wealth, and Happiness*. New Haven, CT: Yale University Press.

Thompson, John. 1995. *The Media and Modernity*. Stanford, CA: Stanford University Press.

Tilly, Charles. 1975. *The Formation of National States in Western Europe*. Princeton, NJ: Princeton University Press.

Tilly, Charles. 1990. *Coercion, Capital and European States, AD 990-1990*. Oxford: Basil Blackwell.

Tilly, Charles. 2009. 'Grudging Consent'. Social Science Research Council. 27 May.

Timmerman, Kenneth, R. 1992. *The Death Lobby: How the West Armed Iraq*. London: Bantam.

Tooze, J. Adam. 2006. *The Wages of Destruction: The Making and Breaking of the Nazi Economy*, London: Allen Lane.

Tooze, J. Adam. 2014. *The Deluge: The Great War, America, and the Remaking of the Global Order, 1916-1931*. New York: Viking.

Truman, Harry S. 1945. 'Radio Report to the American People on the Potsdam Conference' 9 August. Delivered from the White House at 10 p.m. Retrieved from http://trumanlibrary.org/publicpapers/viewpapers.php?pid=104.

Tucker, Patrick. 2014. 'The Military Is Already Using Facebook to Track Your Mood'. *Defence One*. 2 July. Retrieved from http://www.defenseone.com/technology/2014/07/military-already-using-facebook-track-moods/87793.

Tufekci, Zeynep. 2014a. 'Big Data: Don't Let the Billions of Data Points Blind You to the Problem of Too Few Sources to Check the Results'. The Brookings Institution. 21 April. Retrieved from http://www.brookings.edu/blogs/techtank/posts/2014/04/21-big-data-can-blind-tufekci.

Tufekci, Zeynep. 2014b. 'What Happens to #Ferguson Affects Ferguson: Net Neutrality, Algorithmic filtering and Ferguson'. *Medium*. Retrieved from https://medium.com/message/ferguson-is-also-a-net-neutrality-issue-6d2f3db51eb0.

Turing, Alan. M. 1950. 'Computing Machinery and Intelligence'. *Mind* 49.
Turse, Nick. 2015. 'The Stealth Expansion Of A Secret U.S. Drone Base In Africa'. *The Intercept*. 21 October. Retrieved from https://theintercept.com/2015/10/21/stealth-expansion-of-secret-us-drone-base-in-africa.
Turse, Nick. 2016. 'Commandos without Borders'. *TomDistach.com*. 18 December. Retrieved from http://www.tomdispatch.com/post/176223/tomgram%3A_nick_turse,_washington's_america-first_commandos_in_africa.
Turse, Nick. 2011. 'America's Secret Empire of Drone Bases'. *TomDispatch.com*. 16 October. Retrieved from http://www.tomdispatch.com/archive/175454/nick_turse_america%27s_secret_empire_of_drone_bases.
Turse, Nick. 2012. 'The New Obama Doctrine'. *TomDispatch.com*. 18 June. Retrieved from http://www.tomdispatch.com/blog/175557.
The U.S. Army Robotic and Autonomous Systems Strategy. 2017. 'Maneuver, Aviation, and Soldier Division Army Capabilities Integration Center'. U.S. Army Training and Doctrine Command. March. Retrieved from http://www.tradoc.army.mil/FrontPageContent/Docs/RAS_Strategy.pdf.
US Congress. 2014. 'National Defense Authorization Act for Fiscal Year 2015'.
US Department of Education. 2014. 'US Department of Education Releases List of Higher Education Institutions with Open Title IX Sexual Violence Investigation'. 1 May. Retrieved from http://www.ed.gov/news/press-releases/us-department-education-releases-list-higher-education-institutions-open-title-i (accessed 23 June 2014).
United States Government Accountability Office. 2012. 'Financial Stability: Report to Congressional Requesters'. GOA-12-886. September.
US Department of Health & Human Services. 2015. 'The ACA is Working for the African-American Community'. Retrieved from http://www.hhs.gov/healthcare/facts-and-features/fact-sheets/aca-working-african-american-community.
US Senate Select Committee on Intelligence. 2014. 'Committee Study of the Central Intelligence Agency's Detention and Interrogation Program'. Declassification Revision. 3 December. Retrieved from https://www.amnestyusa.org/pdfs/sscistudy1.pdf.
Van Buren, Peter. 2014. 'Drone Killing the Fifth Amendment: How to Build a Post-Constitutional America One Death at a Time'. Retrieved from http://www.tomdispatch.com/blog/175872/tomgram%3A_peter_van_buren,_undue_process_in_washington.
Van Creveld, Martin. 1999. *The Rise and Decline of the State*. Cambridge: Cambridge University Press.
Vander Brook, Tom. 2013. 'Army Plows Ahead with Troubled War-Zone Program'. *USA Today*. 28 February.
Vogel, Kenneth P. and Arnsdorf, Isaac. 2016. 'Trump's Campaign Dwarfed by Clinton's'. *Politico*. 21 May. Retrieved from http://www.politico.com/story/2016/05/trumps-campaign-dwarfed-by-clintons-223438#ixzz4IzcezjP5.

Waldhauser, Thomas, D. 2017. 'United States Africa Command 2017 Posture Statement, Testimony to US Senate Committee on Armed Services'. 9 March. Retrieved from https://www.armed-services.senate.gov/hearings/17-03-09-united-states-central-command-and-united-states-africa-command.

Wasko, Janet. 2014. 'The Study of the Political Economy of the Media in the Twenty-first Century'. *International Journal of Media and Cultural Policy* 10(3).

Weaver, Nicholas. 2013. 'Our Government Has Weaponized the Internet. Here's How They Did It'. *Wired*, 13 November. Retrieved from http://www.wired.com/2013/11/this-is-how-the-internet-backbone-has-been-turned-into-a-weapon.

Weigley, Russell. 1960. *The American Way of War: A History of United States Military Strategy and Policy*. Bloomington, IN: Indiana University Press.

Weinberger, Sharon. 2011. 'Pentagon Cultural Analyst Helped with Interrogations'. *Nature*. 18 October.

The White House. 2013. 'Fact Sheet: U.S. Policy Standards and Procedures for the Use of Force in Counterterrorism Operations Outside the United States and Areas of Active Hostilities'. Press Release. 23 May. Retrieved from http://www.whitehouse.gov/the-press-office/2013/05/23/fact-sheet-us-policy-standards-and-procedures-use-force-counterterrorism.

Whitlock, Craig. 2011. 'U.S. Drone Base in Ethiopia is Operational'. *The Washington Post*. 27 October.

Whitlock, Craig. 2012. 'U.S. Expands Secret Intelligence Operations in Africa'. *The Washington Post*. 13 June.

Whitlock, Craig. 2014. 'Pentagon Set to Open Second Drone Base in Niger as it Expands Operations in Africa'. *The Washington Post*. 31 August.

Whitlock, Craig and Miller, Greg. 2011. 'U.S. Assembling Secret Drone Bases in Africa, Arabian Peninsula, Officials Say'. *The Washington Post*. 20 September.

Whitlock, Craig and Miller, Greg. 2013. 'U.S. Moves Drone Fleet from Camp Lemonnier to Ease Djibouti's Safety Concerns. *The Washington Post*. 24 September.

Wilson, H. T. 2004. *The Vocation of Reason: Studies in Critical Theory and Social Science*. Leiden: Brill.

Wilson, William. 1978. *The Declining Significance of Race: Blacks and Changing American Institutions*. Chicago, IL, University of Chicago Press.

Wilson, William. 1987. *The Truly Disadvantaged; The Inner City, The Underclass and Public Policy*. Chicago, IL, University of Chicago Press.

Wolf, Amelia Mae and Zenko, Micah. 2016. 'Drones Kill More Civilians Than Pilots Do'. *Foreign Policy*. 25 April. Retrieved from http://foreignpolicy.com/2016/04/25/drones-kill-more-civilians-than-pilots-do.

Wolf, Eric. [1982] (2010). *Europe and The People Without History* Berkeley, CA: University of California Press

Wood, Ellen Meiksins. 1997. 'Modernity, Postmodernity or Capitalism?' *Review of International Political Economy* 4(3).

Wood, Ellen Meiksins. 2001. 'Contradictions: Only in Capitalism'. In Panitch, L. and Leys, C. (Eds), *A World of Contradictions, Socialist Register*. 2002. London: Merlin.

Wyden, Ron, Udall, Mark, and Heinrich, Martin. 2013. 'End the N.S.A. Dragnet, Now'. *New York Times*, 25 November. Retrieved from http://www.nytimes.com/2013/11/26/opinion/end-the-nsa-dragnet-now.html?_r=2&

Zhao, Yuezhi and Duffy, Robert. 2008. 'Short-Circuited? The Communication and Labor in China'. In *Knowledge Workers in the Information Society*. Catherine McKercher and Vincent Mosco (Eds). Lanham, MD: Lexington Books

Zinn, Howard. 2003. *A People's History of the United States, 1492-Present*. New York: HarperCollins.

Zucman, Gabriel. 2015. *The Hidden Wealth of Nations*. Chicago, IL: University of Chicago Press.

Index

9/11   3, 67, 106, 108, 112, 114, 116, 121
1033 Programme   87
2008 Recession   xiv, 2, 7, 9, 51, 82, 93

A

Acxiom   72
Adorno, Theodor   127
Affective Servitude   16
Affirmative Action   48, 79, 81, 96, 152
Afghanistan   xi, 59, 73, 105, 107, 108, 112, 114, 115, 116, 119, 152
Afghan War   102
Africa   26, 34, 35, 102, 105, 117
Alabama   42
Albright, Madeleine   104
Alexander, Keith   68
Alexander, Michele   84
Algorithmic Regulation   xvii, 23, 134, 135, 136

Al-Harethi, Salim Sinan   60
Alienation   82, 96
Al-Maliki, Nouri   109
Al-Qaeda   61, 105, 106, 116
Al-Shabab   117
Amazon   14
American Anthropological Association   71
American Civil Liberties Union, the   87
American Civil War   xiv, 40, 41, 42
American Colonial Trade   37
American Expeditionary Force   56
American Federation of Labour   44
American Medical Association   72
American Psychological Association   72
American Revolution   36, 37, 38
Amiriyah Shelter   103
Anderson, Tanisha   96
Antiterrorism and Effective Death Penalty Act   67

Arab Spring   109, 110
Arpanet   9
Artificial Intelligence   129, 131, 134
Assad Regime   110
Assange, Julian   75
Atlantic Charter   45
AT&T   72, 73, 74
Authoritarianism   70, 113
Automation   22

B

Baghdad   100, 109
Balance of Power   6
Baltimore   88
Barker, Dean   53
Bates, John   70
Baudrillard, Jean   103
Becker, Gary   132
Beckert, Sven   37
Bell, Derek   80
Bernanke, Ben   52
Big Data   xvii, 19, 20, 67, 72
  Law Enforcement   70
  Metadata   68
  Mining   69
  Policing   72
bin Laden, Osama   105, 106, 115
Bio-mimicry   60
Black
  Culture   80
  Elites   80
  Emancipation   41
  Political Consciousness   82
  Poverty   42, 80, 93
  Subjugation   82
Black Lives Matter   23, 77, 92, 93, 94, 96
Booz Allen Hamilton   73
Bordeaux   36
Boston   39
Boston Dynamics   xiv, 60
Boyd, Rekia   96
Bransburg v. Hayes 1972   75

Brazil   34, 113
Brennan, John O.   116
British Army   152
Brown, Barrett   75
Brown, Michael   85, 92, 96
Brzezinski, Zbigniew   106, 115
Bumpurs, Eleanor   96
Bureaucratic Agency, the problem of   4
Bureau of Applied Social Research   58
Burundi   61
Bush, George H. W.   103, 104
Bush (George H. W.) Administration   105
Bush, George W.   107, 111
Bush (George W.) Administration   67, 72, 108, 121

C

Capital Accumulation   xvi, 1, 2, 6, 7, 13, 37, 82, 106, 107, 108, 145, 148
Capital Flight   14
Capitalism   1, 24, 108, 145, 147, 148
  Digital   13
  English   30, 32
  International Affairs   99
  Problems of   24
  Racial   41
Capital-State Relationship   4
Caribbean, the   35, 37, 101, 112
Carnegie, Andrew   41
Carney, Mark   52, 53
Carter Doctrine   101, 105
Carter, Jimmy   101, 115
Centralization of Power   3
Cheney, Dick   103
China   99, 105, 112, 115, 121, 122, 147
ChoicePoint   72

Chomsky, Noam   128, 129
Churchland, Paul   139
CIA   xii, 59, 62, 68, 72, 73, 75, 105, 112, 116, 152
Civil Rights   xii, 48, 70, 74
  Civil Disobedience   135
  Digital Rights   13
Civil Rights Movement   48, 79, 80
Class Decomposition   14, 83
Class Struggle   xiv, 31, 147
  From Above   49
  From Below   12, 44, 46
Climate Change   xiii
Clinton Administration   67, 75, 83, 111, 121
Clinton, Bill   49, 83, 84, 105, 112
Clinton, Hillary   111, 113
Coates, Ta-Nehisi   79
Coburn, Tom   72
Cognitive Behaviourism   125, 126, 127, 140, 142, 143
Cold War   57, 58, 67, 71, 99, 103, 105, 111, 145
Colonialism   26, 31
  in the Americas   xvi
Commission on Industrial Relations   44
Commodification   10, 31, 45, 108
Commodification of Data   76
Communications Assistance for Law Enforcement Act   67
Compton, James   103
Computation   57, 60, 129, 137, 142
Computational Turn, the   128, 131, 135
Confederacy   41
Consumerism   47
Counterterrorism   70, 118
Cuba   44, 113
Cusseaux, Michelle   96
Cybersecurity   70
Cybersecurity Information Sharing Act   73

D

Dar es Salaam   105
DARPA   22
DARPA (Defense Advanced Research Projects Agency)   xiv, 60
Data
  Commodification   21
  Labour market   21
  Metadata   72
  Mining   21, 61, 134, 135, 138
Datafication   20
Debt Bondage   50, 85, 145, 147
Decentralization of the Workplace   15, 16
Defence Intelligence Agency   71
Deferred Action for Parents of Americans   115
Demilitarisation   148
Democratization   15, 30, 39, 47, 146
Department of Defense   57
Department of Homeland Security   67
Deregulation   50
Derrida, Jacques   130
Deskilling   15
Digital Accountability and Transparency Act   73
Digital Coercion   xiv, 23
Digital Divide   14
Digital Mode of Production   8, 13
Digital Repertoire of Contention   23, 92
Displacement   36
Dispossession   xiv, xvi, 7, 26, 31, 40, 45, 99, 111, 145, 146, 147
Division of Labour   30, 44
  International   116
DoD   xiii, 71, 75, 86, 105, 107, 112, 116
Dodd-Frank Act   52
Dow Jones Industrial Average   106

Drone Warfare   60, 61, 62, 64
Du Bois, W. E. B.   41, 42, 44, 45, 91
Dutch East India Company   34
Dutch West India Company   34
Dyson, Michael   88

E

East Asia   26
Economic Crisis   42, 44, 106, 145
Economies of Bondage   8, 25
Egypt   100, 103, 112, 117
Ehrlichman, John   82
Elsevier   72
Emancipation Proclamation   41
Emerging Market Economies   14
Empire
  American   106, 107, 108, 110, 145
  British   31, 32, 34, 37, 40, 100
  Dutch   34
  French   37
  Rule in   6
  Spanish   32, 34
  Systematic Cooperation   6
  USSR   100, 115
English East India Company   34
English, the   35, 36
Enron   16
Equality of Opportunity   21
Espionage Act
  1917   45, 66, 75
Europe   26, 36
European   xvi
Exploitation   26, 104

F

Facebook   xiii, 20, 71, 74
Fair Sentencing Act   97
Fall of the Berlin Wall   12
FBI   67, 68, 70, 72, 83
Federal Reserve Bank   46
FICA   69
Fifth Amendment   66

Financialization   82
Financial Stability Oversight Council   52
First World War   45, 55, 100
FISA   69
Flynn, Michael   71
forced labour tradition   36
Foreign Intelligence Surveillance Court   68, 70
Fourteenth Amendment   43
France   34, 56, 100
Free Blacks   40
Free Labour   7, 40, 99, 147, 150
Free Trade   112
Frege, Gottlob   128
Frey, Shelly   96
Fuchs, Christian   9, 14

G

Garner, Eric   89, 92, 96
Genocide   3, 40, 112
  of Native Americans   43
  violence   40
Georgia   42
Germany   56, 100, 112
Global South   12
Global War on Terror   69
Google   20, 74, 137
GPS   22, 68
Gray, Freddie   96
Great Depression   46
Great Society   48, 51, 81, 82
Greenwald, Glenn   73
Guantanamo Bay   90, 111, 113
Gulf War   7, 102, 103, 105, 116

H

Haass, Richard   107
Hay, Colin   4
Hayden, Michael   60, 68
Hegemony   34, 59, 76, 115, 123
  American   124
  British   45, 46

Western Pacific   122
Heinrich, Martin   73
Higher Education Act, The
    of 1965   48
Highway of Death   103
Historical Materialism   11, 85
Holder, Eric   65, 66, 75, 97
Honduras   113
Hoover, J. Edgar   67
Horkheimer, Max   127
Human Terrain System   59, 69
Huntington, Samuel   48
Hurricane Katrina   82
Hussein, Saddam   103, 108

I

Idealism, in Communication
    Studies   11, 12
Ignatieff, Michael   64, 107
India   8, 34, 35, 56, 112
Indigenous Populations   33, 34
Industrialization   25, 42
Industrial Revolution   37, 41
Industrial Workers of the
    World   44
Institutional Oppression   85
Intellectual Property   13
Intelligence Committees   67
International Humanitarian Law   63
International Monetary Fund
    7, 106
International Trade   12
Internships   17
Interstate Commerce
    Commission   43
Iran   75, 100, 101, 102, 103, 105,
    108, 109, 110
Iranian Revolution   101
Iraq   xi, 59, 100, 101, 102, 103, 104,
    105, 108, 109, 110, 112, 116,
    119, 121, 153
Iraqi Army   109
Iraq invasion   102

ISIS   109
ISMI catchers   88

J

James, C. L. R.   32, 36
Japan   62, 99, 112, 122
Jessop, Bob   4, 6, 7
Joint Task Force   102
Justice Department   xii, 75

K

Kahneman, Daniel   132
Katz, Elihu   58, 59, 141
Keller, Bill   67
Kerry, John   108
Keynes, John Maynard   51
Krugman, Paul   46
Ku Klux Klan   42
Kuwait   101, 102, 104

L

Labour
    Military   119
Labour Power   1, 7, 28, 36, 99, 147
Labour Regimes   xvii, 14, 22, 116,
        146, 147
    Change   35
    Docility   16, 22
    Emerging   9
    International   146
    Reserve Army of Labour   147
    Rotating labour force   16
    Unfree   153
    Union membership   22
Latin America   33, 49, 99, 101, 113
Lazarsfeld, Paul   58, 59, 141
Lerner, Daniel   58
Levi, Edward   67
Libya   117
Lichtblau, Eric   67
Lloyd George, David   55
Los Zetas   114

M

Madison, James   36
Mahan, Alfred   45
Management Revolution, Critique of   19
Manifest Destiny   56
Manning, Chelsea   23, 75
Marcuse, Herbert   127, 136
Marshall, Thurgood   81
Martin, Trayvon   92
Marxist Political Economy   25
Marx, Karl   1
Mass Communication   141
Mass Deportation   115
Mass Protest   8
mass surveillance   60, 61, 66, 68
Mechanization   15, 43, 81
Mellon, Andrew   46
Mellon, James   41
Mercenaries   119
Middle East   58, 64, 99, 100, 102, 105, 110, 112, 116, 118, 121
Miliband, Ralph   3
Militarization   10, 99, 146
Mills, C. Wright   2, 47, 141, 142
Minerva Research Initiative   71
Mohammed, Nek   60
Monroe Doctrine   99
Morgan, J. P.   41
Mosaddegh, Mohammed   100
Mosul   100, 109

N

Nagel, Thomas   139
Nairobi   105
Nantes   36
National Capitalism, decline of   13
National Science Foundation   71
National Security Strategy   106, 111
NATO   109, 112
Neurosociology   126

New American Way of War   xv, 64, 146
New Deal   46, 48, 51
New York   39, 89, 106
Niger   62, 112, 117
Nixon Administration   121
Nixon, Richard   49, 82, 101
NSA   xi, 61, 67, 68, 69, 70, 71, 72, 73, 74
Nudges   133

O

Obama Administration   60, 61, 62, 65, 75, 93, 97, 115, 118, 121
Obama, Barack   78, 79, 98, 113, 117, 120
Occupy Movement   23
Odierno, Raymond   118, 119
Okinawa   111, 114
Oklahoma City Bombing   67
Oman   110, 112
OPEC   101
Operation Merlin   75
Ottoman Empire   100

P

Pakistan   xi, 62, 64, 112, 116
Panette, Leon   120
Patriot Act   67
Paul, Rand   65
Pentagon, the   23, 60, 71, 86, 120, 121
Pershing, John   56
Persian Gulf   113, 114
Petraeus-Broadwell scandal   59
Petraeus, David   59, 152
Philadelphia   39, 81
Philippines   44, 61, 62, 122
Plait Amendment   44
Police
  Brutality   77, 89, 90, 92, 96, 97
  Racial Profiling   90
Police Militarization   85, 86, 87

Policing
  Labour boycotts   89
Post-Racial Society Thesis   79, 80
Poverty   xiv, 8, 46, 82, 84
PRISM   74
Procedural Democracy   105
Progressive Period   47
Psychological Warfare Division   58
Psychologism   125, 142

Q

Quantification   135, 139

R

Racial Inequality   8, 81
Racism   50, 78, 80, 85, 97
  Institutional   89, 92
  Systematic   81
Rawls, John   51
Reagan Administration   105
Reagan, Ronald   49, 67, 102
Reconstruction   43, 91
Reed, Adolf   80
Refugees   109
Rent Economy   13
Republican Party   48
Reserve Army of Labour   17, 22
Resistance   29, 30, 32, 56
Revolutionary War   38, 39, 40, 41, 99
Rice, Tamir   92
Risen, James   67
Robinson, Cedric   41
Rockefeller, John D   41
Roosevelt, Franklin D.   46
Rorty, Richard   128
Rule of Law   22
Ruling Class   2, 22, 111, 133, 146, 147
  American   23, 42, 101, 106, 108, 143, 145
  Ideology   36, 73
  Neoliberalism   48
  Spanish   33

Rumaila Oil Field   102
Russell, Bertrand   128
Russia   100, 109, 110, 112, 115

S

Saudi Arabia   100, 101, 102, 103, 105, 109, 110
Schiller, Dan   7, 10
Schwarzkopf, H. Norman   103
Searle, John   129, 139
Second World War   xiv, 45, 57, 99, 100, 111, 127, 128
Security State   xvi, 3, 5, 8, 23, 67, 73, 74, 116, 118, 119, 124, 146
Securocrats   5
Segregation   43, 78, 82
Senate Armed Services Committee   104
Servicemen's Readjustment Act 1944   58
Shannon, Claude   128
Silicon Valley   xiii, 9, 16
Skinner, Burrhus Frederic   127
Skocpol, Theda   3, 4
Slave Rebellions   36
Slavery   xiv, 26, 36, 38, 40
  British Dependence upon   32
Smith, Yvette   96
Snowden, Edward   23, 68, 73, 74, 75
Social Inequality   xii, 8, 27, 39, 40, 46, 49, 81, 92, 143
Social Policy   127
  Neuroscience   134
  Nudges   133
Social Reproduction, struggle of   13
Social Stratification   21, 57, 131
Somalia   61, 64, 112, 116, 117
South Africa   12
Southern Border Plan   115
South Korea   62, 112, 122
Sowell, Thomas   81
Spanish   111

Spanish-American War   45
Special Forces
  Africa   121
Stamp Act   37
State Department   xii, 62, 107, 120
State Formation   xvi, 4, 26, 28, 29, 32
Stuxnet   70
Sudan   105
Supreme Court of the United States   xiii, 47, 74
Surplus Value   26, 145, 146
Surveillance
  Capitalism   xv, 21
  Chilling Effect   69
  Combat   62
  Corporate   22, 73
  Counterintelligence operations   70
  Digital   67, 74
  Global   62
  in Afghanistan   73
  Law Enforcement   67
  Mass   65, 68, 75
SWAT Teams   86, 87
Syria   xi, 100, 101, 103, 109, 110

T

Tax Havens   14
Tennessee   42
Terrorist Attack Disruption Strikes   61
Thirty Years' War   34
Thomas, Clarence   81
Tilly, Charles   27, 29
Timmerman   102
Tobacco Cultivation   34
Training and Doctrine Command   59
Trilateral Commission   48
Truman. Harry   47
Truth, Sojourner   41, 94
Tufekci, Zeynep   20
Turing, Alan M.   128

U

Udall, Mark   73
Uganda   61
UN Compensation Commission   104
Under-Consumption, crisis of   153
Uneven Development   xvi, 1, 5, 25, 106, 111, 148
Unfree Labour   xvii, 26, 42, 146, 147, 148
United Arab Emirates   109, 110
United States   xiii, 13, 66, 106, 127
United States Government Accountability Office   52
United States Reserve Bank   52
UNSC 687   104
UN Security Council   102
Urbanization   30, 42, 58
US, Arms Trade   110
US Army   43, 59, 60, 114, 118, 119
US, bases in Saudi Arabia   105
US, Involvement in Afghanistan   105
US Marines   60
US Navy   22, 60, 62, 124
USSR   46, 57, 100, 101, 102, 103, 105, 109, 111, 112, 121
US Strategy   107
US, support of Iraq   102

V

Value Theory   9
Verizon   74
Vietnam   8, 49, 61, 101
Violent Crime Control and Law Enforcement Act   84
Virginia Company   34
Voting Rights Act   97

W

Wage Labour   25, 30, 49, 147
War
  Invasion of Afghanistan   106

Invasion of Iraq   108
Low-visibility   117
On Drugs   82, 83, 113
Washington   167
Welfare State Liberalism   51
West, Cornell   81
whistleblowers   xii, 23, 66, 74
Wilson, Darren   85
Wilson, William   81, 82
Wilson, Woodrow   44, 45
Wolfowitz, Paul   105
Worker Analytics   21
Working Class   28, 40, 49
  American   50
  Consciousness   39, 45
  Rebellion   39, 42, 43, 46

World Bank   7, 106
World Trade Organization   7, 106
Wyden, Ron   73

X

XKeyscore   74

Y

Yemen   60, 61, 62, 64, 66, 110, 116
Yom Kippur War   49, 101
Yoo, John   66

Z

Zinn, Howard   34
Zinni, Anthony   104

CPSIA information can be obtained
at www.ICGtesting.com
Printed in the USA
LVOW13s0411140917
548684LV00021B/1566/P